D0688281

UMBRIA

PHILIP'S TRAVEL GUIDES

UMBRIA

JONATHAN KEATES

PHOTOGRAPHY BY JOE CORNISH

Acknowledgements

I should like to thank my brother Timothy for undertaking to drive me on all the journeys mentioned in this book.

British Library Cataloguing in Publication Data
Keates, Jonathan *1946–*
Umbria. – (Philip's travel guides)
1. Italy. Umbria – Visitors' guides
I. Title
914.56504829

ISBN 0-540-01231-9

First published by George Philip Limited,
59 Grosvenor Street, London W1X 9DA

Printed in Italy

Contents

To Jon, Caroline, Philip and Alice

Half-title illustration In the cloister of San Pietro in Valle, near Spoleto.

Title-page illustration Looking across the hills north of Monte Subasio and Assisi.

Opposite A grove of young birch trees near San Giustino.

Città di Castello
Serra di Burano
Scheggia
Gubbio
Umbertide
Tuscany
0 10 20 km
Gualdo Tadino
Marche
Lago Trasimeno
Perugia
Nocera Umbra
Assisi
Monte Petrarvella
Spello
Foligno
Città della Pieve
Tiber
Montefalco
Trevi
Monti Sibillini
Monte di Melonta
Castelluccio
Norcia
Todi
Valnerina
Orvieto
Spoleto
Cascia
Monti Martani
Monte Croce di Serra
Nera
Terni
Amelia
Narni
Abruzzo Molise
Lazio

Introduction

Does Umbria really exist? It is not a political entity, like Tuscany, which was once a grand duchy, it is not bound together by history or tradition, and it is not even a particularly apt geographical expression. We may talk glibly about 'the Umbrians', but this will not mean very much in terms of a sharply defined cultural identity, and the local styles in painting, architecture or vernacular building are far too diverse to bind the region together.

Yet Umbria has an extraordinarily powerful sense of its own separateness, as a place which is happy to be neither Tuscan nor Roman and whose individuality dawns upon the traveller by degrees, if only because he will always have entered it via some other part of Italy. There are no major airports, the region is entirely landlocked, and the largest cities, Perugia and Terni, hardly rival such centres as Milan, Bologna or Florence in their urban sprawl. Thus, in the long history of Italian travel, towns like Trevi, Spoleto and Narni have been visited more often by accident than by design. Tourists stumbled across them on their way somewhere else or because they had somehow turned aside off the old road to Rome which ran straight out of Tuscany into Latium, avoiding Umbria altogether.

The terrain was never easy to cross. Four distinct ranges of hills dominate the Umbrian landscape, stretching south and east of Lake Trasimeno. The most westerly of these is the series of tall bluffs, Monte Petrarvella, Monte di Melonta, Monte Croce di Serra and others, which runs along the Latian frontier and overhangs the valley of the lower Tiber. The central spine of the province is formed by the Monti Martani, bounded by the horseshoe curve of the plain south of Perugia and Assisi, nowadays littered with light industrial installations and the only dull interval in an otherwise infinitely varied landscape.

To the east you begin the steep climb towards the Sibylline Mountains, the Monti Sibillini, which form a natural frontier with the Marche region stretching to the Adriatic. As for the northern corner of Umbria, around Gubbio, Città di Castello and Umbertide, this is more obviously a southern spur of the Apennines, with the same scatter of remote villages and deeply incised valleys rising to the long, almost dead straight line of the Serra di Burano and the nature reserve east of Scheggia.

These are not necessarily gentle prospects, but their colours are a good deal subtler and softer than those in parts of Italy more frequented by tourists and photographers. One of the lasting delights of Umbria is the simple pleasure of not finding that everywhere has been crawled over by coach parties. Even Assisi somehow restrains the visiting hordes and reminds you continually of its existence as an ordinary town, whose everyday life not merely absorbed the experience of Francis but could indeed be said to have

A detail from the romanesque portico of Santa Maria Assunta, Lugnano in Teverina.

given him the very character that makes him so universally beloved.

This sublimely unvisited quality of Umbrian towns, the sense of places too deeply preoccupied with their immediate lives to give much thought to self-conscious public relations exercises, has its roots in the more depressing realities of history. The past, amid these thickly wooded slopes, rolling pastures and steep-sided valleys, has not been an especially happy one, and the annals of cities, monasteries, castles and villages make you wonder why the people who now live here preserve the extraordinary charm of manner, equanimity and good humour for which they are famed throughout Italy.

Their earliest recorded ancestors, the people who gave the region its name, left little more to the traveller's eye than the dramatic sites of ancient settlements like Narni, Amelia and Gubbio, perched on the tops and flanks of the hills, and the stretches of Cyclopean wall surrounding them which still survive here and there. That they spoke their own language is clear to us from the remarkable Eugubine Tables, the set of religious ordinances written in a parallel Umbrian and Latin text and originally composed for the citizens of Iguvium (Gubbio) during the early years of the Roman empire.

The Eugubine Tables are specific on the subject of enemies, and a list of these includes a people called the 'Turce' – none other than the wealthy and aggressive Etruscans, whose territory, by 600 BC, stretched all the way from the banks of the River Po almost to the gates of Rome itself. The Etruscans are always represented as a shadowy and mysterious people about whom little enough is known, but in fact an immense amount has been discovered regarding their customs and social organization, if only because the importance they accorded to death and burial rites means that many of their ornately decorated tombs, painted with scenes and figures from everyday life, have survived. Some of the most significant, such as the Ipogeo dei Volunni at Perugia, are to be found in Umbria itself.

Perugia indeed formed one of the lynchpins of Etruscan power during the gradual rise of Rome as a serious challenger for dominion in central Italy. In 309 BC the city was vanquished by the Roman consul Fabius, and during the next hundred years its autonomy and that of other Etruscan settlements was gradually chipped away. So far from accepting defeat with a bad grace, however, the Umbrian communities were soon noted for their conspicuous loyalty to Rome, a loyalty they were given a chance to prove at a truly nail-biting moment in the history of the republic.

In 217 BC the great Carthaginian general Hannibal (247–182 BC), spearhead of his nation's desperate bid to fight off the Roman stranglehold on their Mediterranean trading bases, crossed the Alps with his elephants and swept victorious through northern Italy. His arrival in Umbria was as the destroyer of

The Oratory of San Bernardino in Perugia, designed by Agostino di Duccio.

AVGVSTA PERVSIA MCCCCLXI

Roman legions under the veteran commander Flaminius at Lake Trasimeno, but any hopes he might have had of raising the malcontent locals against their so-called oppressors were disappointed. Umbria not only failed to revolt, but actually saw Hannibal off under the walls of Spoleto, still justifiably proud of repulsing the Carthaginians at a gateway known for several centuries as the Porta Fuga, the Gateway of Flight.

Partly as a reward for such fidelity, Rome showered benefits on the region. There is a far more obvious Roman presence here than in neighbouring Tuscany, for example, and it often seems as if every country town has got its surviving traces of a theatre, an amphitheatre or baths. Only Perugia, fatally backing the wrong side in the civil war of 41 BC between Octavius Caesar and Mark Antony's brother Lucius and destroyed by fire as a partial result of its rebellious defiance of Octavius, never fully recovered in status or substance during the Roman era.

It was when the empire began to fall apart under the constant threat of barbarian invasion in the fifth and sixth centuries AD that Umbria took on a geopolitical significance with which it can hardly have been very happy. The Via Flaminia (now the *statale* no. 3), the highway linking Rome to Rimini on the Adriatic, cut across the southern corner of the region, and it was this road which formed a rough boundary between two territories, that of Byzantium, controlling the Roman Empire, and that of the invading Germanic Longobards.

During the early sixth century the Byzantine emperor Justinian (527–565) decided once and for all to crush the power of the Goths, who had swept into Italy fifty years before, seized Rome and established powerbases at Ravenna and Verona. His invincible general Belisarius (505–565) faced the toughest challenge of his career in the person of Totila, the last great Gothic leader, ruthless in battle yet generous to his enemies in their defeat. The war dragged on for nearly twenty years, much of it fought up and down the valleys of Umbria, and it was only when Belisarius had been replaced by the valiant eunuch Narses (480–574) that Totila was finally overcome beneath the walls of Gualdo Tadino in 552.

As if this were not enough, a fresh horde of Germanic invaders descended on the land. The Longobards (their name actually does mean 'long beards') left a lasting imprint on the language and institutions of Italy, and it was in Spoleto that they established a powerful dukedom, carving out a slice of Umbria for themselves against the renewed ambitions of Byzantium which dominated the remainder of the region.

While this strife went on, a quiet revolution was taking place in the religious life of Europe, under the guidance of a man from Norcia on the edge of the Monti Sibillini. St Benedict (480–547) and his sister St Scholastica developed the earliest western form of monastic life, in which groups of monks and nuns, guided by a strictly enforced code of conduct, strove to live out a disciplined existence within the shelter of a settled community. Though the ideals of the Benedictine Rule were entirely spiritual, it was not without its practical considerations: the earliest monastic buildings could easily be defended against barbarian attack, and the order imposed by the contemplative life brought an element of harmony and continuity to the atmosphere of an age torn by discord and anxiety.

Spirituality is in the very air and rocks and waters of Umbria, and the region has produced more saints, hermits, pastors and religious teachers than any other part of Italy. Christianized very early, its towns boasted glorious throngs of martyrs to successive waves of Roman imperial persecution, its woods and caves provided a refuge for anchorites seeking solitude for meditation, and its hills were scattered with sanctuaries and pilgrimage chapels.

The holy men and women of Umbria come in a fascinating diversity of guises. There are warrior heroes like the great Herculanus, Bishop of Perugia, captured while organizing the defence of the city

The Via Flaminia still runs through the ruins of Carsulae.

The romanesque apse and campanile of Santa Maria Maggiore, Assisi.

and executed on Totila's orders; missionaries like Felicianus, patron saint of Foligno, martyred at the staggering age of 94 for preaching Christianity among the Emperor Decius's military prisoners; and from the same city mystics such as the Blessed Angela, who died in 1309 leaving a remarkable account of her visions. Then there are the poets, finest being Jacopone da Todi, author of the *Stabat Mater*; the intensely practical characters like the much loved Rita di Cascia; and of course the most popular of all, the man who has been called 'the human being nearest to Christ himself', St Francis of Assisi.

By the time of Francis's birth in the late twelfth century the whole of northern and central Italy was fragmented into warring city states, themselves often riven by civic factionalism of the kind familiar to us from Shakespeare's vivid portrayal of the furious street battles between Montagues and Capulets in *Romeo and Juliet*. The broader political spectrum of a jostle for power between the Pope and the Holy Roman Emperor (their respective parties known as Guelph and Ghibelline after two German castles) involved the destiny of Umbria itself, which fell very gradually under Rome's sway.

Though some cities, such as Assisi and Spoleto, passed comparatively early into papal hands, others, such as Terni and Orvieto, lurched between a variety of overlords before becoming part of 'the Patrimony of Saint Peter', and one or two, like Gubbio, were absorbed as late as the seventeenth century. By 1600, however, nearly all of the area we now call Umbria had been subsumed into that extensive sovereign territory known as the Papal States. It was not especially prosperous, and as the eighteenth century wore on, foreign travellers tended to notice the disparity in living conditions between 'progressive' Tuscany to the north and its more reactionary Roman neighbour.

The fact is, nevertheless, that the papal government was for the most part just and benign, and there was little genuine resentment of its stricter ordinances and exactions. What is most noticeable even today, in all the territories forming part of the wide domain once governed by Cardinals and sheltered by the privileges and prerogatives of Mother Church, is the extraordinary handsomeness of the gates and walls and palaces of every town, large or small. Many of them no doubt were the wretched, disease-ridden, beggar-swarming holes conjured up for us in the pages of Victorian travel literature, but there is a serene beauty in their piazzas, fountains and porticoes which is hard to match elsewhere in Italy.

What Umbria had also produced meanwhile was a substantial and continuing tradition of local painting and sculpture. Much worthwhile re-evaluation of her artists has taken place during the present century, and recent pioneering exhibitions have invited us to appreciate a wealth of talents at which earlier ages have unjustly sneered. It may be true that the really great renaissance artists who worked here were either

The cloister of San Pietro in Valle, near Spoleto.

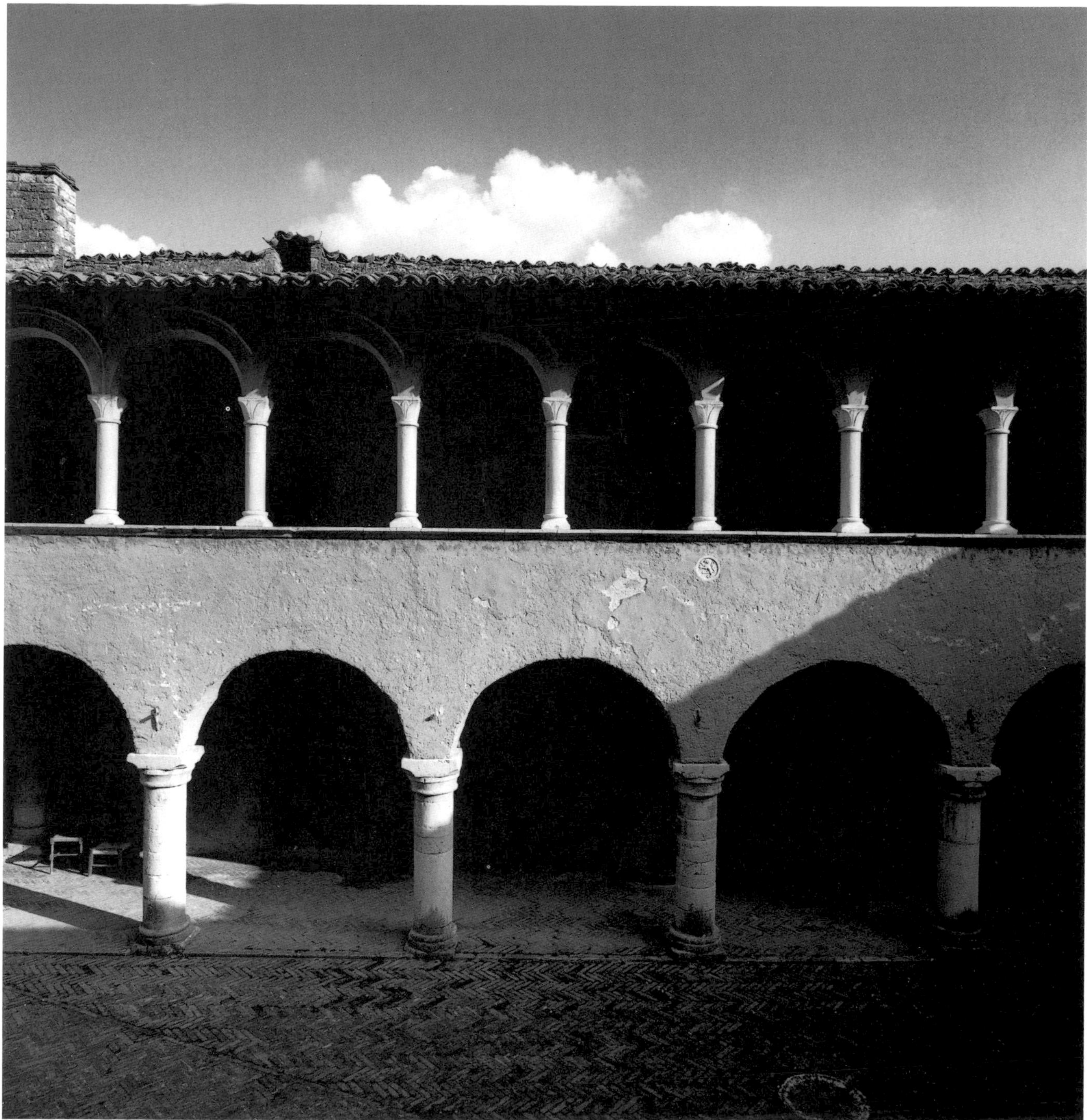

visitors from Tuscany such as Fra Angelico and Filippo Lippi, or else natives like Perugino and Pinturicchio who had to look further afield for wealthy patrons, but there is a distinct identity to the loosely-named 'Umbrian School' of the fourteenth and fifteenth centuries, numbering painters such as Nicolò Alunno and Bartolomeo Caporali and neatly characterized by the anonymous writer in *Baedeker's Italy 1890*, who notes its typical features as 'reverie, tranquillity and gentleness of sentiment'.

The awakening to a regional consciousness in fields other than painting began while the Papal States were in their last decades as an independent territory. The great movement towards Italian unity known as the Risorgimento, which gripped the hearts and minds of everyone during the early nineteenth century, duly set its mark upon Umbria. In the bitter armed struggles between the Papal forces and an increasingly fractious and resentful populace in other areas of the state such as Romagna and the Marche, many Umbrians remained touchingly loyal to the Church's temporal authority, and except in Perugia, which reacted with characteristic turbulence to the government's show of force, the region was hardly noted for its revolutionary heroism.

Modern Umbria has followed the fluctuating destiny of united Italy. The dreams and hopes of the Risorgimento were often doomed to disappointment, and in the years before World War I many left in search of a better life in the north or emigrated to America. Now, even if Umbria does not always blossom like the rose, the effects of Italy's booming industrial economy have brought increasing prosperity to the territory. The little factories and workshops down the Tiber plain may look unsightly, but they generate the money and employment which has preserved both the beauty and the prosperity of places like Città della Pieve and Spello.

Tourism has been slow in overtaking Umbria and its worst excesses have been most effectively restrained. Though many of the old farmhouses and cottages throughout the countryside are now being converted to holiday homes, there is as yet no sense that the land is losing its identity and turning into a bijou theme park for the affluent. What instantly strikes the visitor is the unforced friendliness and civility of the Umbrians. After the boorish Romans and the arrogant Florentines, the welcoming embrace of Spoleto, Narni or Montefalco seems almost miraculous in a late twentieth-century context, and it becomes easy to comprehend the personal attractiveness of Umbria's saints.

Even food and wine – perhaps especially food and wine – reflect this integrity and straightforwardness. Here and there in Italy, outside the smaller, more old-fashioned *trattorie*, you see the phrase *cucina sana e genuina*, which literally means 'healthy and genuine cooking', but really says so much more about the love of the cooks for their work, the tact and charm of the waiters and the no-nonsense decor of establishments dedicated to the serious business of eating and drinking without snobbery or pretence.

Umbrian restaurants possess this down-to-earth attitude to a marvellous degree. Except once, in a lugubrious hole in Orvieto where I was the sole customer and the exorbitant bill seemed calculated to cover the cost of the fussy wall decorations, they have never disappointed me. The whole landscape comes to the table, lamb from the mountain pastures, trout from the swift streams of the Valnerina, the lentils of Castelluccio, black truffles from the woods and sausage from pigs that rootle in the oak groves.

As for the wines, these seem all the better for being so little known. You will not find most of them outside Umbria (only the white Orvieto has ever had an international fame), but their limited local production has a distinctly favourable influence on quality. Try, for example, the excellent fruity red Sagrantino of Montefalco, the ruthlessly dry Chardonnay from the same region and the Bianco d'Arquata, in my view one of the finest of all Italian white wines for sheer engaging variety of savour.

The village of Castelluccio in the Monti Sibillini on Umbria's eastern border.

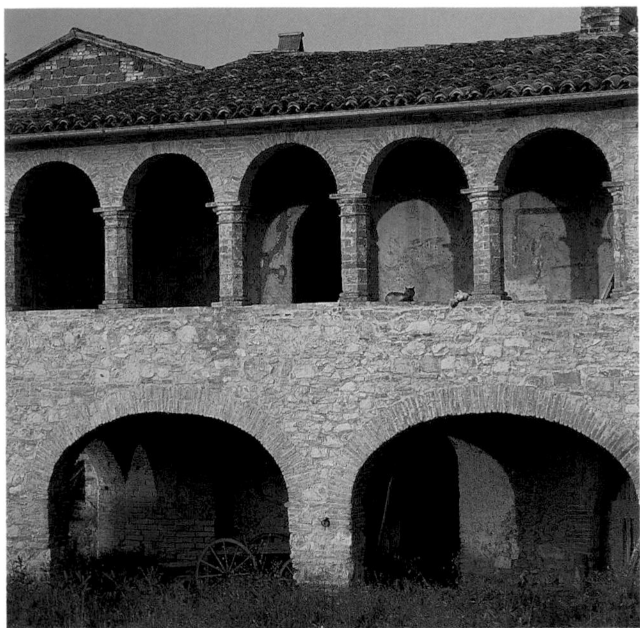

The last glow of sunset strikes the loggia of a farmhouse near Trevi.

Though it is quite impossible to explain why, the food and wine of Umbria seem much more closely connected than in other regions of Italy with the nature of the landscape which produces them. This obviously has something to do with the traditional character of Umbrian agriculture and economy. In any area which historically lacked a wealthy and enlightened aristocracy which was prepared to experiment in new farming methods and to build itself grand villas on rural estates, there is bound to be a sense of a life more simply lived, more closely linked to seasonal rhythms and prepared to make the best of limited resources.

Beyond the Tiber valley, whose fertile plain has been heavily scarred by the operations of modern industry and transport, Umbria is nearly all hills of one sort or another, and the look of its towns and villages in the context of the landscape is that of places which have sprung up like growing things from the rocks and soil around them. What makes these ancient settlements so attractive to the modern traveller is their sympathy with their surroundings. Apart from Terni, Cascia and Foligno, and the outlying suburbs that have sprawled beyond the historic city limits of Perugia and Narni, it is hard to think of a single inhabited spot in Umbria that is not instantly striking in its beauty or which fails to lure you towards it up some winding road, through a narrow medieval gateway and into its warren of steep streets and dark alleys.

The building materials of the region provide an obvious range of contrasts. Some may not instantly take to the harshly bright, undressed stone of the Assisi region; others may regret the notable absence, in certain towns and cities, of those elegant stucco palace façades which are such a winning feature of Tuscany and Lazio (though Orvieto provides an outstanding exception to this rule). Certain travellers will feel at once the sense of warmth conveyed through the use of volcanic tufa as a building material for cathedrals and citadels, and most of us, after visiting Bevagna, Bettona and Città della Pieve, will appreciate the subtlety and versatility of brick. In Città della Pieve, a town I can scarcely write about without a certain racing of the heart, brick indeed strikes the keynote. The colour of the city, seen from a distance, is a kind of rose pink, turning golden as the sun strengthens during the day and flushing to something almost like madder red in the sunset. The brick here is not that kind of harsh mud brown or rusty hue with which we are familiar in northern Europe, but softer by far, so much so indeed that some of the buildings in the town look almost cream-coloured until seen at close quarters, when the delicacy of the pointing is revealed.

Sympathetic blending between Umbrian towns and their surroundings has of course a great deal to do with their actual siting, and even if this was always initially a purely practical consideration, time has generally achieved the happy result of making each one look as if

Città della Pieve, among the loveliest of Umbrian hill towns.

UN VIAGGIO

it were intended for its particular spot. Most of them, understandably, are strategically located on hilltops, and the profusion of these hill towns in their landscape can seem bewildering in the sense that each, viewed from afar, has such an attractive air of completeness about it, as though it alone were worth looking at.

It would be quite wrong, however, to imagine that Umbria is a case of see-one-and-see-the-lot. As soon as you get close to any of these towns – Todi, Spello, Bevagna, Nocera – you begin to grasp the intrinsic uniqueness of each and to see why the fierce individuality of these places, over which they often came to blows with one another, put down such ancient roots. Umbrian cities are enormously proud of their local celebrities, and this is a genuine admiration, not just small-town special pleading. One of the official histories of Todi features at least fifty pages of potted biography, listing every minor Renaissance cleric, seldom-commemorated martyr saint and insignificant eighteenth-century poet. Here as elsewhere in Italy the implication is that the tradition which produced great men and women like these is still firmly alive and demanding respect.

A greeting to travellers on the gate of a forsaken garden near Orvieto.

The ultimate delight of wandering in Umbria is that the journey never grows predictable. Surprise is the keynote, and you should always be prepared, just at the moment when the fields and trees and streams appear at their most seductively gentle, for something truly odd and unexpected to catch the eye. This is a country for the imaginative explorer, and armed with a decent car and a strong pair of walking legs, which of us can possibly resist it?

Before you begin your journey, a note or two on some Italian building and historical terms which will frequently recur in this book. A cathedral, for instance, will often be referred to by its Italian name of *duomo* (literally 'house of God', from the Latin *domus*), a small fortified town or village is called a *borgo*, from the Germanic *burg*, and a fortress or citadel is known as a *rocca*, from which, in medieval times, a *podestà*, or mayor, might have ruled. (This last term was revived, largely for its patriotic sonority, by Mussolini.) Armed with technical labels like these and an unquenchable appetite for exploring, you cannot really go far wrong on your Umbrian expeditions.

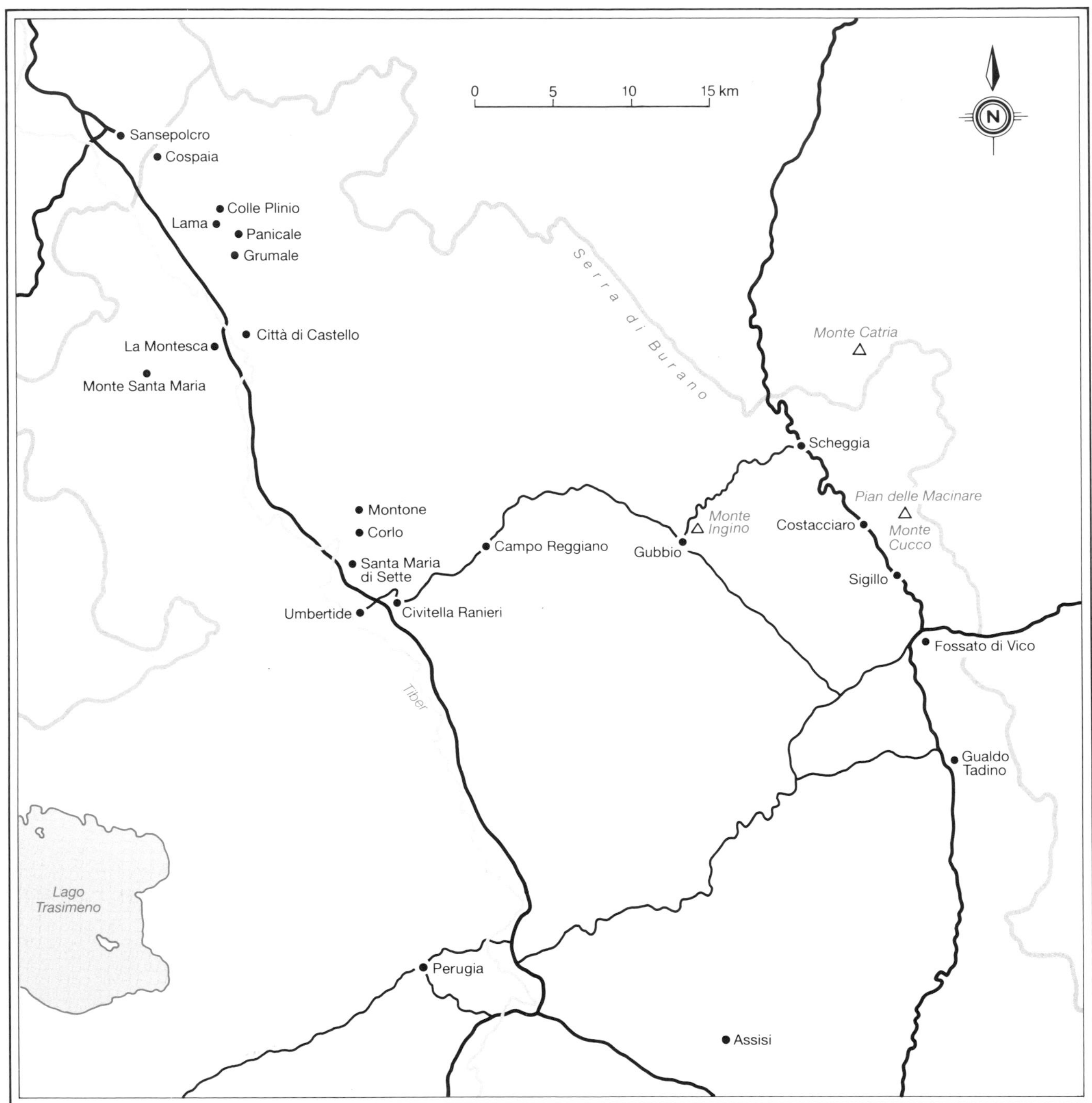
0
5
10
15 km
N
Sansepolcro
Cospaia
Colle Plinio
Lama
Panicale
Grumale
Città di Castello
La Montesca
Monte Santa Maria
Serra di Burano
Monte Catria
Scheggia
Pian delle Macinare
Monte Ingino
Costacciaro
Monte Cucco
Gubbio
Sigillo
Montone
Corlo
Campo Reggiano
Santa Maria di Sette
Umbertide
Civitella Ranieri
Fossato di Vico
Tiber
Gualdo Tadino
Lago Trasimeno
Perugia
Assisi

1
Down the Tiber Valley

Città di Castello – Umbertide – Gubbio – Gualdo Tadino

The wisdom of the ancients, seeking out the indwelling essence of created things and assigning a tutelary spirit to each, gave the rivers of the earth their patron gods and goddesses. Now and then in Italian museums you are likely to come across recumbent statues of the River Tiber, personified as a hale old man with flowing locks and a bushy beard. His air of slightly ponderous solemnity is somehow appropriate to the river itself, one of the essential facts of the Umbrian landscape, threading south-west in a stately, sometimes positively turgid progress towards Rome.

It is Father Tiber who leads you south out of Tuscany into Umbria. As you follow this valley, it is worth counting your blessings that you are no longer required, as in the days of disunited Italy, to bribe a throng of greedy customs officials so as not to have the contents of your baggage flung upon the road and thoroughly searched, or to pay the various taxes on imported goods from which the inhabitants of villages on either side of the border creamed off a cosy living.

At least one of these hamlets enjoyed the privileges of an anomalous status as neither Tuscan nor Papal; as the so-called 'Republic of Cospaia', it remained independent from 1440–1826. When Pope Eugenius IV (1431–47) handed over Sansepolcro to the Florentines, somebody made a small but crucial cartographical error over the existence of a certain ditch, and the little pocket of land around Cospaia suddenly achieved the complete autonomy proclaimed in the inscription above the doorway of the parish church, which reads: 'To the perpetual and established liberty of Cospaia'.

This is tobacco country, and you can see its dark green bunches chequering the fertile plains among the yellow squares of sunflower. When Italy acquired the smoking habit (and Italians are still unrepentant smokers), Cospaia survived as a kind of 'safe house' or no-go area for smugglers of either cigars or plugs of the raw leaf. Even after the Grand Duke of Tuscany and the Pope finally decided to bring the cheeky little republic's independence to an end, it was allowed to go on planting and selling its tobacco.

The enchantments of this countryside, a succession of rolls and ridges above streams feeding the gradually broadening river, captivated that most engagingly personal of Roman letter-writers, Pliny the Younger (*c.*62–113), who probably acquired his villa here during the final years of the first century AD. You can visit the site, traditionally called Colle Plinio, by following the little valley beyond the village of Lama. Archaeologists are, as usual, rather reluctant to identify these scattered remains of what was evidently a wealthy colonial administrator's 'desirable and commodious country residence' as the villa mentioned in the famous letters, but since tiles and bricks stamped

with Pliny's initials have been discovered, authentication seems irresistible.

The villa itself was a large country house, perhaps not quite the Roman equivalent of Chatsworth or of one of the châteaux of the Loire, but impressively proportioned nevertheless. There were frescoed walls, cool colonnades, little courtyards with gently plashing fountains and suites of rooms specially adapted to changes in the weather. The bath-house, besides its steam-room and three plunge baths, had a court for ball games attached, and below the main buildings lay a race-track, where riders could be watched from an open-air dining room in which dishes floated to and fro across the waters of a marble basin. Beyond stretched the avenues and parterres of the great garden, with its rose-beds and cypress alleys and box hedges clipped into fantastic topiary shapes.

From Lama take the minor road via Panicale and Grumale down to the junction with the main highway to Città di Castello, nowadays preferable to the noisy *superstrada* which runs beside it right the way along the river valley to Perugia, Todi and beyond. The town itself is folded in the embrace of the Tiber where it veers slightly eastwards, with the enclosing hills and some exceptionally fine stretches of sixteenth-century fortification girdling three sides of the neatly proportioned oblong stretching along the river.

Nobody, it seems, can quite make up their minds about Città di Castello, and the customary unison chorus of praise for the beauties of a small Italian town is surprisingly mute. Old Edward Hutton, who trotted Edwardian armchair travellers so obligingly round Italy with the aid of his rhapsodic prose style and an infectious enthusiasm for medieval art, called it 'one of the most charming towns in the upper valley of the Tiber', but the more recent writer of a very well informed guidebook concludes that 'when all is said and done, Città di Castello is a second-division town of little real interest'.

A farmhouse near Cospaia on the Tuscan frontier.

A furious satyr guards a door at Città di Castello.

There is more than a little to be said about the place, and in terms of artistic interest, quite a lot to be done. So at least thought Raphael (1483–1520) when he arrived here as a young man in 1504. Still an adolescent, he was already the most admired pupil of the great Pietro Perugino, though Giorgio Vasari, in his *Lives of the Artists* (1568), tells us that 'it was impossible to make a clear distinction between Raphael's own works and those that were Piero's'.

Città di Castello, to which Raphael came with a group of young friends while Perugino was in Florence on business, was thus crucial in the development of his personal style. Here he painted the *Crucifixion*, now in the National Gallery in London, and the austerely dignified *Marriage of the Virgin* which found its way to the Brera in Milan, and these, whatever their debts to his master, rank as the first major statements of a talent which became one of the benchmarks of European art.

His patrons were the city's ruling family, the Vitelli, whose precarious hold was maintained by a series of

shrewd deals with the Pope, the Medici family and the dukes of neighbouring Urbino (Raphael's birthplace). Vitellozzo Vitelli had not reckoned, however, with the malign ascendancy of Cesare Borgia, who, having invited him to a conference at Sinigaglia on the Adriatic coast, had him strangled, an act greatly commended for its ruthless practicality by Machiavelli. Vitellozzo may after all have earned the lukewarm appraisal of the Italian historian who tells us that 'as a prince and soldier he made men fear him, but they were not sorry at his death': he so despised guns for the power they gave mere footsoldiers to unhorse mounted knights that he used to blind all the musketeers he took prisoner.

Vitellozzo and his family are recalled by the splendid palace in the Via della Cannoniera built for them between 1521 and 1532 by the inspired Florentine architect Antonio da Sangallo the Younger, its façade decorated by Giorgio Vasari himself. This now houses, besides an archive and a library of 50,000 volumes, the civic picture gallery, which gives you an excellent perspective of the shifting artistic currents in the days when the Vitelli themselves had both money and political clout.

Tuscan influences predominate. Here are a *Maestà* in Sienese style by an anonymous local fourteenth-century master, two gilt-bronze statuettes attributed to Lorenzo Ghiberti (1378–1455), creator of those miraculous Florentine Baptistery doors, and a *Coronation of the Virgin* from the warmly sympathetic brush of Domenico Ghirlandaio (1449–94). By common consent the glory of the collection is the *Martyrdom of St Sebastian* by Luca Signorelli (1441–1523), painted in 1490 for the church of San Domenico. As always with this highly individual artist, we feel him defining his own terms, heedless of anyone else's aesthetic or the impression he is likely to make on younger painters. The saint is confronted by five athletic archers, two of them stripped for action, eagerly stringing their bows.

Cypresses punctuate the landscape near San Giustino.

Luca Signorelli's *Martyrdom of Saint Sebastian*, at Città di Castello.

In the distance citizens gather to watch, while far away in the ruined amphitheatre the soldiers rally. The poignancy of the whole episode is somehow heightened by a sense of detachment, as if Sebastian, ignored by a wider world, was himself transcending that world by his death. Alas, this has recently been removed for restoration.

From the gallery walk up the Via dei Casceri and across the Via San Florido to the *duomo*, dedicated to

Saints Floridus and Amantius, bishops during the sixth century, when the town was still known by its Roman name of Tifernum. Practically nothing remains of their cathedral or of the romanesque building which replaced it. Nearly everything here is either baroque or rococo, starting with the incomplete but still highly elegant façade created by Francesco Lazzari in 1632. The decorated niches surrounding the porch contain not statues but painted escutcheons with the arms of the see.

Inside, the nave, flanked by a sequence of interlinked chapels, is harmonious, if not especially arresting; but look up at the late eighteenth-century frescoes in the dome by Tommaso Conca, whose father Sebastiano, a spirited and fanciful Neapolitan, has had something of a revival in recent years. The apse has paintings by the equally able hand of Marco Benefial (1684–1764), most of whose work is found much further south. In the left transept you should certainly not miss Rosso Fiorentino's *Transfiguration*. Or, if you do miss it, it will not miss you, for everything of Rosso's is arresting in its gloomy, hectic individuality, reflecting the violence of his life and death. Hag-ridden by his obsessive jealousy of a rival, he committed suicide in 1541 at the age of 47, while working for François I of France at Fontainebleau.

To the left of the *duomo* stands a curious tubular campanile of the thirteenth century, rather like an Irish round tower. Behind the church it is worth strolling into the public gardens, rather neatly tucked into an angle of the ramparts, to gaze across the Tiber towards La Montesca with its villa and Monte Santa Maria with its ruined sixteenth-century castle.

Otherwise walk back towards Piazza Matteotti, east of the cathedral, where the history of Città di Castello, politically confused and often dramatic, is charted in some most impressive buildings. The sprawling Palazzo del Podestà looks baroque, but it may originally have been built by Angelo da Orvieto, an Umbrian architect who flourished between 1334 and 1352. Angelo certainly designed the gothic portico and double-arched windows of the Palazzo Comunale immediately behind it, but typically the whole grandiose scheme, involving a third storey crowned with battlements, somehow never got finished, because the citizens were too busy squabbling and nobody quite knew where the next penny was coming from.

Your choice is now, as in nearly every old Italian town of any consequence, between the Franciscans and the Dominicans. Whatever the good relations binding St Francis to St Dominic (and several are the places in Tuscany and Umbria where the pair are said to have met), their two orders cordially loathed one another, and thus tended to site their churches as far away from each other as possible within the confines of the city walls.

To reach San Francesco, turn down Via Angeloni to find the church in Piazza Raffaello Sanzio. The building, begun in 1273, retains its traditional 'preaching barn' shape, but was much worked over during the sixteenth and seventeenth centuries. Many of its treasures disappeared in 1797 when, soon after Pope Pius VI (1775–99) had been compelled to sign a peace treaty with the invading French at Tolentino, Napoleon's commissioners arrived with the express object of plundering the Umbrian cities of their art treasures. One of these was Raphael's *Marriage of the Virgin*, which at least stayed in Italy, since it was claimed as a reward by General Giuseppe Lechi, who had come to Città di Castello on behalf of the French to proclaim the town's so-called independence from the Pope. He later presented it to the Brera in Milan, where, in spite of numerous requests for its return, it has remained.

The most beautiful feature of San Francesco is undoubtedly the Cappella Vitelli, designed for the family at some time during the mid sixteenth century by Giorgio Vasari (1511–74). Concord and contrast between the various architectural elements – heavy Corinthian pilasters lightened by the slender cornice linking the capitals and the delicate scallop-shell

An Umbrian roofscape at Montone.

niches below – create an ideal ensemble. This is set off by Pietro di Ercolano's wrought-iron gates, by the marquetry of the stalls showing scenes from the life of the Madonna and St Francis, and by an imposing *Coronation of the Virgin* by the omnicompetent Vasari himself.

At San Domenico, which you reach by walking up Via Angeloni to Piazza Matteotti, and then down Corso Vittorio Emanuele and along Via Signorelli, the chief delight is not so much the medieval church itself (though there are some decent fresco fragments, including an ambitious Crucifixion on the right-hand wall) as the lovely cloister, once part of the adjacent convent, which is now a home for the blind. Under the baroque frescoes by the local painters Sguazzino and Abbatini, showing scenes from the life of the blessed Cieca della Metola (*cieca* means blind, but the connection is surely coincidental), you can sit quietly for a moment in the shade of the round renaissance arches, which contrast with ornate triple-headed gothic windows on the inner walls.

On the road south towards Umbertide there is little to engage you until the left turn towards Montone. This will be your first experience of something which soon becomes an Umbrian *sine qua non* – the winding mountain road, with its perilously sharp curves, on which you despair of ever reaching your destination, though you can see it hanging tantalizingly on the distant hillside.

Montone, however, is worth the haul. Its position and the way it has retained its Umbrian essence unchanged lend it a far greater charm than some of the towns closer to the Tiber. The property of all the local dynasties in turn – the Del Monte, the Fortebraccio, the Vitelli – it eventually passed into papal hands in 1546. It was Carlo Fortebraccio who in 1473 presented the church of the Collegiata with one of the thorns from Christ's crown, which, if you happen to visit Montone on an Easter Monday, you will see publicly displayed. Of the other churches, the best is San Francesco, reached by a scramble up a flight of steps which leads to a magnificently comprehensive view of the north Umbrian countryside. Behind its inlaid doors, the work of Antonio da Mercatello (1476–1530), also known as Bencivenni, there are some tolerable frescoes by Bartolomeo Caporali (1420–1503), painted in 1482 (notice the Archangel Raphael and the boy Tobias over the first altar to the right) and the remains of a painting by the fascinatingly elusive Antonio da Ferrara (1390–1449), whose rather conservative style has its own distinctive charm.

Unless you wish to try the hairpin bends all over again, it is probably better to push eastwards from Montone and take the turn which leads down Via Corlo and Santa Maria di Sette to Umbertide. Once again this is a town which has had a worse press than it merits from guidebook writers, though its fortunes never ran very smoothly from the start. As Roman Pitulum it was sacked by the Goths, only to be rebuilt in the ninth century as Fratta degli Uberti (*fratta* means thicket, or spinney) and destroyed once more by the *condottiere* (soldier of fortune) Braccio Fortebraccio, master of Perugia in the early years of the fifteenth century. Heavily bombed during World War II, it preserves a handful of elegant buildings and a most engaging central piazza, with a fourteenth-century Palazzo Comunale which was once the town house of the Ranieri di Sorbello, still the grandest family in these parts. There is also a neo-classical post office from the years following Italian unification in 1860, when the town chose to rename itself Umbertide after King Vittorio Emanuele's eldest son Umberto.

If you follow Via Cibo out of the square and cross the railway line, you eventually reach the church of Santa Croce, whose early rococo high altar acts as a somewhat incongruous setting for an impressive *Deposition from the Cross* which Luca Signorelli painted in 1516. He was already 75 years old, but seems to have undertaken the whole work unaided, with all his customary sense of deep personal involvement with the subject. The emphasis here is on the physical effect of emotion:

The castle of Civitella Ranieri seen across summer cornfields.

the Apostles steady themselves with the ladders they hold, the grief-crazed Mary Magdalen reaches out for support to the Cross itself and Christ's Mother faints away. Below the picture is a masterly series of predella panels showing the discovery of the True Cross by St Helena, the mother of Constantine.

From Umbertide follow the road eastwards over the hills towards Gubbio. The landscape here is dotted with castles, many of them romantic ruins, such as Monte Cavallo above the romanesque abbey of Campo Reggiano, some, such as the noble pile at Civitella Ranieri, which is a private residence, still very much alive. Suddenly the steep slopes open out around *la conca di Gubbio*, a small valley which was obviously once the bed of a lake, and reveal the first views of the town, hanging off the mountainside in a spectacularly precipitous tumble of medieval roofs, walls and towers.

One modern art historian has called Gubbio 'among the most remarkable single feats of civic planning in the history of medieval Italy'. Some of us may feel that the wonders of Gubbio are due precisely to the fact that civic planning has nothing whatever to do with it. For a start, the city as a place of settled habitation is one of the oldest in Italy. We may discount the charming fable which says that it was among the first five cities built after the Flood, and that its founder was Noah's grandson, a certain Gomero Gallo, but whatever civic planning might have been necessary was well advanced by the time the Etruscans established their authority here during the fifth century BC.

Ikuvium or Igubium was an important Roman city, with temples to all the gods, a sizeable theatre, bathhouses and basilicas. What is more, it was plainly regarded as a major centre of religious activity of various kinds for the entire region. The details of at least one elaborate set of rituals have come down to us through the discovery in 1444, in an underground chamber near the ruined theatre, of seven bronze plaques engraved with extensive inscriptions in Latin and Umbrian describing the various acts of a corporation of priests known as the Attidian Brotherhood. Their ceremonies included augury through careful observation of birds in flight ('the hawk and the raven should fly in advance, the woodpecker and magpie behind'), a sequence of prayers to local gods – Gabovius, Cerfius and Volfionus – and an involved series of sacrifices ('three oxen before the Trebulan gate, three fat sows behind') as the priestly college moved in procession around the city.

There is something singularly moving about these Eugubine Tables, as they are called, when you see them today in the museum of the Palazzo dei Consoli. They place us in touch with a vanished language and a long-extinct solemnity whose meticulous observance was designed to protect the city and ensure its survival. They also remind us of Rome's wisdom in not suppressing the alien cultures it dominated, but absorbing them into the fabric of an expanding empire. There is a kind of providential magic in the Tables' continuing existence, though it would be interesting to know whether, as some hold, there were originally another two which have somehow got lost.

What endured of Roman Gubbio was sacked by Totila's Goths in the sixth century AD, and an embassy of its citizens apparently went all the way to Byzantium to seek aid from the Emperor. The rebuilt city had learned its lesson, and during the centuries immediately following, Gubbio achieved a reputation for sturdy independence and fiercely courageous fighting men. By 1000 she had her own code of laws and a freedom upheld by two annually elected consuls on the Roman model. She assisted the ruthless, domineering Holy Roman Emperor Frederick Barbarossa (1155–90) to sack the city of Milan in 1163, and brought back a number of expert Milanese clothworkers who established the wool trade as the mainstay of Gubbio's independent power in the fretful, cutthroat, competitive world of the Italian city states.

After a spell of resentful subservience to the Papacy, Gubbio surrendered the last of her independence in 1384 to the Montefeltro family, whose chief seat was at Urbino, over the mountains to the east. They were among the few great dynasties of renaissance Italy whose members possessed something approaching moral principle. True, Dante places one of them in Hell

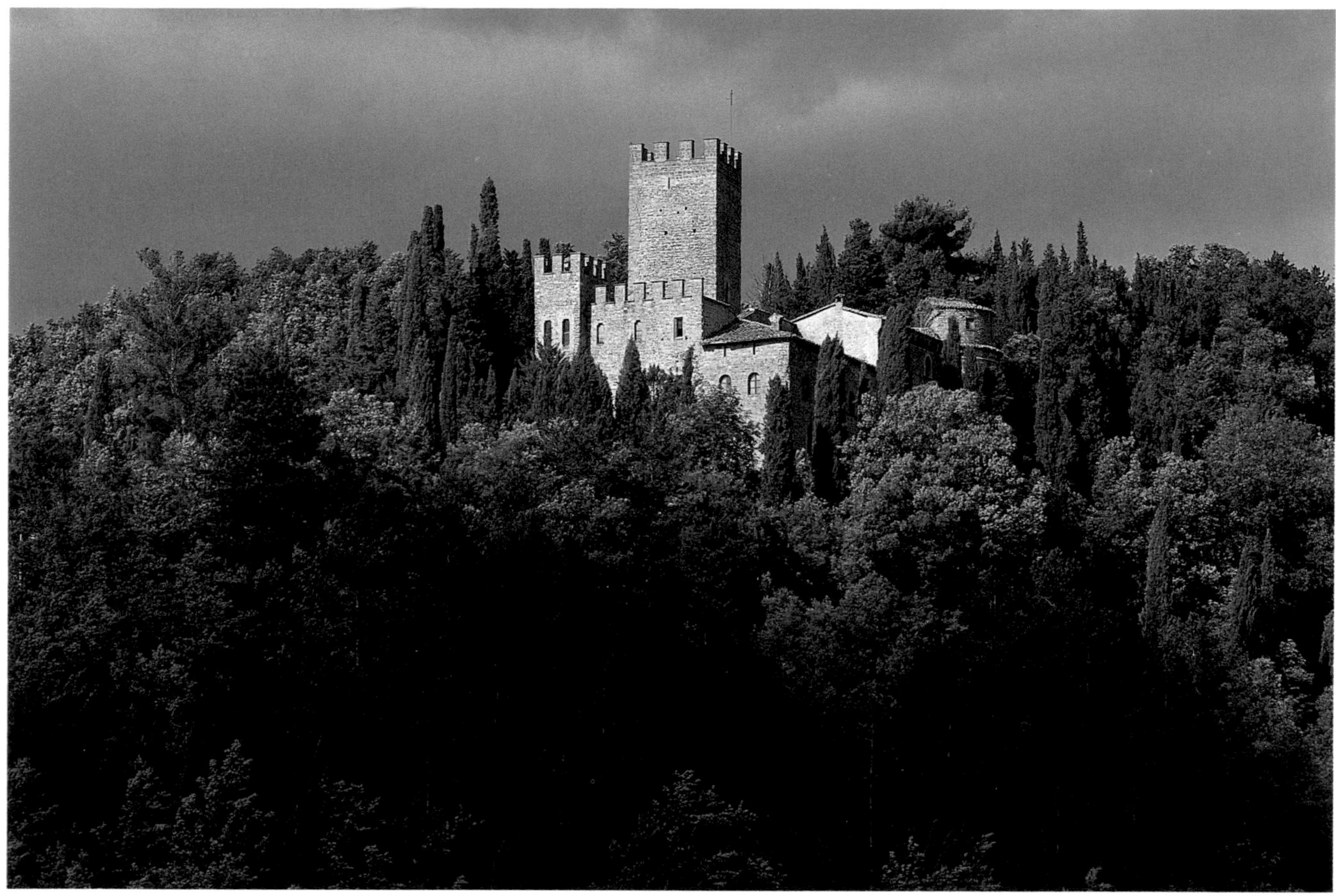

The towers of Monteleto, north-west of Gubbio.

for giving evil counsels to the Pope, but for the most part history bears out the praises of the nineteenth-century historian Dennistoun, who said that 'in the territories earned by their good swords, and their faithful services to the Church, it was their pride to foster the lessons of peace, until their state became the cradle of science, of letters and of art'.

When in 1504 the Montefeltro line of succession was extinguished and Gubbio passed, along with the rest of the ducal domains, to the Della Rovere family, successive popes, preoccupied as so often with worldly ambition and temporal power, made efforts to grab the territory for themselves by force of arms. The citizens of Gubbio, with their habitual valour, held out for their dukes. No wonder that Don John of Austria, watching the Gubbians in action against the Turks at the battle of Lepanto in 1571, asked 'What then is this Gubbio? Is she greater than Naples or Milan, or what is she?'

The Papacy, however, was not to be baffled. Having tried and failed with military invasions, the Church now used her ultimate sanction of religious blackmail, persuading Duke Francesco Maria II that the loss of his only son was an act of God and that he had better

Left The Palazzo dei Consoli dramatically dominates the town of Gubbio.

Above A rainwashed Piazza della Signoria in the heart of Gubbio.

sign away his inheritance for the sake of his immortal soul. He was allowed to remain nominal ruler of the dukedom of Urbino and its towns, including Gubbio, until his death, but Pope Urban VIII (1623–44) sent in his own men to take possession when the ink on the transfer documents was scarcely dry. Francesco Maria died, brooding and despondent, in 1631, and Gubbio became part of the Papal States, within whose boundaries it stayed for another two and a half centuries.

The embodiment of Gubbio's municipal independence, which even the Montefeltro and the Della Rovere made some show of respecting, is the Palazzo dei Consoli in the Piazza della Signoria. Built between 1332 and 1337, as the inscription in gothic characters above the central porch indicates, this is one of the great statements of medieval civic power, worthy to set beside its more grandly conceived equivalents in Florence and Siena. Both a fortress and a palace, it is a symbol of firm but always detached and impartial government.

Architecturally the building's unity of design, setting tall buttresses against arched windows and castellated battlements, is due to the genius of two Umbrian masters, Angelo da Orvieto and Matteo di Giovanello, known as Gattapone, a Perugian whose major achievements are assigned to the 1360s. It was probably Angelo who created the triple-arched main doorway and the staircase sweeping away from it so majestically, but Gattapone is likely to have been responsible for the main structural framework, as well as for the massive supporting arches which underpin the whole fabric (you can see them by going into Via Gattapone, immediately behind the palace).

Inside, the immense vaulted chamber on the first floor was designed for important gatherings of the townspeople, and is still known as the Salone dell'Arengo (literally, the 'Harangue Room'). This is where you will find the Eugubine Tables, as well as Roman sarcophagi and inscriptions, one of them taken from the façade of the theatre, telling us of the good works of Gnaeus Satrius Rufus, who renewed the roofs of the basilicas, restored the temple of Diana and contributed to the games in honour of the Emperor

Gubbio's Palazzo del Bargello overlooks the famous 'Madman's Fountain'.

Augustus in the first century BC. There is also a set of 26 medieval lavatories, revealing Italy to have been a good deal more sophisticated than England in the field of domestic plumbing.

On the second floor you will find the civic picture gallery, five rooms displaying Umbrian, or more specifically Gubbian, art arranged in chronological sequence, from the fourteenth-century work of painters such as Guido Palmerucci (1316–45), to renaissance masters like Timoteo Viti (1465–1523) and Ottaviano Nelli (b.1375), and Perugino's pupil Sinibaldo Ibi (1475–1548). There are two saints by the Spanish baroque painter Jusepe Ribera (1591–1652), unlovely but convincing as always, and an elegantly worked *St Francis in Ecstasy* by Andrea Sacchi (1599–1661), a Roman whom the see-saw of taste has recently brought back into critical favour.

Do not expect masterpieces here. Those who cannot share my pleasure in these small Italian collections of minor talents and want a perpetual array of big names will be disappointed. But anyone will enjoy the view from the loggia on top of the palace, which gives you a capital prospect of all the notable buildings in Gubbio rising from a sea of red-tiled roofs spotted with grey and yellow lichen and clumps of house-leek.

Gattapone also worked on the Palazzo Pretorio, the piazza's other main component, begun in 1349 as a series of single chambers raised one above the other on a sturdy central pillar. The building was never properly finished and has been much pulled about ever since, but you can get at least some idea, from its overall shape, of how the architect saw it in relation to the rest of the square.

Now take the Via dei Consoli, which runs down the hill from the north-west side of the square. This is one of the best streets in Gubbio in which to see the characteristic medieval *porte dei morti*, marked features in the architecture of Umbrian and south Tuscan towns. These 'doors of the dead' are said to have been specially created for passing coffins out of the house, but it seems more likely that their function in these fortress-like dwellings was defensive, since their long, narrow apertures, with the step raised above street level, could be easily guarded in the event of a street fight.

About half-way down Via dei Consoli is the Bargello, built as a prison in the late thirteenth century and preserving its original windows with their pointed arches, and the tower from which Gubbio was once governed. The fountain in front of the little church of San Giuliano is connected with a sinister legend which says that anyone who walks around it three times will go mad. Has anybody tested the experience and kept their sanity? Opposite the rather dull San Domenico further down the hill, the Palazzo Beni conveys a good idea of aristocratic Gubbio's mood of proud austerity at the close of the fourteenth century.

The street, which eventually becomes Via Cavour, turns a sharp corner and widens into the broad oval Piazza Quaranta Martiri. On the north-eastern side of the square stands the Loggiato dei Tiratori dell'Arte della Lana, a long portico under which the weavers on whom the town's prosperity depended used to stretch their skeins of wool. Next door is the church of Santa Maria dei Laici, once the chapel of the hospital before it moved to the eighteenth-century building opposite, and founded in 1313. Of the wealth of frescoes within, the most arresting are surely those in the crypt, by Giacomo di Benedetto Bedi (1432–75), painted around 1460 and featuring a gruesome Crucifixion in which an ugly old man drives a massive bolt into Christ's feet.

Walk round the piazza to the church of San Francesco, completed after the Pope's appeal for sponsorship from other Umbrian cities in 1292, to designs by the Perugian architect Fra Bevignate (1259–1305). Here is one of the most harmonious of Gubbio's gothic structures, with a beautiful pilastered apse and a broad nave and aisles separated by tall columns. In the apse itself you will find a series of scenes from the life of the Virgin by Ottaviano Nelli, who was born here around 1375 and worked on this dignified fresco sequence between 1408–13.

St Francis himself visited Gubbio on several occasions, the most famous of them providing a well loved scene in the countless episodes from his life depicted by medieval artists. The town and its neighbourhood, we are told, were terrorized by 'an exceeding great wolf, terrible and fierce', of whom even armed men were afraid. Typically fearless and trusting, the saint went out to meet the brute, making the sign of the Cross and saying 'Brother Wolf, I command thee in the name of Christ that thou do no harm', whereupon the animal lay down at his feet as quiet as a lamb. Francis then preached a gently reproving sermon, which the wolf showed signs of having understood, and got the beast to promise good behaviour in exchange for regular feeding by the citizens, the deal being clinched by a shake of the right paw.

Wolves are unjustly maligned, and it was probably the first time this one had experienced kindly treatment from a human being. He became the citizens' pet, welcomed in every house, and died two years later in venerable lupine sanctity. His skull is rumoured to have been discovered near the little church of San Francesco della Pace in Via Savelli, on the site of the lair

21

Simple gothic arches frame the ornate apse of the *duomo* at Gubbio.

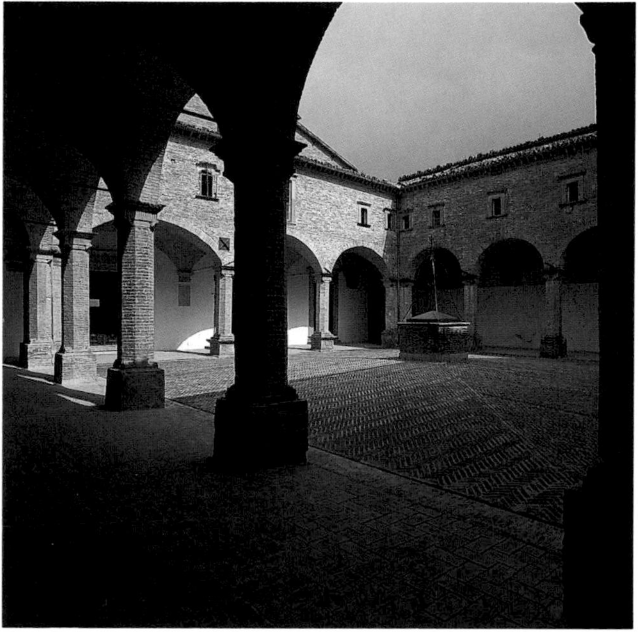

The austere brick cloister of Gubbio's basilica of Sant'Ubaldo.

allotted him by the saint (a quaint renaissance inscription on the front of the building tells the whole story).

If you walk up Via della Repubblica and take the steps behind Palazzo Pretorio, you come to Via Ducale, which takes you to the handsome renaissance palace built in 1476 on the site of a Longobard fortress by Federico da Montefeltro (1422–82), Duke of Urbino. The fate of the Palazzo Ducale has been rather mixed. When Laura McCracken wrote her excellent *Gubbio Past & Present* in 1905, the place was derelict, having been used for fifty years as a silk mill and stripped of all its fittings. 'In a few years', she wrote, 'it will drop into a heap of ruins.' Well, perhaps not quite, though a later spell as a private dwelling can hardly have helped, and careful restoration has involved a painstaking recovery of its former splendour. The magnificent arcaded courtyard designed by Francesco di Giorgio Martini (1439–*c.*1501), architect of the more famous palace at Urbino, can already be enjoyed; decorations here include reliefs of the Order of the Garter presented to Federico in 1474 by Edward IV, King of England, as a tribute to his international renown as a warrior.

A medieval back street in Gubbio frames a view of rocky hills.

Opposite the palace is the modest gothic cathedral, begun in the thirteenth century, where the line of ogival arches across the nave, supposed to imitate praying hands, leads towards a frescoed presbytery containing sixteenth-century organ lofts by the brothers Luca and Giacomo Maffei, local craftsmen. Here, too, rare enough in Italian churches, are some vivid panels of early medieval stained glass.

If you leave Gubbio by the western approaches you ought on no account to miss the Roman theatre, reached across the fields from the Viale del Teatro

Romano and exceptionally well restored. As has been noted, the building was already in use by the first century BC, when Gnaeus Satrius Rufus restored it, but in modern times it was not unearthed until 1789, when much of its decoration was removed and the structure was re-covered. Another excavation in 1826 simply provided local people with an opportunity to make free with the stonework, and the stage, till then intact, promptly disappeared. More recent work has uncovered some fine mosaic flooring and the auditorium, now the venue for an annual dance festival.

At the opposite end of the town, a cable-car will take you up the steep hillside to the basilica of Sant'Ubaldo, built in 1512 as a thanks-offering for the recovery of their cousin Pope Julius II (1503–1513) by Elisabetta and Eleonora della Rovere, wife and mother of the Duke of Urbino. Gubbio's much-loved patron St Ubaldo, whose body was brought here in 1194, lies in a glass coffin under the high altar. A member of the noble Baldassini family, he attracted early admiration for his devout life and self-denying manner, once travelling to Rome in order to ask the Pope not to make him Bishop of Perugia. As spiritual leader in Gubbio he was an invaluable peacemaker and 'beyond everything pleasing in conversation, his speech flavoured with the salt of wisdom, benignant and affable'. He it was who dared to stand up, on the citizens' behalf, against the repulsive Emperor Frederick Barbarossa, busy devastating Umbria. So taken aback was Barbarossa at being reproved by the pious, frail old man that he presented John the Baptist's finger as a holy relic to the town.

Every year, on 15 May, the vigil of the saint's death, his body is brought down to the *duomo* as part of a singular ceremony, the Corso dei Ceri, whose origins are plainly in an ancient pagan phallic cult. Three immense poles shaped like Christmas crackers and called *ceri* (candles), each bearing the statue of a saint, are carried through the city by men in black, yellow or blue shirts and white trousers, who whisk them up and down the steep, narrow lanes in a kind of helter-skelter race which involves getting St Ubaldo's *cero* up to the basilica doors before either of the others. The occasion sends the town into a fever of excitement, and the day, with its feasting, toasts, gorgeously robed clergy and surging, laughing crowds, is a manifestation of something truly Italian in a way that many of the better-known traditional *feste* no longer are.

North-east of Gubbio the landscape takes on just the kind of grandeur and drama you might expect, as the road curves sharply to and fro up the slopes of Monte Ingino towards Scheggia. Though there is nothing to see in Scheggia itself, it forms an adequate base for exploring this mountain frontier of Umbria and the Marche. The road north-east (no. 360) leads along the edge of Monte Catria, running through forest to the romanesque abbey of Santa Maria di Sitria. The community was founded by that intensely energetic Tuscan saint, Romualdo (950–1027), the patron saint of stammerers and known in medieval England as St Rumbold, whose monks locked him up for six months in a little cell next to the church. The crypt here is especially impressive, centred as it is on a Roman column with a Corinthian capital.

You can easily get lost on these mountain roads and wander all the way over the provincial frontier to Sassoferrato, so, rather than trying to explore further, it is probably better to turn back to Scheggia and go south down the narrow valley as far as Costacciaro, with its ruined fortress and medieval walls, lying under the shadow of Monte Cucco, Umbria's highest peak. The whole area is very popular with hang-gliders and cavers, eager to penetrate the grotto which runs nearly a kilometre into the mountain, the fifth deepest cave in the world. If you want to climb Monte Cucco itself, take the road east out of Costacciaro and carry on until you get to the turn towards Pian delle Macinare, whence a footpath leads to the summit.

Less energetically, you may take the Roman Via Flaminia south to Sigillo, once an important town on the so-called Byzantine corridor, by which Rome maintained links with Ravenna across Longobard territory. It was utterly destroyed in 1230 by the Holy

Clustered rooftops at Gualdo Tadino.

Brightly glazed tiles decorate a window at Gualdo Tadino.

Roman Emperor Frederick II (1220–50), and only rebuilt thanks to the generosity of the Perugians, who gave the townspeople a set of statutes decreeing that Sigillo was 'to be defended as though it were our own city of Perugia'.

Beyond Sigillo, turn off the main road and up the hill to the pleasant old town of Fossato di Vico, which, like its neighbour, was refounded in the Middle Ages on the site of a Roman settlement. You should try to get here on Good Friday, when the local people perform an ancient Passion play in full costume, with the various incidents from the gospel story taking place along a sort of Via Crucis through the oldest part of the town, culminating at the castle. All three churches deserve a glance: gothic San Benedetto contains a frescoed portrait of Pope Urban V (1362–70), the Cappella della Piaggiola has a cycle of miscellaneous scenes (including the Mystic Marriage of St Catherine) and San Pietro is good, solid, rustic romanesque.

From Fossato, go south to Gualdo Tadino, which lies on a hillside overlooking a fertile plain, not unlike Gubbio. This is the Tadinum mentioned in the Eugubine Tables: Gualdo, from the German *wald* (wood), was added by the Longobards. Before they arrived in the sixth century, the town had been the scene, in 552, of a ferocious and decisive battle between the ever valiant Totila, leading his apparently invincible Goths, and the Byzantine army commanded by the one-eyed eunuch Narses.

Totila was no mere barbarian brute. As depicted by Edward Gibbon in his *Decline and Fall of the Roman Empire* (1776–88), he emerges as a dashing, spirited, imaginative hero, the Napoleon of the Goths, 'chaste and temperate', 'the gallant and accomplished youth'. For twelve years, from 541 to 552, the fortunes of Italy lay in his hands, and barely a town in Umbria escaped a visitation from his horde. While the high command of the Emperor Justinian's Byzantine armies was torn in half with intrigues, jealousies and suspicions, Totila seized every advantage lying in his way, until Narses the eunuch, 'ranked among the few who have rescued that unhappy name from the contempt and hatred of mankind', gained control of the imperial forces.

Narses succeeded where others had failed in uniting various factions and races into a convincing battle array. When at last the two armies faced each other below Gualdo Tadino, the eunuch cunningly rode to and fro among his host of Greeks, Persians, Longobards and Huns dangling gold chains and bracelets before them as an earnest of the fruits of victory. Six thousand Goths were slaughtered in the battle and Totila himself was killed with a savage lance-thrust by Asbad, prince of a Germanic tribe called the Gepids who nurtured an ancient grudge against the Goths. The jewel-encrusted bonnet and bloodstained robe of the self-styled 'King of Italy' were carried in triumph to Justinian at Constantinople.

Gualdo was sacked in 996 by the Emperor Otto III (983–1002), out of spite at its support of a rebellious Roman nobleman and, like most of the other towns in this part of Umbria, which have had similarly chequered careers, was rebuilt during the twelfth and thirteenth centuries, when the centre of the town was moved up the hill for greater safety. When Napoleon annexed the Papal States to his French empire in 1808, he gave Gualdo Tadino important privileges, which its citizens were determined not to forget when the papal *ancien régime* was restored by the Congress of Vienna in 1815, and the town became a thorn in the side of the Vatican during the Risorgimento

Gualdo, with its brightly patterned local pottery and its tasty sausage known as *soppressata* (not so much 'suppressed' as 'compressed'), is the more attractive for having retained so much of its medieval essence intact. The cathedral of San Benedetto, however questionable the appeal of the modern paintings and furnishings inside, has kept its elegant fourteenth-century stonework on the arches of the doorways and the double rose window. From here, walk along Corso Italia, past the fountain by one of my favourite Tuscan architects, Antonio da Sangallo the Elder (1453–1534), and mount the hillside towards the citadel, known as the Rocca Flea and built by Emperor Frederick II in 1237. This now contains the town archives and a small museum, but the sense of its beginnings as a fortress and look-out post is still very strong.

Back along Corso Italia, you come at last to the church of San Francesco, most intelligently restored during the 1960s to its earliest form as a gothic building of the early fourteenth century and now the town's picture gallery. It was already rich in frescoes, especially in the apse, which was decorated around 1460 by Matteo da Gualdo, the highly talented and idiosyncratic local master born here in about 1435, whose work became so widely sought after throughout Umbria.

His *Madonna with Saints* (1477) forms one of the true glories of what is in any event a fascinatingly diverse little collection. Framed in an ogival arch, the Virgin sits on a grandly classical throne which is faintly disappearing into the forest of gilded tendrils behind. She and her attendant saints have curiously elongated faces and bodies, draped in robes which recall much earlier medieval and even byzantine models, yet it is impossible to apply simple terms like 'old-fashioned' to anything as personal in style as this. Compare it,

This expansive rose window dominates the façade of the *duomo* at Gualdo Tadino.

while you are here, with the ornate polyptych painted six years earlier by Nicolò Alunno (1430–1502), an equally arresting master – surely the two must have known each other – whom you will meet again on your travels across these Umbrian hills.

Though they dedicated a church to him, the citizens of Gualdo Tadino were not particularly welcoming to St Francis of Assisi. When he first arrived here with his brethren, he was jeered at and stoned, so that he felt justified in obeying Christ's command to wash the town's dust from his feet; on his return some years later, though, he was allotted a small hermitage, which alas no longer survives. Nowadays you will find Gualdo a good deal more hospitable, especially if you hunt out the Gigiotto restaurant in Via Morone. They have been serving hungry wanderers here since 1875, and you can eat delicious local lamb, home-made green ravioli and *bruschetta* (thick slices of toast soaked in olive oil) spread with Umbrian black truffles.

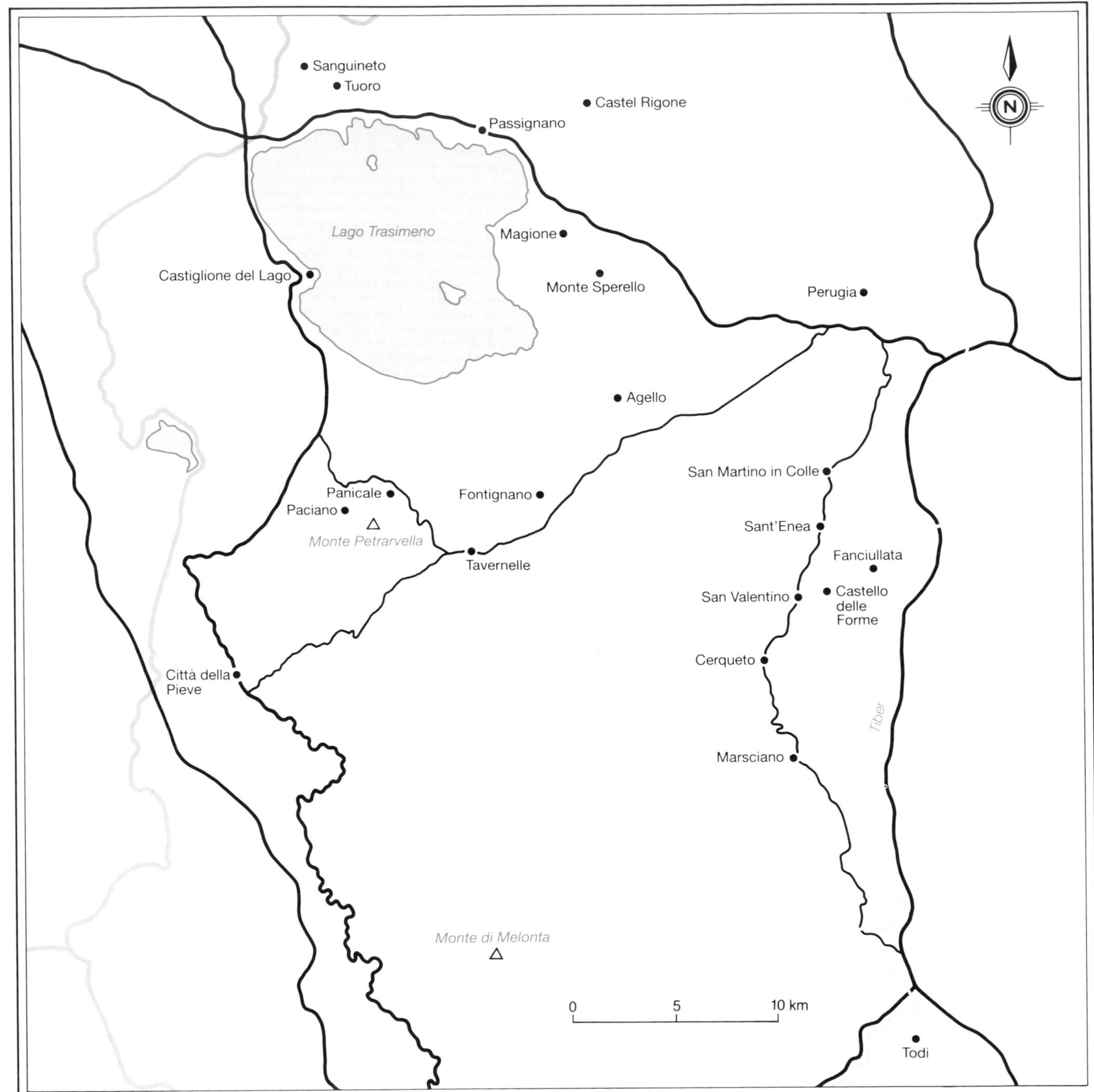
Sanguineto
Tuoro
Castel Rigone
Passignano
Lago Trasimeno
Magione
Castiglione del Lago
Monte Sperello
Perugia
Agello
San Martino in Colle
Panicale
Fontignano
Paciano
Sant'Enea
Monte Petrarvella
Tavernelle
Fanciullata
San Valentino
Castello delle Forme
Cerqueto
Città della Pieve
Tiber
Marsciano
Monte di Melonta
0
5
10 km
Todi

2
City of Popes and Painters

Lake Trasimeno – Perugia – Città della Pieve

Natural frontiers are the key to Umbria, and none is more definitive than Lake Trasimeno, the fourth largest lake in Italy after Garda, Como and Maggiore. It does not, of course, possess their advantage of a majestic Alpine setting, and it is far shallower (barely eight metres at its deepest), but it has the same quality of romantic expansiveness, an inland sea if ever there was, with bays and capes and islands, and a certain undeniable grandeur in the suddenness with which its surrounding little hills crowd up to the shore.

Like other Italian lakes, it has been substantially tamed by man. Its still relatively unpolluted waters support commercial fishing for local restaurants (eels were, and indeed are, the classic speciality) and the lakeside is dotted with jetties for boating and sandy bathing places. What ought to be stressed, however, is that none of this human intrusion on the serenity of nature is ugly or uncontrolled. Even at the popular little summer resorts of Passignano or Castiglione del Lago, there is none of the rowdiness and vulgarity of the seaside, and the placidity of the lake is rarely troubled.

On one never-to-be-forgotten occasion its waters really did run with blood. In 217 BC the great Carthaginian army of Hannibal, which had already defeated the Romans among the vineyards of western Lombardy, swept southwards into central Italy. Relying on what turned out to be inaccurate information regarding the willingness of the Umbrians to rebel against Rome, Hannibal arrived on the shores of Trasimeno, having outmanœuvred the Roman forces at Arezzo and Cortona and preserved his international army (including the only elephant to have survived the Alpine passes) intact and raring for combat.

The pursuing Romans were led by the consul Flaminius himself, ready to take any sort of risk in his desperation to head off the biggest threat to her power that republican Rome had ever faced. There can be no doubt as to who was the better general, and Hannibal in any case had time on his side in which to take stock of the terrain and set the perfect lethal trap for Flaminius as his legionaries marched between the mountains and the lake. In the natural amphitheatre of hills west of the village of Tuoro on Trasimeno's northern shore, Hannibal stationed his Libyan and Iberian troops, leaving a small body of men at the eastern end as if to suggest an army marching away towards Perugia.

Once Flaminius had advanced through the defile and into the valley, on the morning of 24 June 217 BC, a band of Celtic warriors descended from the hillside to cut off his retreat. The rising mists revealed Hannibal's main force prepared to strike, and the Carthaginian horsemen, falling upon the Romans, drove them back

towards the lake as the Libyans and Iberians closed in to finish them off. The battle lasted a mere three hours, with Flaminius cut to pieces by a Gaulish spearman and fifteen thousand of his men slaughtered as they struggled in the reeds and mud of Trasimeno itself. Only the vanguard initially sent forward in pursuit of the pretended fugitives managed to escape with the news to Rome. The city was literally stunned into silence by the shock of the defeat.

The battle left its mark on the landscape. Not only does the name of the hamlet Sanguineto, reached up a turn off the lakeside road, preserve the memory of a reeking massacre, but the ground continues to yield its harvest of weapons, helmets, horse-harness and skeletons, over 2000 years after the fray. Apart from the hurriedly dug mass graves and the tombs of the thirty Carthaginian noblemen killed in the fight, archaeologists have discovered the special cremation pits in which Hannibal ordered the burning of the corpses for fear of epidemics. You can see many of the finds in local museums, such as that at Perugia.

East of Tuoro the road loops southwards to pass through Passignano, a sedate little bathing place from which you can take one of the ferries across Trasimeno to the islands. Of these three, the Isola Minore is what its name suggests, very small indeed, and Polvese, the largest, is a vast olive grove, whose old sandstone church of San Secondo has been re-opened in recent years. Most rewarding and seductive, to a point at which the traveller has little wish to return from it to the mainland, is the Isola Maggiore.

On its eastern shore, what first catches your eye is the pretty castellated nineteenth-century Villa Isabella, built from a suppressed Franciscan convent (the saint is said to have spent forty-two days of Lenten fasting here in 1211, eating only half a loaf of bread), and as the boat rounds the island the little village comes into view with its brick-paved streets and houses of friable golden stone. On the way to an excellent fish luncheon at the Sauro restaurant at the north end of the village, it is worth looking into the church, with its delightfully primitive icing-sugar baroque decoration and a not unpleasing air of slow decomposition. After lunch, walk up the hill to the church of San Michele Arcangelo, built in the early fourteenth century, decorated with anonymous frescoes of evangelists and saints and containing, over the altar, a *Crucifixion* by Bartolomeo Caporali. From outside San Michele you gain a splendid prospect across the lake towards the rolling border country of southern Tuscany.

The colours of sunset transform Lake Trasimeno.

If you can force yourself to leave the Isola Maggiore, there is a scatter of those little *borghi*, or fortress villages, to be explored on the mainland. Typical of the Umbrian landscape, these are also eloquent of the historical experience of small communities in Italy between the fall of the Roman empire and the growth of stable government during the Renaissance. The village, perched watchfully upon its hilltop, could turn at a moment's notice into a defensible stronghold, shutting the gates on its approach roads and manning its walls and towers.

At Castel Rigone, which you reach by taking the Umbertide road out of Passignano, the *rocca*, or citadel, in which the inhabitants could make their last desperate stand, is in ruins, but in compensation there is the Madonna dei Miracoli. This church is an outstandingly beautiful example of the northern Italian architectural styles which spread to Umbria during the late fifteenth century, with a graceful portico adorned with a lunette showing the Madonna with Saints Augustine and Bartholomew, carved by the Florentine Domenico Bertini in 1512.

Magione, on the way to Perugia from Passignano, is less immediately attractive but far more obviously imposing, since it was here in 1420 that the Knights Hospitaller, now known as the Knights of Malta, built their great four-towered castle, incorporating the remains of a Benedictine abbey. Magione, incidentally, is a medieval word meaning the same as the English 'mansion' or French *maison* – the knights' house. It was the birthplace of that fearless monkish explorer

Giovanni da Pian di Carpine, who carried the Franciscan rule into Germany in 1221 and went thence to Hungary, Poland and Spain. Finally, seized with a chronic wanderlust, he set off to bear St Francis's teachings to the Khan of Tartary, and stayed for eighteen years among the Mongols before returning in 1248 to write the *Historia Mongolorum*, dying in 1252 on yet another journey, this time to the wild mountains of Dalmatia.

From Magione, you can take a pleasant southerly detour past Monte Sperello and the medieval castle of Monte Melino before turning back on to the main road. The hills grow softer, the colours on their slopes more subtly varied, Umbria in short becomes more Umbrian and Tuscany is left behind for ever as you cover the final stretch of the highway to Perugia.

No sensitive tourist in Italy ignores the travellers who have come before him across the centuries, or fails to reflect that not all of them were enchanted with the surrounding prospects or pleased with the welcome they received. When General Sir George Whitmore KCH, Commandant of the Royal Military Academy at Woolwich, travelled northwards along this very road in July 1830, he did so in a state of mounting rage at Italian customs. At Passignano he and his family were provided with an atrocious meal since it was a religious fast-day:

> If the *vetturino* [coachman] had not brought some potatoes with him from Perugia we might have starved. The eggs were not eatable from having been fried in bad oil – the wine was quite sour – a steak defied all attempts at mastication – the female waiter was woefully seamed with scrofula, and a starved cat and mangy cur haunted us during the whole of our halt.

Sunlight and shadow in the main square of Castel Rigone.

Typical rustic Umbrian stonework surrounds a doorway at Castel Rigone; a roman head has been incorporated in the wall.

Whitmore had nevertheless been greatly taken with Perugia. 'Who is not enchanted' he wrote 'with the high-towering city, when, having climbed with the assistance of quadrupedal oxen the ramps of a steep mountain, its long line of houses first greets the view?' The oxen are no longer necessary, and an initial encounter with the town is nowadays not quite so enchanting. Few places in Italy possess more unpromising approaches: the whole of the plain below the long ridge on which old Perugia lies is scattered with an unsightly rash of early 1960s high-rise blocks and factories, whose position and design reflect a complete lack of sympathy with the landscape.

Do not be put off. Once you have escaped the suburban mess at the foot of the hill and hauled yourself up the zigzagging roads from the *superstrada* or taken the somewhat protracted bus-ride from the station, one of the most rewarding, lively and potently individual of Italian cities awaits you. Here, some visual delight or other always crowns the scramble up an interminable flight of steps or the weary trudge against the gradient of yet another steep slope.

The prevailing colour of Perugia is a kind of soft dove grey, which seems appropriate to a place of such venerable seniority. It was there on top of the bluff by the time the Etruscans arrived in the seventh century BC, to make it into one of the chief strongholds of their confederation of twelve cities. The ruler of the league was not, as once thought, a hereditary king, but an elected leader known as the *lucumo*, whose principal role was to command the army in battles against neighbouring peoples, more especially the Romans. In 309 BC Rome finally seized Perugia, wielding a somewhat uneasy authority over her, which received its severest test when Hannibal, fresh from his victory at Trasimeno, marched under the walls of the town but decided there was no time to be wasted on a siege.

Perugia has been historically unlucky in its relations with conquerors, rulers and governors. In 41 BC, when Mark Antony had left Rome for Egypt and the embraces of Cleopatra, his rejected wife Fulvia and his brother Lucius rebelled against his fellow triumvir Octavius Caesar, and Lucius sought refuge at Perugia. Octavius's siege successfully reduced the town to starvation and submission, but his inflexible harshness condemned 300 of the chief citizens to a mass execution which he witnessed personally. Pleased with the results, he decided to sack the city on the following day.

In the intervening hours a noble Perugine, Caius Cestius Macedonicus, set fire to his house and stabbed himself within the burning ruins. As most of the town was built of wood, the fire spread swiftly, and by morning the hotly contested Perugia was a heap of ashes. All Octavius was able to take back to Rome was a statue of the goddess Juno, the city's patroness, whom the Perugines promptly abandoned in favour of Vulcan, god of fire, whose temple remained appropriately unscathed. To his eternal credit Octavius, when he became the Emperor Augustus, rebuilt everything on a more lasting and substantial scale, and gave orders that the town was to be called Augusta in addition to its own name.

After the empire's fall, Perugia survived sieges by Goths, Longobards and Byzantines, only to grow harder and more determined than ever to hold onto some sort of independence at whatever cost. Her people were – and probably still would be, if again put to the test – noted for their ferocity and bravery in combat, and during the early Middle Ages neighbouring cities like Assisi, Gubbio, Spoleto and Todi learned this to their cost, as did Perugia's Tuscan trade rivals, Arezzo and Siena. When the Aretines hanged some Perugine prisoners with dead cats round their necks and their tunics stuck with the little fish from Lake Trasimeno of which they were notoriously fond, Perugia struck back with a bloody revenge, and when the Sienese tried conclusions with her, some fifty of their flags were captured and tied to horses' tails.

Only the papacy played for time with Perugia, a prize plum which must one day drop into its lap. Freedom, prosperity, a strong currency and a university to rival those of Bologna and Pavia made the

---

A Perugian townscape from Via del Acquedotto.

Perugines vain and over-confident, and the popes were now able to exploit the factional rivalry between the ordinary citizens and the increasingly powerful nobility. Perugia's story during the fourteenth and fifteenth centuries is almost a parody or a pastiche of our wildest fantasies of violence and passion in renaissance Italy, *The Duchess of Malfi* crossed with *The Mysteries of Udolpho*, and its scenes and personalities flash upon the inward eye like moments from some relentlessly melodramatic newsreel. Biordo Michelotti is cut down by conspirators and his blood collected in a silver basin by the citizens; Braccio Fortebraccio gives his wife Nicolina a casket telling her not to open it until after his death or his return home – when he dies under the walls of Aquila, she unlocks the box only to discover a black veil and a sceptre; the Oddi fight the Della Corgna and the Staffa do battle with the Arciprete, while jugs and pitchers are hurled into the street from the windows above, and the clergy and university professors bustle out from their houses to persuade the brawlers to lay down their arms.

The *ne plus ultra* of savagery, egoism and tyranny was reached with the rise, during the early 1400s, of the Baglioni family. Everyone was afraid of them, but even the many who hated them admired their physical courage, and their beauty was a legend throughout Italy. Where they walked, crowds gathered to marvel at their handsome faces and lofty stature. Their very names – Gismondo, Astorre, Grifonetto, Atalanta, Zenobia – have the dimension of romance. Many were put to death in the apalling sequence of murders and revenges known as *il gran tradimento* ('the great betrayal') which took place in 1500, when Grifonetto tried to wipe out his entire clan and was himself killed by order of his cousin Gianpaolo.

It was time for the popes to close in, as one by one the remaining Baglioni picked each other off. In 1535 Paul III (1534–49), one of the most ruthless and uncompromising of holy fathers, drove out Ridolfo Baglioni (1518–54) and took over Perugia at the head of fourteen cardinals and 1300 troops. When the city later dared to revolt against his imposition of a salt tax, he abolished its former privileges, tore down the old Baglioni palaces, along with nine churches, twenty towers and over a hundred houses and, as the ultimate symbol of his authority, raised on top of them (literally, since whole walls and pavements were incorporated within the building) a colossal fortress designed by Da Sangallo the Younger, known as the Rocca Paolina. One of its courtyard walls bore the grimly triumphant inscription *Ad coercendam Perusinorum audaciam* ('To subdue the audacity of the Perugines').

The citizens went on hating the Rocca Paolina for three centuries, whatever the benefits of Papal rule, until, during the tumult and uncertainty of the revolution of 1848, when Perugia was in the hands of a provisional government, the chance at last arrived to do away with it for ever. On 13 December, a procession with flags and military bands, led by Count Benedetto Baglioni, a direct descendant of Ridolfo, marched to the fortress and began the laborious task of dismantling it. Through the faulty operation of explosives, four people were killed and thirty-two injured, but the work went steadily on until political events, in the shape of an Austrian regiment sent by the newly reinstated Pius IX, halted the demolition. But the Perugines detested their Bastille enough to want everything down, and in 1860, when the city was finally annexed to a united Italy, they started again on what was left. Thomas Adolphus Trollope, brother of Anthony the novelist, watched 'a number of people gloating over the progressing destruction of the detested walls, as crowbar and pickaxe did their work'. He noticed an old man with a flowing white beard, who sat watching the slow destruction intently, and asked who he was. 'That old man,' replied Trollope's companion, 'comes here at break of day, and remains till the workmen knock off at night. He was many years a prisoner in the fortress, and was liberated at the fall of the Papal Government.'

By no special irony, the site of the Rocca Paolina, now the Piazza Italia which acts as the city's bus terminus, is the ideal point from which to begin a walk through the centre of Perugia. What remains of the fortress itself upholds the eastern side of this elegant rectangular piazza, and tucked into an angle of one of

Perugia's bitter struggles against nineteenth-century popes commemorated in a noble war memorial.

its bastions is the Porta Marzia, part of the Etruscan rampart cast around the town, of which substantial portions still endure. This gateway was simply blocked in by Antonio da Sangallo when he built the *rocca*, but its original arch with its cross-hatched pilasters remains. The three figures in the niches, between horses' heads, are Jupiter, Castor and Pollux, but Perugian legend always declared that they were members of a family who died from eating poisoned mushrooms.

A door in the wall leads to an extraordinary subterranean experience, that of wandering through what used to be a street of Baglioni palaces, on top of which Paul III simply flung his fort. Here in the lamplit gloom you can see the remains of houses, churches and towers, with the old passageways and cannon emplacements of the *rocca* thrust amid them.

Up above in Piazza Italia is the by no means unpleasing array of late ninteenth-century civic buildings in a style redolent of the confidence (misplaced though this turned out to be) of the newly united Kingdom of Italy. From here, walk down Corso Vannucci, broadest and liveliest of Perugia's central streets, along which the city strolls on its evening *passeggiata*. There is no proper translation for this word, which means the sauntering up and down which takes place on every fine evening of the year in every town and village the length and breadth of Italy. Margaret Symonds and Lina Duff Gordon, barely out of their teens when they published their excellent history of Perugia in 1897, tell us that 'the place is gay enough in spring and summer; indeed the Corso is a good specimen of an Umbrian Piccadilly on a fine May evening, and there are plenty of carriages and good motors in the tourist season'. The carriages and motors have gone, since the street is mercifully restricted to pedestrians, but you need merely to replace today's crowd of students, businessmen and a discreet scatter of tourists with the women in humming-bird hats and moustachioed men in boaters whom Lina and Margaret saw, and you can say that nothing has really changed.

Vannucci was the surname of Perugia's greatest painter, who since his death has always been known as Pietro Perugino, though in fact he was born (in 1445 or 1450) at Città della Pieve, on the other side of Lake Trasimeno. The Vannucci were themselves on the edge of poverty, and took little Pietro, aged eight, to the workshop of a Perugine artist as an apprentice, presumably as much to save money as to foster his gifts, but the boy prospered and was soon sent to study in Florence. By 1490 he had become one of the most celebrated painters in all Italy, though many of his commissions were carried out by students and merely given their finishing touches by the master's hand. He died of the plague at Fontignano, west of Perugia, in 1523, and is rumoured to have been bundled into a hastily dug grave by the roadside, having refused the last rites, but this detail seems at odds with his always reverent handling of religious themes.

His reputation endured throughout the seventeenth and eighteenth centuries, when he was often preferred to Raphael. Oliver Goldsmith, in *The Vicar of Wakefield*

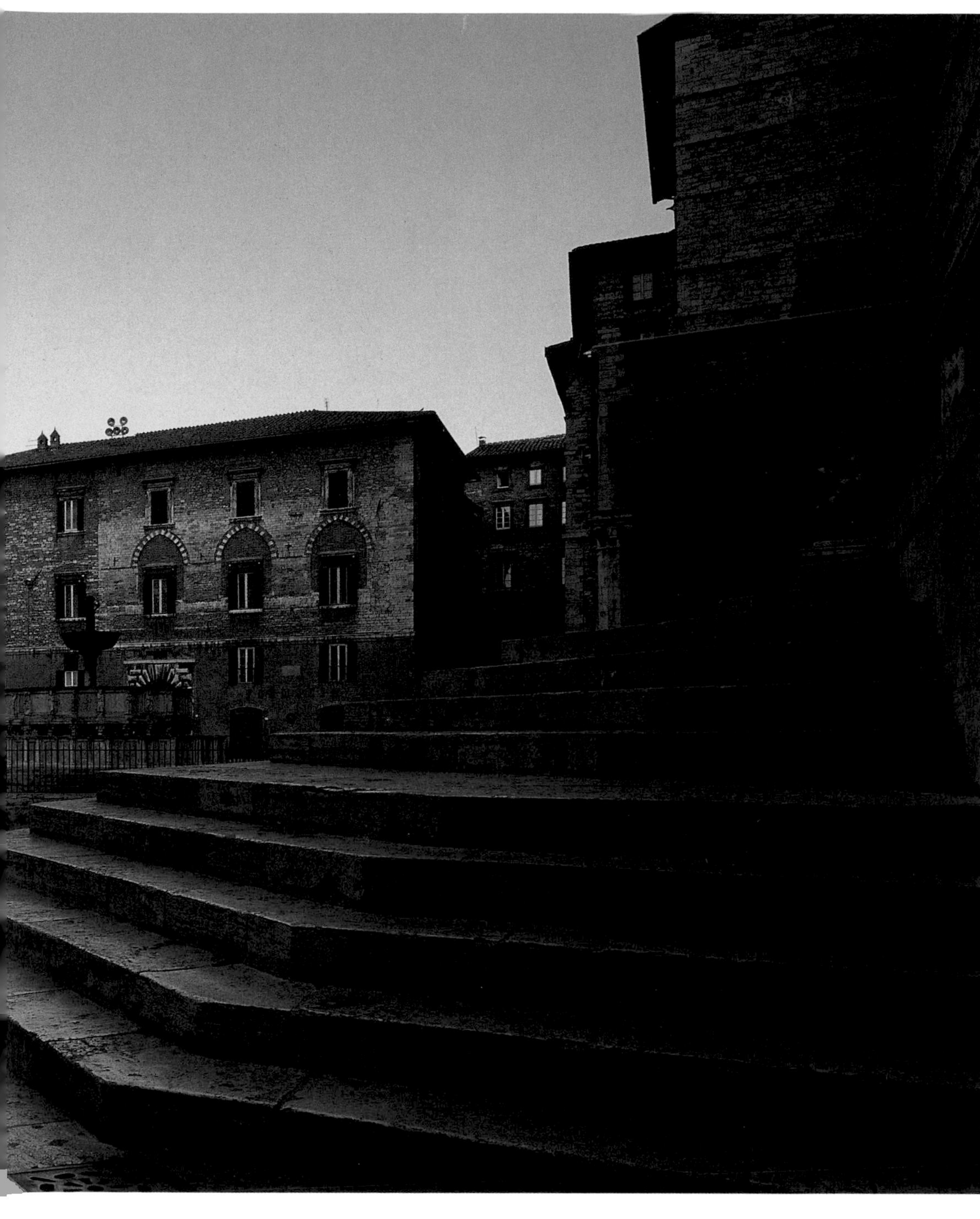

Perugia's majestic Palazzo dei Priori at sunrise.

(1766), wittily tells us that the secret of passing for a 'connoscento' consists of adhering to two rules, 'the one always to observe that the picture might have been better if the painter had taken more pains; and the other, to praise the works of Pietro Perugino'. He was a favourite with Napoleon Bonaparte (1769–1821), whose pillaging of Italian works of art had such a drastic effect on the churches and religious houses of Umbria, and much of his best work is now scattered around European galleries as a result of its enforced wanderings over the Alps after the French invasion. It was only in the nineteenth century that Perugino's achievement was severely depreciated. Critics, especially English and American, thought of him as an insincere lightweight, and it comes as no surprise to find Henry James (writing in 1909 but reflecting a taste formed thirty years earlier) complaining of 'the uniform type of his creatures, their monotonous grace, their prodigious invariability'.

Maybe Perugino was rather too in love with his own facility, and perhaps there is something a trifle too saccharin-sweet in the melting softness of his brushwork, but when he is good, he is so very good that you understand at once why the rich merchants and nobles and ecclesiasts of the Renaissance courted his talent so readily.

It was merchants, the Perugine Moneychangers' Guild, who commissioned him in 1496 to paint the walls of their Sala del Collegio del Cambio, an immense hall within the Palazzo dei Priori, which stands at the northern end of Corso Vannucci. The *palazzo* itself is an outstanding example of late medieval civic architecture, an immense, crenellated, gothic fortress-palace of positively inescapable grandeur, begun in 1297 and carried on during the whole of the following century, to be completed in 1423. Down the ample flight of steps below its north doorway would come the *podestà* and the four mace-bearers, with their silver staves each decorated with the griffin emblem of the city, followed by the ten priors with their gold chains, the whole procession being heralded by the six state trumpeters, whose silver trumpets were hung with red-and-white silk banners.

High above this door you can see the griffin, together with a lion, from whose paws once dangled the keys to the gates of Assisi, raided in 1321, and the chains from the gallows of Siena, spoils from the battle of Torrita thirty years later. These were carried off for ever by unruly pro-Austrian militiamen in 1799, and all that remains are the metal bars from which they hung.

Inside the Palazzo dei Priori is a sequence of magnificent rooms, some of them still used for public meetings. The Sala dei Notari, from 1583 onwards, was a lawyers' office (*notaro* means an attorney), but the ceiling frescoes here are older than this, dating from the end of the thirteenth century and assigned to Giotto's contemporary Pietro Cavallini (1273–1308). Other adjacent rooms are not always visitable, but you can occasionally get a glimpse of the Sala del Consiglio Comunale, with a fresco by Pinturicchio, *Madonna and Child between Two Angels*, and the Sala Rossa. This contains a painting by the sixteenth-century Assisian artist Dono Doni showing the historic moment when Pope Julius III, in February 1553, returned to Perugia all the privileges which Paul III had peevishly stripped from it thirteen years earlier.

It was in the Sala del Consiglio Comunale that in 1375 a typically Perugine episode took place. After a battle in the Tiber valley, the citizens returned with a number of English prisoners, members of the dreaded mercenary 'White Company' led by the great *condottiere* Sir John Hawkwood (*c*.1320–94), known to the Italians as Giovanni Acuto. The prisoners wrote pathetically enough to their captors, saying 'We also are Christians, and perishing of thirst. Have mercy on your wretched English vassals.' Foolishly, the Perugines let the English go free, only to find themselves attacked afresh by Hawkwood's band, who killed 1500 men and took the *podestà* prisoner. After that, so they say, this room where the decision to release the English

Variegated bands of medieval carving surround the portal of Palazzo dei Priori, Perugia.

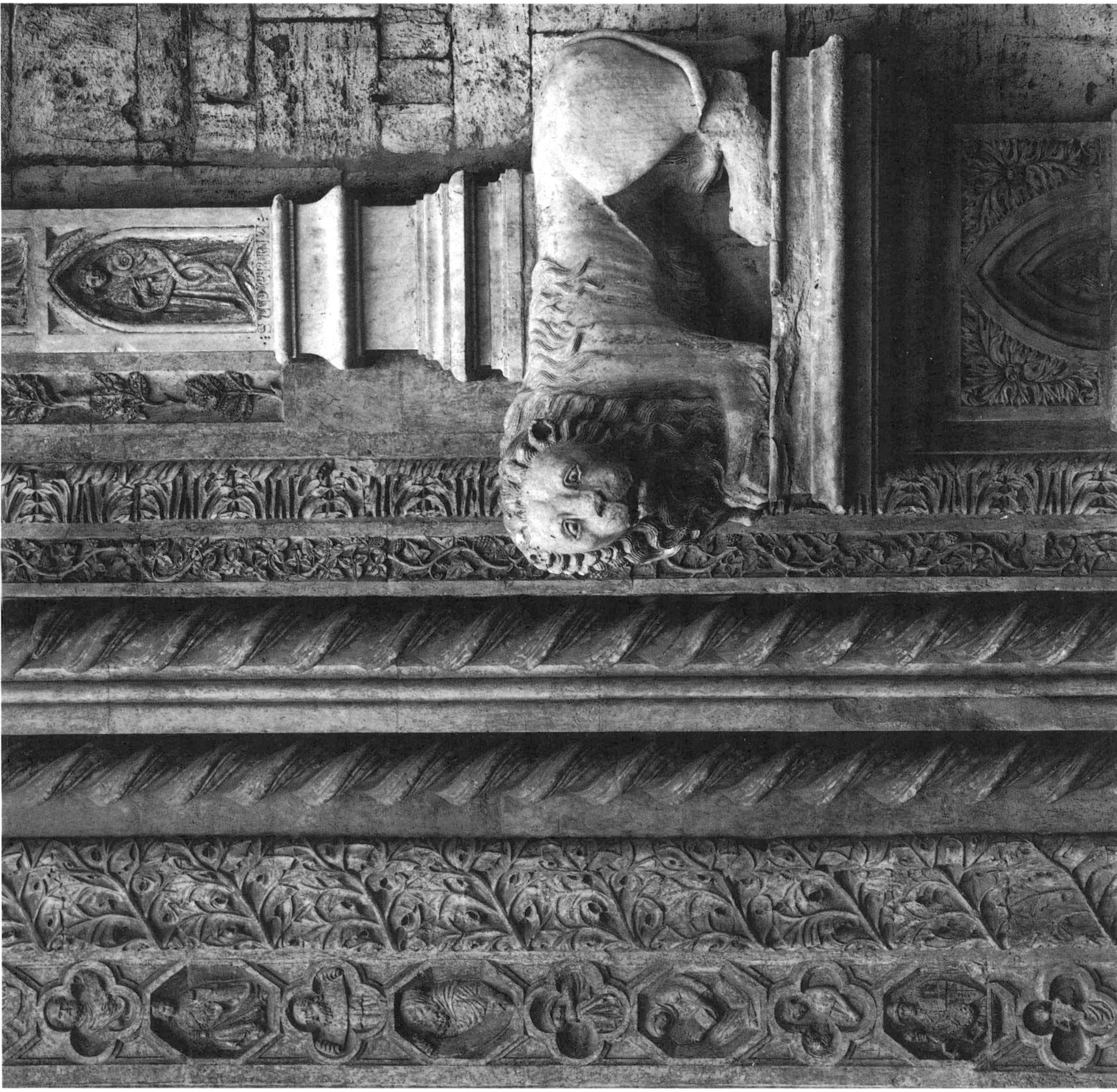

ɪore the name 'Sala del Malconsiglio' (Room ısel).

ıird floor of the Palazzo dei Priori is the :ionale dell'Umbria, the most important ·e showcase of regional painting in all its appealing diversity, but also displaying works by artists more obviously associated with nearby Tuscany, some of whom carried out major commissions in the Umbrian towns. One of these was Fra Angelico (1387 or 1400–1455, referred to in Italian guidebooks and labels as 'il Beato Angelico'), the Dominican monk from Fiesole, above Florence. His polyptych, *Madonna and Child with Angels and Saints*, is one of the glories of the gallery for the miraculous way in which its radiant reds and blues and the mottled marble of the steps to the Virgin's throne seem to vie in brightness with the gilt ground against which the figures are placed.

A painter considered as much Umbrian as Tuscan is Piero della Francesca (1420–92). His great altar-piece, showing the Madonna with attendant saints, would be magnificent enough in itself, but the predella panels below, showing the miracles of St Anthony and St Elizabeth and the receiving of the stigmata by Francis, reveal a freer hand at work, and the *Annunciation* above, with a setting of idealized renaissance architecture, is one of Piero's most deeply personal utterances, the clue, as it were, to the whole ensemble.

As for the native Umbrians themselves, what warmth, what intimacy and gentleness! Here is Marino da Perugia, an artist of whom we know nothing beyond the *Madonna in Majesty* which he signed in 1309 on the sword carried by St Peter at the bottom left-hand corner, and the airily graceful Benedetto Bonfigli (1420–96), in whose *Annunciation* the blond-ringletted Angel Gabriel is crowned with a garland of pink roses, and Fiorenzo di Lorenzo (1440–1522), one of those painters whom you will never see reproduced in art histories, but who become instantly attractive when met in contexts such as this.

The Palazzo dei Priori is really several buildings in one, and a separate entrance will take you into the Collegio del Cambio, the hall of the moneychangers, begun in 1452 by Bartolomeo di Mattiolo and Lodovico di Antonibo. It was here, in the vast vaulted audience room surrounded by inlaid wooden benches, that Pietro Perugino set to work on his splendid fresco cycle in 1496.

The idea for this sequence of paintings is, you might say, the central concept of renaissance humanism, that of an attempt to fuse the best impulses of classical antiquity with the essential values of the Christian world, whether through a genuine belief that the latter represented a culmination of the former, or through a covert nostalgia for a romanticized Greek and Roman past without the dimension of Mother Church. At Perugia the inspiration belonged to Francesco Matarazzo, the city's greatest chronicler, a lecturer in the university and secretary to the ten priors. He it was who devised the sequence of ancient worthies (Cato, Socrates, Trajan, Horatius and Pericles), the allegorical figures (Temperance, Fortitude and Prudence), the pagan gods and goddesses and the six sybils whose prophecies were held to have foretold Christ's birth. It was Matarazzo also who devised the series of Christian icons (Isaiah, Moses, Daniel and David), and the scenes of the Nativity and the Transfiguration.

It is hard to imagine a better guide than this to what the men and women of the Renaissance set out to achieve, and the poignancy of this vision of a peaceable kingdom of pagan and Christian is all the greater when we consider that it was planned and painted during one of the most turbulent and bloodthirsty moments in Perugia's history, when the city's inhabitants were violating almost daily the sanctity of those ideals implied by the Collegio del Cambio's frescoes. This was the time of Grifonetto Baglioni's *gran tradimento*, and of his cousin Gianpaolo's terrible revenge, when he decorated the *palazzo* with traitors' heads and with portraits of them hanging upside down, a time when the streets ran with blood and no man knew who might next be his enemy.

Yet Perugino's frescoes, in which he was assisted by his pupils Andrea d'Assisi (1484–1516) and the young Raphael, are suffused with an extraordinary gentleness and choreographic elegance. The sybils pose like women just leaving a dance-floor, still feeling, as it

Garlands of fruit surround a heraldic emblem on a Perugian door.

were, the pattern of the steps they have been treading. The emperors and generals and prophets have slender, feminine hands and, as one Victorian commentator remarks, 'their long, limp bodies would have fallen as field flowers fall before the scythe or even a summer shower'. They are far removed in spirit from the worldly, bullying churchmen who were keenly eyeing Perugia with a view to catching it up into their domains.

You can see Perugino's self-portrait in a panel on the right-hand wall, pug-nosed, thin-lipped, triple-chinned and not at all like the kind of person modern cliché has taught us to think of as artistic. This is fulfilled instead by the representation, among the prophets, of the youthful Daniel, with his straggling blond curls and immense brown eyes, a figure convincingly claimed to represent the young Raphael.

Outside the Palazzo dei Priori, in Piazza IV Novembre (it used to be called Piazza San Lorenzo), stands one of Perugia's best-loved works of art, the Fontana Maggiore, designed in 1275–7 by Nicola Pisano (1220–78) and his son Giovanni (1245–1314), working with Fra Bevignate. The fountain's outer basin is decorated with twenty-four white marble bas-reliefs, showing the months of the year (January's pig-killer is strong enough to carry his dead boar on his shoulder, August is vigorously flailing the newly harvested corn and so on), a wimpled dame out falconing, Romulus and Remus being suckled by the she-wolf, and scenes from Aesop's fables. The inner basin carries Giovanni Pisano's beautiful series of caryatids, two of which are portraits of contemporary figures, Matteo da Correggio, the *podestà* of the day, and Ermanno de Sassoferrato, another civic official known as the Capitano del Popolo. The work is crowned by Giovanni's group of three water nymphs, apparently the oldest piece of bronze casting to survive from the Middle Ages.

Now climb the steps to the baroque porch of the cathedral of San Lorenzo. The platform in front of the doorway is a favourite Perugine meeting-place and an excellent spot from which to photograph the fountain and the *palazzo* beyond. To your right you will find a dramatically executed statue of Perugia's beloved Julius III, Giovan Maria Ciocchi del Monte, who was welcomed during his short papacy (1549–55) with almost abject delight by the citizens. This is the work of Vincenzo Danti (1530–76), said to be only nineteen when he undertook it. He was a locally born sculptor and you can see other works by him in the Palazzo dei Priori and in the basilica of San Francesco at Assisi.

The cathedral itself, begun in 1345, replaces an old building pulled down over a hundred years earlier, but even once the foundation stone was laid, there was no serious attempt to carry on the new work for several decades, and the whole enterprise was only completed in 1490. It is not especially striking from any architectural viewpoint: a series of tall octagonal pillars rises towards shallow gothic ribbed vaults, crossed, as nearly always in Italy, by iron stanchions. The ceilings are covered in mediocre late eighteenth-century frescoes, and the columns of the nave have a stucco cladding painted to achieve a sort of mock marble

effect. Yet there is something oddly, inexplicably comforting about the homely gloom of this place, lit only occasionally by the cluster of candles in front of an altar or by the feeble glimmer of day filtering through the stained glass, which makes you want to linger within it as an anonymous shadow.

Directly to your right as you enter is the chapel of San Bernardino. This belonged to the Merchants' Guild, who bought the rights to it in 1515 and later installed the handsome set of wooden stalls, made by Ercole del Tommaso del Riccio and Jacopo Fiorentino in 1567. To paint their altar-piece, a *Deposition from the Cross*, they chose Federico Barocci (*c*.1535–1612), the last really distinguished artist produced by the city of Urbino. Barocci is best known by his buoyantly exalted *Madonna del Popolo* which hangs in the Uffizi at Florence, but a recent comprehensive exhibition of his work allowed us to see why he achieved such celebrity in the late sixteenth century as the heir to Titian, Raphael and Michelangelo. He loved Perugia and adopted two orphan boys here, to whom he taught painting. One of them established himself successfully as his foster-father's pupil, but the other was simply noted as a good-looking idler with a devastating effect on women, which brought him his death at the hands of a jealous rival.

Professional rivalry is said to have caused Barocci's own death from the effects of a slow poison while painting this very altar-piece, but this is mere fancy, since he is known to have completed it in 1569 and lived on for another forty-odd years. The assured, vibrant, highly imaginative treatment of the subject is hardly the work of a dying man. A storm is blowing up, and the wind snatches at the robes of the women as they strain to catch the swooning Virgin, and at the cloaked figure on the left holding the dead Christ, while another man toils down the ladder with a pair of pincers and the Crown of Thorns. The whole ensemble is doubtless rather too carefully posed and full of allusions to earlier treatments of the scene (had Barocci seen Rosso Fiorentino's account of it at Volterra, I wonder?), but the subtleties of colour and the sense conveyed of a drama of physical movement and effort make this one of the most memorable works of art in all Perugia.

Further along the right side of the nave is the Cappella del Sacramento, designed by Galeazzo Alessi (1512–72) and containing the remains – or parts of them – of three out of four popes who died at Perugia. Urban IV's death in 1264 after a reign of just three years was from natural causes, but since he was morbidly obsessed with plots to poison him, it is no wonder that for many years he was believed to have succumbed to a basket of figs tainted with a mixture of arsenic and boars' grease. Martin IV (1281–5) killed himself with a surfeit of eels, and Dante placed him among the gluttons in Hell: 'for his breakfast he is purged of the eels of Bolsena and *vernaccia* wine'. The most distinguished and powerful of them was Innocent III (1198–1216), scourge of the Albigensian heretics, giver of the Church's official blessing to the Franciscans, architect of papal authority and enemy of King John of England, whose kingdom he placed under an interdict in a prolonged dispute over the appointment of Stephen Langton as Archbishop of Canterbury. When Innocent died at Perugia on 16 July 1216, while trying to patch up a feud between the towns of Gubbio and Città di Castello, the French diplomat Jacques de Vitry tells us that 'it was then that I appreciated the vanity of worldly pomp, for on the night before the funeral, thieves broke into the cathedral and despoiled the Pope of his precious vestments. With my own eyes I beheld his corpse, half naked, lying in the middle of the church, already beginning to stink'.

On the opposite side of the cathedral you will find the chapel which houses Perugia's most precious relic, the wedding ring of the Blessed Virgin which was stolen from the Tuscan town of Chiusi and brought here by Fra Winter of Mainz in 1472. The ring is made of agate and apparently changes colour according to the disposition of those who look upon it, though it

The medieval Fontana Maggiore, Perugia, the work of Nicola and Giovanni Pisano.

strikes most people as being yellowish-blue in tone. It is kept locked inside fifteen boxes within a gilt bronze and silver tabernacle, and exhibited to the faithful once a year. The altar-piece here is a pallid nineteenth-century copy of Perugino's *Marriage of the Virgin*; the original was looted by the French in 1797 and now hangs in the gallery at Caen in Normandy.

Walk through the sacristy, with its pompous late sixteenth-century frescoes by Giovanni Antonio Pandolfi (d.1581), into the Canonica, the chapter buildings of the cathedral, gathered around two very pretty cloisters, the first of which is lined with a scatter of sculptured fragments from churches and Etruscan tombs. This used to be known as the Vatican of Perugia, since so many popes stayed here, and at least five were elected by conclave here during the thirteenth century. To the left as you emerge into the first cloister, you find the door leading to the Museo Capitolare (or Museo dell'Opera del Duomo). Here, among the glow of illuminated manuscripts, the gleam of monstrances and the lustre of copes and chasubles, you will come upon one of Luca Signorelli's outstanding early achievements, *The Madonna Enthroned among Four Saints*, one of whom is St Onuphrius, in whose chapel in the cathedral the picture formerly stood. Certainly the figures themselves are as good as we might expect from Signorelli, but the most attractive detail lies in the wealth of flowers – lilies, jasmine, violets and convolvulus – with which the artist has bedecked the picture.

From the Canonica, go back into the cathedral square and round behind the Palazzo dei Priori into Via dei Priori, which gives you an excellent introduction to the steeply pitching, narrow streets which are the essence of the Perugine experience. Cars are useless here, and walking, however breathless some of the hills may leave you, offers the only way of really getting to know the colours, textures and layout of the ancient city.

Umbrella pines in the fields near Paciano.

Half-way down Via dei Priori on the right stands the elegant Roman baroque church of San Filippo Neri, designed by Paolo Marucelli (1594–1649) in a style appropriate to the cult of this sixteenth-century saint, founder of the Oratorian Fathers and the Chiesa Nuova in Rome. The brilliantly adorned high altar boasts an *Immaculate Conception* by Pietro da Cortona (1596–1669), whose flamboyant colouring and audacity of composition brought him phenomenal success in Florence and Rome. Next to the unfinished façade of the rather dull church of Santa Teresa, further along to the left and begun during the same period, you can see the Torre degli Scirri, a twelfth-century tower which is one of the last of those medieval family fortresses from which the rival clans of Italian cities used to menace each other in the days of Guelph and Ghibelline bloodshed.

An improving story attaches to the renaissance church on the corner of the square beyond. On 12 September 1512, some young men were playing cards outside a butcher's shop here. When one of them, a barber named Fallerio, swore a dreadful oath on losing the game, the picture of the Madonna in its shrine nearby closed its eyes in shame and kept them shut for four days. The miracle caused special prayers to be said before the precious image which, on 7 April 1513, was installed in the new church, known as the Madonna della Luce, the work of a Perugine goldsmith named Cesarino del Roscetto (d.1527). The fresco over the altar, which we know to be by Perugino's pupil Tiberio d'Assisi (1470–1524), is said to be the picture in question but there is, as so often, some confusion over dates among the historians.

Out under the erstwhile Etruscan Porta Trasimena, nowadays called the Arco di San Luca, you come upon a broad, grassy piazza, dominated on the right by the Franciscan convent (currently occupied by the municipal art college) and the half-ruined gothic pile of San Francesco, begun in 1230. The church's interior is closed (restoration has been going on for more than ten years), but the façade is a weird decorative compromise between gothic and romanesque which looks like the very worst sort of vulgar architectural doodling.

It seems designed, in fact, to throw into relief the exquisite taste and charm of the building on the opposite side of the piazza, the Oratorio de San Bernardino, among the most captivating of Perugia's works of art. Created in 1461, it was intended as a memorial to Bernardino of Siena (1318–1444), who had many times preached in this open space to the citizens, and here, as in his native Tuscany, had become a deeply revered spiritual force among the people. In Perugia his role was not unlike that of his contemporary Savonarola at Florence, inspiring repentant sinners to make bonfires of such worldly vanities as packs of cards, books of astrology, obscene pictures, jewels and cosmetics, but his message, unlike the grim Dominican's, was essentially one of redemption and reconciliation through God's love, and he was swiftly canonized after his death in 1450.

The front of the little oratory is essentially a renaissance *tempietto* (small temple-like building), of the kind on which its architect Agostino di Duccio (1418–81) had already worked at Rimini in the famous Tempio Malatestiano. Here the overall impression is of a conscious blending of Christian images with an exuberant appeal to the classical past of 'Augusta Perusia'. The bishops and angels in shell niches on either side are combined with garlands and a Roman arch and a wonderful sequence of female allegories and dancing angels, their hair and draperies flying in the breeze, their mouths open in song as they beat drums and triangles and sound the lute and violin. The colours too – mottled pink marble, terracotta, green and blue painting – enhance the pervading sense of joy. There is really nothing like it in the whole of Umbria.

Inside the oratory, the altar is a fascinating illustration of the way in which antique Roman art was adapted to Christian imagery. It is made out of a fourth-century marble sarcophagus which once contained the bones of the Franciscan friar Egidio, carved with reliefs of Old Testament scenes, including Noah's Ark and Jonah and the Whale, but in a style that had remained unchanged over hundreds of years spent in depicting the gods and heroes of pagan mythology.

Now walk along Via Pascoli, which winds across the hillside and then slopes suddenly downwards towards Via Sant'Elisabetta, whence you start to climb once again, under one of the innumerable arches which span the narrow Perugine lanes. This brings you out onto the busy, lopsided Piazza Braccio Fortebraccio, with the Italian University for Foreigners to your left, housed in the massive late baroque Palazzo Gallenga Stuart. Built in 1754 by the architects Francesco Bianchi and Pietro Caratoli, it originally belonged to a branch of the great Tuscan Antinori family. Local guidebooks are hopelessly uninformative on the Gallenga Stuarts, but all of them will tell you that the comic dramatist Carlo Goldoni (1707–93) began his acting career here as a little boy, playing a female role in a farce called *La Sorellina di Don Pilone*. Goldoni says that 'the subtle air of the mountainous city' did not agree with his doctor father, so the family moved on, but he might have had some further success here as an actor, since the townsfolk were notoriously stage-struck, and there were theatres not only in noble palaces but at all the colleges and convents as well.

Opposite the palace stands the megalithic Arco d'Augusto, an Etruscan arch made of massive travertine blocks, and crowned by a frieze probably added by the Romans. From the piazza you should now follow the long Corso Garibaldi, which leads you gently up the hill through an outlying quarter of the city formerly celebrated for the evil living and rebelliousness of its inhabitants, but now most agreeably tranquil and sedate. The gothic church of Sant'Agostino, on your right, is worth inspecting for its beautiful choir, whose inlaid woodwork was executed between 1502–32 by the Florentine Baccio d'Agnolo (1462–1543) to a design by Perugino.

The object of this long walk – and you should resist all temptations to abandon it – is one of the loveliest churches in Perugia, and certainly one of the oldest in Italy. On its green lawn between cypress trees, with the open countryside falling away beyond, the temple

Etruscan and Roman masonry combine in the Arco d'Augusto, Perugia.

of Sant 'Angelo has that irresistible savour of antiquity which has somehow survived all attempts by successive epochs to mask or destroy it. Legend says that this was the very temple of Vulcan which survived the fire of 40 BC and was then pulled down and rebuilt by the early Christians using columns from a nearby temple of Flora, and there is no reason to doubt that something of the kind took place during the early fifth century.

The pillars of this round church are indeed a fascinating jumble of marble oddments, with Corinthian capitals supporting a drum of alternating stonework and brick courses, above which is the plainest of beamed roofs. The ambulatory behind the inner ring of columns is surrounded by small altars and chapels, several of which are decorated with very early medieval fresco fragments, and the quiet simplicity of everything here makes it the ideal retreat for meditation and repose after a morning's wander.

Before you leave the city, however, two further places deserve a visit, though they are in quite the opposite direction from Sant 'Angelo, on a spur of the hill to the south-east of Piazza Italia, in Corso Cavour. The first is the church of San Domenico, a gothic building of 1305 whose interior was entirely rebuilt in 1614, but has recently been restored to something more like its earliest gothic form. Behind the high altar you will find that comparative rarity in Umbrian churches, an exceptionally colourful and grandly conceived renaissance stained-glass window, showing twenty-four richly garbed saints in vivid greens, reds and blues. The largest stained-glass window in Italy after those in the *duomo* at Milan, it was begun in 1411 by the Perugine Fra Bartolomeo di Pietro and the Florentine Mariotto di Nardo.

Below this, in the right transept, is Perugia's best piece of gothic sculpture, the superb tomb of Pope Benedict XI, who died here in 1304, some say – yes, once again – as a result of eating poisoned figs brought to him in a basket by a young man disguised as a nun, sent by certain jealous cardinals. The monument, commissioned by his fellow Dominicans, shows the thin-featured Pope lying asleep under a canopy whose curtains are being drawn back by attendant angels, beneath a tabernacle supported by marble columns. These were once adorned with mosaic, much of which was hacked off by members of a French cavalry regiment quartered in the church during the Napoleonic invasion. Nobody knows who carried out this composition, but it was almost definitely none of the three illustrious artists, Giovanni Pisano, Arnolfo di Cambio and Lorenzo Maitani, to whom it has been enthusiastically attributed.

The lovely cloister of the former Dominican convent next to the church was designed by the fifteenth-century Perugian architect Leonardo Mansueti; from here you enter the Umbrian National Archaeological Museum. This is the easiest way of making the acquaintance of Perugia's Etruscan rulers, whose idiosyncratic funerary sculptures, with their reclining married couples, chased bronze mirrors and heavy gold pendants, form the central exhibits of a display reflecting three centuries of archaeology among the tombs and ruins of Umbria.

Beyond San Domenico, Corso Cavour turns into Borgo XX Giugno, in which stands San Pietro, unquestionably Perugia's grandest church. Started as a cathedral by the nobleman Pietro Vincioli in 963, it retains the shape of a romanesque basilica in its round-arched nave of marble colonnades and the deep roof of its apse, but later ages have added a whole series of delightful embellishments. The courtyard of 1614 through which you enter is early baroque, with alternate square and oval windows above a small cloister. The campanile above was based on a design by the Florentine architect Bernardo Rossellino (1409–64), whose signature, as it were, is the ornate garlanded cornice below the pinnacle.

Inside, the nave ceiling was exuberantly gilded during the late sixteenth century, when the fine sequence of large biblical scenes was added by Antonios Vassilakis (1556–1629), a Greek from the island of Milos who italianized his name as Vassilacchi

A stained glass panel from the basilica of San Domenico, Perugia.

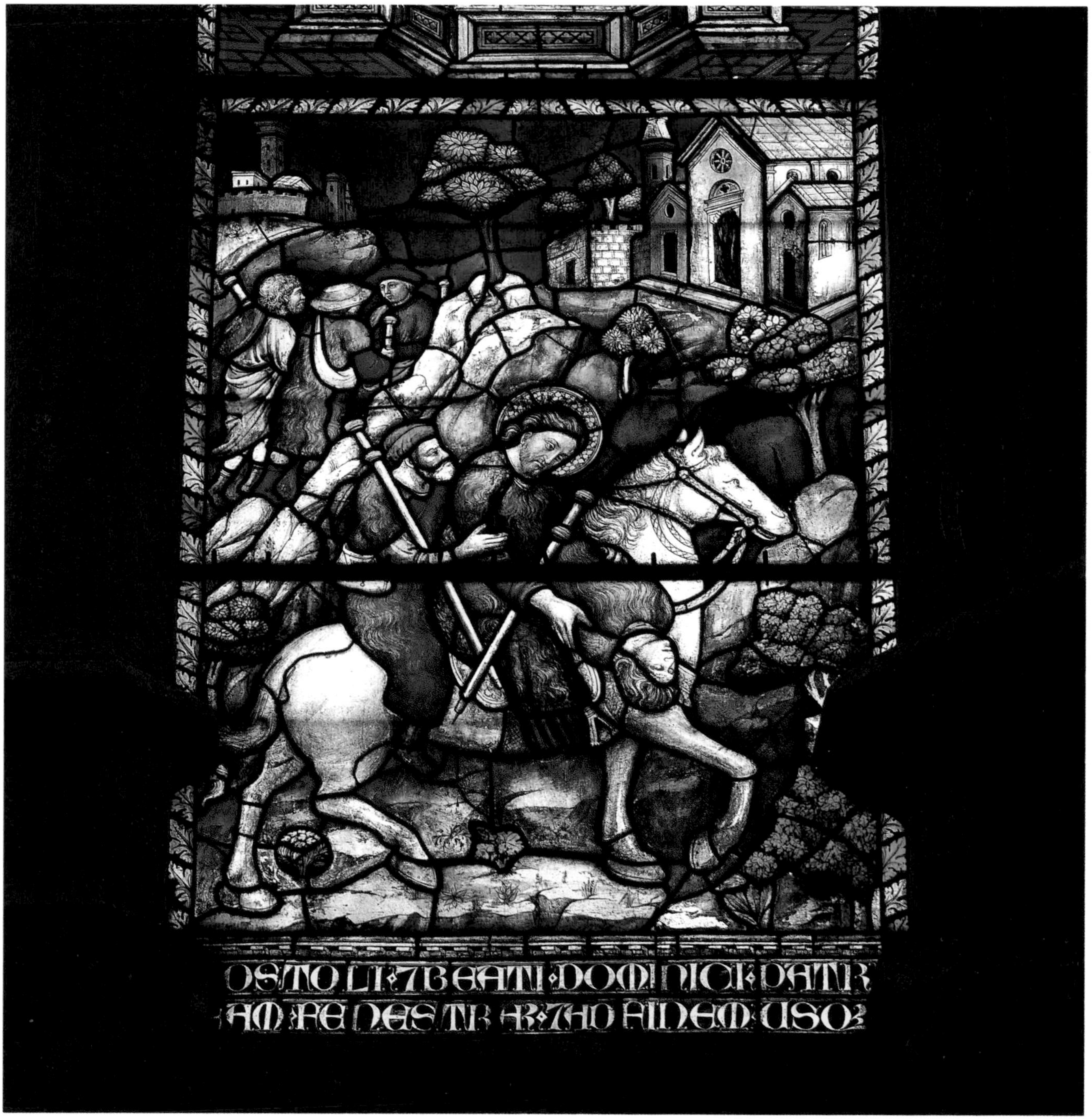
OSTOLI 7 BEATI DOMINICI PATR

and became a talented pupil of Veronese. In fact, the whole basilica is rich in good late renaissance painting and magnificent furnishings from the same period, from the majolica floors of the sacristy, with its four saints from the hand of Perugino, to the domed and gilded marble tabernacle of the high altar and the gorgeous set of inlaid choir-stalls by a group of craftsmen from as far away as Bologna and Bergamo, thought to have been influenced by Raphael and at work between 1526–35.

San Pietro makes a fitting close to a tour of Perugia, though if you travel by train, you will surely relish the railway station, with its nineteenth-century gothic brass timetable stands and the painted panels of the waiting rooms. I am always reluctant to quit this city, which appears to me to have sorted out better than most that conflict between the life of the present and the burden of the past which perplexes so many towns in modern Italy.

From the city, the Umbrian countryside beckons you to go exploring. The road south towards Marsciano and Todi takes you out among eighteenth-century villas of the Perugine nobility towards San Martino in Colle, within its medieval ramparts, where the parish church is a by no means unattractive piece of work by that indefatigable nineteenth-century theatre architect Giovanni Santini. Beyond Sant'Enea (who is actually not Aeneas but simply an Umbrian form of Agnes), turn up the hill at San Valentino, through Castello delle Forme, and down again to Fanciullata ('the village of the girls'), where the church boasts a rich array of frescoes from the always interesting brush of Bartolomeo Caporali. Further along the spine of the hilltop lies Cerqueto, where you will find the first precisely dated work by Perugino, a powerfully drawn St Sebastian painted for the parish church in 1478.

Perugino is still with you on the road westwards from Perugia through the valley south of Lake Trasimeno towards his birthplace at Città della Pieve. This is often written off as a dull highway with nothing on it, but the verdict is hardly fair. The countryside is, as ever, most attractive, with olives clustering the gentle slopes and a string of villages along the hilltops beckoning you to turn aside. Agello, where some of the wretched Roman victims of the slaughter at Lake Trasimeno lie buried, has a ruined castle with sweeping vistas over to Tuscany in one direction, out across the Tiber valley in another, and on clear days taking in Assisi and the southern Apennines. Further west at Fontignano, under its turreted fortress, you will find one of Perugino's last frescoes, a *Madonna and Child* painted in 1522, in the little church of the Annunziata.

When you reach Tavernelle, try to find the right turn for the sanctuary of the Madonna di Mongiovino. It is not well signposted, but you can see it perched tantalizingly on the hill, a stately domed church of pinkish sandstone, built in 1513 by Rocco di Tommaso (1495–1526), a sculptor and architect from Vicenza, assisted by three other sculptors in his work on the handsome doorways and Corinthian pilasters. Each of the chapels, set at angles to the main body of the church, contains good frescoes, especially those by the Pisan painter Niccolo Pomarancio (1517–96), who seems to have been greatly in demand throughout Umbria.

The villages and hamlets fade away after Tavernelle, and the country grows strikingly empty as the road winds on through the oak groves so typical of western Umbria. When at last you reach the main Orvieto road, a right turn brings you up to Città della Pieve, which would be worth the journey even were the way from Perugia far drearier than it actually is.

Much of the town's visual enchantment, both viewed from afar (it looks like some eye-catching feature in a seventeenth-century landscape painting) or when explored within its walls, is due to the simple fact that there was never any decent building stone to hand, so the inhabitants turned to brick instead. This has weathered over the centuries into creamy pink, soft brown and reddish grey under the slope of the tiled roofs. Città della Pieve means 'town of the parish

Pope Benedict XI lies at rest on his medieval tomb in San Domenico, Perugia.

Above Square and oval windows alternate in the Perugian cloister of San Pietro.

Right The tall campanile of San Pietro on Perugia's southern spur.

church' – *pieve* derives from the Latin *plebs*, people, the name loosely applied, in early medieval times, to any country congregation. Its history is unusually vague, though we know that Emperor Frederick II confirmed the citizens' privileges in 1243, and that the two snakes on the civic coat of arms derive from a league with Milan in 1375, whose ruling Visconti family bore a serpent for their badge. Pope Clement VIII (1592–1605) gave the town a bishop in 1601 and changed its name from Castel della Pieve. Otherwise it has managed to keep its ancient beauty, yet to remain one of the liveliest of Umbria's small cities, in the late twentieth century surely not far short of a miracle.

Arriving from Perugia, you may leave your car outside the city walls near the church of Santa Maria dei Servi, which contains a *Deposition from the Cross*, a much damaged but still eloquent fresco signed and dated by Perugino in 1517. The small baroque church opposite is dedicated to the Blessed Giacomo Villa, martyred here in 1304 while defending the Servite convent against a band of robbers. His body is kept in the silver casket under the altar. The Porta Santa Maria brings you into Via Roma, and to your left you can see the first of those incomparably elegant small aristocratic palaces which are such a notable feature of the city. This once belonged to the Bandini family, who commissioned it from Galeazzo Alessi. Opposite is the altogether more austere Palazzo Orca, built in the seventeenth century.

Should you be seeking the house where Perugino was born, a stone tablet marks the site on the corner of the street. Turning left you enter Piazza Plebiscito, the heart of the ancient settlement on a hill once sacred to Apollo. The cathedral, dominating the square, is dedicated to Saints Gervase and Protase, Roman martyrs, but though its outer fabric is partly medieval, much of the interior was altered during the seventeenth century. Where other north Umbrian churches had their Peruginos purloined by the French, Città della Pieve was lucky to retain a lyrical interpretation of Christ's baptism, painted in 1510 when the artist was at the height of his powers. The composition plays upon the delicately angular posture of the four figures, ranged against just such a green prospect as you may see from the town walls. In the chapel next to this is a starkly eloquent wooden Crucifix by the Florentine sculptor Pietro Tacca (1577–1640).

Next to the *duomo* is the Torre Civica, not, as you might at first imagine, a church bell-tower, but a twelfth-century turret, part of the town's early defences. Milder manners and softer times are evoked by Palazzo della Corgna, built for Ascanio della Corgna, named Perpetual Governor of Città della Pieve by his uncle Pope Julius III in 1550 (nominating papal nephews as this city's rulers became rather a tradition). Even in its current rather battered and weather-beaten state, the palace tells us something about Ascanio's good taste, for he was not only a friend of Galeazzo Alessi who designed it, but also an amateur pupil. If you can manage it, get a look inside at the remarkable mythological ceiling frescoes by the Florentine painter Salvio Savini, completed in 1580, their brilliant panels set within a border of swags and cartouches.

From Piazza Plebiscito, follow Via Pietro Vannucci, which takes you out along the northern spur of this triple-pronged town, with medieval arches over quiet lanes running parallel with the main street, and splendid glimpses of open countryside beyond. If the Palazzo Giorgi-Tacchini to your left looks like an opera house, with its long balcony and triple entrance arches, this is really no accident, for its architect, Giovanni Santini of Perugia, designed theatres at Narni and Orvieto and completed Città della Pieve's Teatro degli Avvalorati in 1834 (you can find this west of the cathedral in Piazza XIX Giugno). Further along on the left, just before you reach the church of the Maddalena, is what purports to be Italy's narrowest street, called (well, somehow it would be) Vicolo Baciadonne, 'Kiss-the-Women Lane'. There is hardly room to walk, let alone kiss.

On the opposite side, in the Oratorio di Santa Maria dei Banchi, is the most impressive of all Perugino's

Delicately carved renaissance details at the sanctuary of the Madonna di Mongiovino.

Left Paciano looks northwards across the fertile Tresa valley.

Above A corner of the piazza at Panicale.

surviving frescoes. Two letters of his, found bricked up in the sacristy along with his terracotta paintpots, tell us, in their crabbed writing, that the painter, like all his kind in an age when artists toiled for gain first and glory afterwards, could drive a hard bargain when he chose. But he was content to settle for less than the going rate with his patrons, the Compagnia dei Disciplinati, who commissioned the work in 1504.

This charitable fraternity, which had begun as a group of flagellants in the Middle Ages, chose an Adoration of the Magi to adorn their oratory. What Perugino produced in response was a sort of romantic fantasy, in which not merely the Wise Men but the Shepherds too play a part, alongside throngs of noblemen and a caravan of travellers winding down a distant road. Loveliest of all is the landscape, a vision of Trasimeno and the Tuscan horizons seen through a faint haze under little whorls of cloud.

Back in the piazza, take Via Vittorio Veneto past the eighteenth-century church of the Gesù, very obviously alluding to its Roman namesake. This street takes you to the *rocca*, with its four tall turrets, built in 1326 with the stated purpose of keeping the citizens in check. It was here, in 1503, that the odious Cesare Borgia, notoriously admired by Machiavelli for his ruthless opportunism, had his political opponents Paolo Orsini and the Duke of Gravina strangled.

On the road north from Città della Pieve towards Castiglione del Lago, take the right turn to Paciano and Panicale. The first is a compact little walled *borgo*, which began life as a feudal castle founded by the invading Charles IV of France (1322–28) during the early fourteenth century. There are some attractive small churches, but the most beautiful aspect of the village, cradled within the surrounding wooded hills, is its setting. As for Panicale, this has the perfect ensemble of little palaces, churches and fountains gathered around two piazzas within the ramparts. To those still on the Perugino trail, I recommend the church of San Sebastiano, which possesses a fresco of 1505 showing the saint's martyrdom.

Panicale crowns a distant hilltop beyond olive-clad slopes.

On the castle ramparts at Castiglione del Lago.

Castiglione del Lago on the Umbrian border is not the most beautiful of towns, on its lakeside promontory with hotels and beach umbrellas, but worth a visit for the splendid ducal palace of the Della Corgna family, who were given the town as a marquisate by Julius III when he made Ascanio governor of Città della Pieve. Galeazzo Alessi once again provided the designs, and Salvio Savini and assistants once more scattered sumptuous mythologies across the ceilings. A glance at this and at the large crenellated medieval castle will make an agreeable prelude to a leisurely Umbrian luncheon at La Cantina in Via Vittorio Emanuele – friendly and unpretentious, which in the increasingly dubious world of modern Italian restaurants means very good indeed.

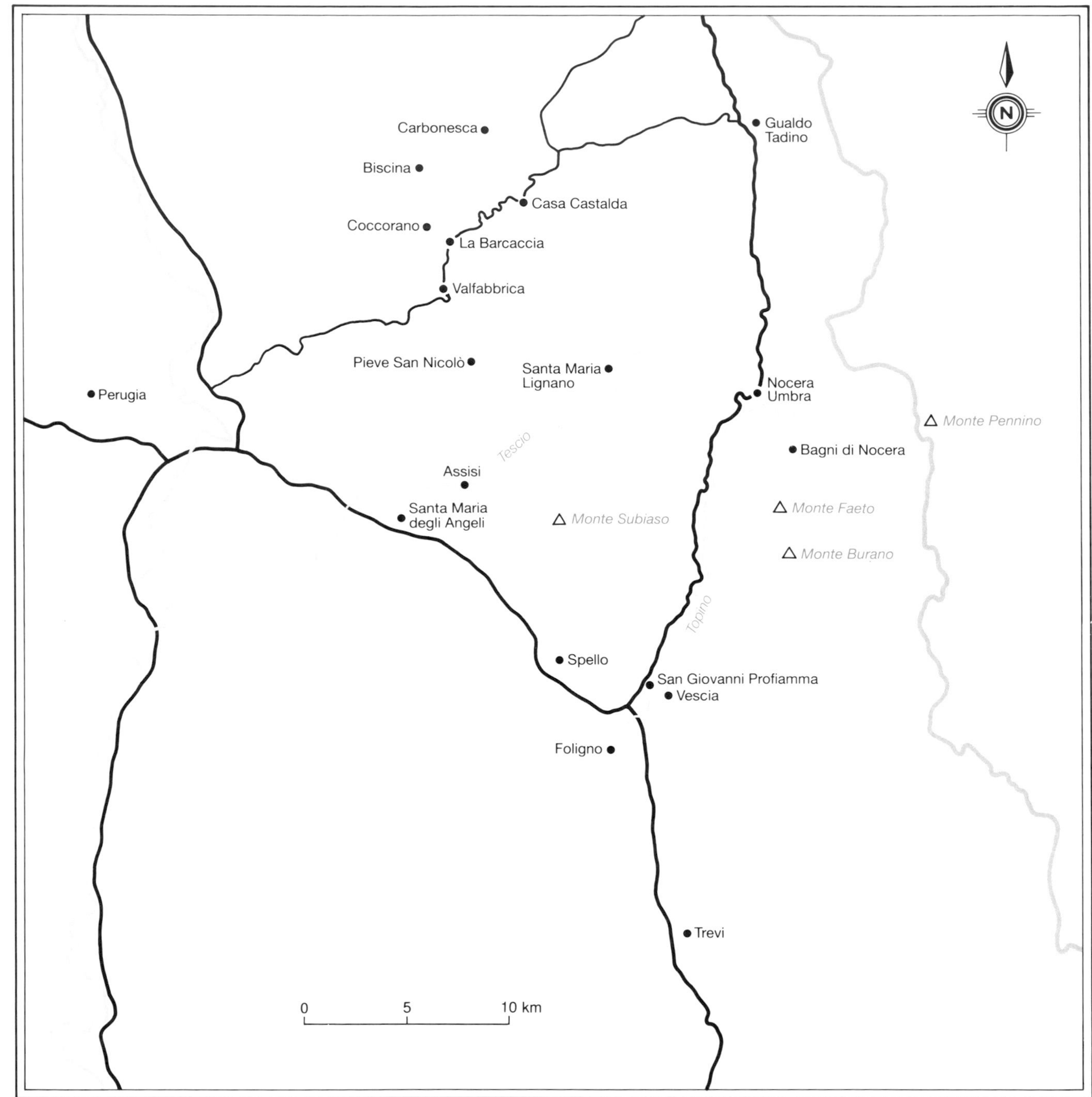
Carbonesca
Biscina
Casa Castalda
Coccorano
La Barcaccia
Valfabbrica
Gualdo Tadino
Pieve San Nicolò
Santa Maria Lignano
Nocera Umbra
Perugia
Monte Pennino
Bagni di Nocera
Tescio
Assisi
Santa Maria degli Angeli
Monte Subiaso
Monte Faeto
Monte Burano
Topino
Spello
San Giovanni Profiamma
Vescia
Foligno
Trevi
0
5
10 km
N

3
In the Footsteps of St Francis

Assisi – Nocera Umbra – Spello

There can be no question as to which is Umbria's most famous city. Perugia and Spoleto are ancient and illustrious, Orvieto has its respectful following among lovers of renaissance art, and Terni, 'the Manchester of Umbria', is, well, big. The wider world, however, has chosen to celebrate a much more modest place, a small grey town crowning one of those hilltops running south-eastwards above the old road to Rome and already historic when, in 1181 or 1182, a boy called Giovanni was born to the wife of a merchant newly returned from France, who added Francesco to the child's baptismal names in honour of his journey.

Would Assisi exist without St Francis? It is his shrine which draws the annual thousands of pilgrims and tourists, and his presence and that of his followers which haunts the surrounding landscape. Yet we might just as easily argue that his achievements would have been diminished without this Umbrian background, so that a glance at that part of the town's story which does not focus upon the saint is essential if we are to understand the true significance of the enduring spiritual force he created.

One of Assisi's most attractive aspects is the feeling it conveys, like such neighbouring towns as Spello and Trevi, that it has somehow sprung organically from the soil of the hillsides and that what you see from a distance clustered there in the shape of churches, houses and walls is really a living thing which, in the blink of an eyelid, might very easily change its form altogether.

Very old the city certainly is, and even if the Trojan Dardanus was not, as legend once had it, her founder, the Umbrians and Etruscans were certainly here and the Romans took possession of the place at the end of the fourth century BC. A Roman presence is strongly marked even today. Apart from the famous Temple of Minerva, there are the remains of an amphitheatre, a theatre, a cistern and several houses, besides such traces as marble tablets and statuary fragments. We know that the citizens of Assisium suffered in the aftermath of the siege of Perugia by Octavius (see p. 50), but that prosperity later returned to the town, governed by its local magistrates, known as *marones*.

One of those who felt the severity of Octavius's confiscations and reprisals was the great poet Sextus Propertius, who was almost certainly born here since so many local inscriptions mention his family name. Propertius is one of those poets whom you may find difficult at first, but whose toughness provokes you into a greater familiarity and respect. Part of the literary circle clustered around the influential patron Maecenas in the first century BC, he knew Virgil and Horace, but his poems, with their sardonic analysis of love and their allusions to Umbrian places and legends, are very different from any of theirs. In at least two elegies he movingly portrays his sense of dislocation as a result of his family's involvement on the losing side in the civil war of 41 BC while he was yet a child.

The fate of Assisi was that of other Umbrian cities when the long peace of the Roman empire came to an end. First she yielded to Totila and his Goths, then in 773 she was sacked by Charlemagne at the head of a Frankish army, though to his credit he ordered her to be instantly rebuilt. The tiresome, bullying Frederick Barbarossa, arriving here in the 1150s, made his lieutenant Conrad of Swabia governor of the city, and it was now that the Pope chose to weigh in as challenger to imperial authority. The fatal strife between Guelphs and Ghibellines broke out in Assisi as elsewhere, and the town, for the next two centuries, wavered to and fro between the cause of the Papacy and the Empire.

Her real hatred, however, was reserved for Perugia, against whom she carried on what now seems a quite phenomenally persistent war of attrition, maintaining her independence in conditions under which any other city would long before have laid down its arms. In 1321 the Perugines even threatened to carry off St Francis's body, and after a siege lasting over a year they captured Assisi and dominated it for the next four decades. Freed by the powerful Papal governor, the Spaniard Gil Alvarez de Albornoz (1310–67), Assisi fell once more to greedy Perugia after an appalling final onslaught, culminating in the burning of the public archives, the sale of numerous citizens into slavery and the rape and slaughter of the nuns of Santa Chiara, who had dared openly to wish destruction by fire upon their detested Umbrian neighbours.

Even then there was no quiet here. The intervention of Pope Eugenius IV (1431–47) was compromised by the revelation that he intended to sell Assisi, lock, stock and barrel, to Perugia. Meanwhile two rival families – that old Italian scenario again – the Nepis, ruling the upper reaches of the town, and the Fiumi, dominating the lower quarters, drove the place senseless with repeated feuding, so that the churches remained perpetually shut, palace gates were barred and chained and a terrible silence reigned in the streets, broken only by the daily skirmish ending in blood. When at last Pope Paul III, he who had 'subdued the audacity of the Perugines' (see p. 52), intervened at the beginning of the sixteenth century, Assisi gave in, on condition that it might be independently governed. Paul, in a rare moment of generosity, chose to agree, and Assisi remained part of the Papal States until 1860.

By the nineteenth century, Murray's *Handbook for Central Italy & Rome* (1875) was asserting that 'no traveller who takes an interest in the history of art, who is desirous of tracing the influence which the devotional fervour of Saint Francis exercised on the painters of the fourteenth and fifteenth centuries will fail to visit Assisi', though it could also declare that 'there are no inns at Assisi worthy of the name'. We should not forget that the town's destiny is ultimately connected with that shift in taste which, during the nineteenth century, brought about the revaluation of medieval art, and that much of the latter-day allure of St Francis's story is due to the fascination which the Middle Ages have since assumed for us.

Francis belongs emphatically to that strife-torn Italy of Emperor and Pope in which his message of peace, charity, love and reconciliation sounded with a clarity all the more startling because it was so unfamiliar. His father Pietro di Bernardone was a wealthy cloth merchant, married to a Provençal lady named Pica, who nurtured in the boy that gift for poetic expression which typified the rich culture of Provence, with its troubadours and 'courts of love'. Francis's early life was just what we might expect from the lively, intelligent child of rich parents with plenty of time and money on his hands. 'First among equals in vanity', says an early biographer, 'he did not shrink from jokes and songs, ridicule and malice. Many, through his pleasant manners and generosity, became wicked and scandalous in their conduct.'

The familiar landmarks of Assisi viewed across a field of poppies.

GELATERIA

The crucial moment in the young man's life came when, aged twenty-six and having survived capture in war and a bout of gaol fever, he began to go through a prolonged spiritual crisis in which the entire focus of his earthly existence was questioned and reappraised. It was during this time that he developed his famous concept of 'Lady Poverty', the equivalent, as it were, of those fair women to whom the troubadours of his mother's Provence dedicated their songs, 'a wife', he proclaimed, 'more lovely than any you have seen, who will outshine all others in her wisdom and beauty'.

His service of Lady Poverty took him among lepers and beggars, brought him, initially at least, the derision of the citizens, and earned him the contempt and anger of his father. The culminating moment came in 1209, when he finally donned the distinctive robe, held by a knotted cord, which embodied his ultimate renunciation. Others now began to join him, such as the nobleman Bernardo di Quintavalle and the poor labourer Egidio, so that very soon the makings of a religious order came into being and he was able to confront the stern and inflexible Pope Innocent III with a request for official recognition of the movement.

Once the papal blessing was given, the Franciscans eagerly carried their message to the towns and villages beyond Assisi, and the Umbrian scene is vividly marked by their presence. It is impossible for even the most hardened and cynical atheist to dislike Francis's personality or to deny the impact of his teaching on the men and women of his time and of ours. The great moments of his later life, such as the sermon to the birds, the visit to the Sultan of Egypt, and the receiving of the Stigmata (the wounds of the crucified Christ), are all touched with a sense of his utter lack of priggishness or dogmatism. From a life of sterile pleasure-seeking amid getters and spenders, Francis had turned to an existence at whose core was a practical goodness healing the wounds of envy, selfishness and hatred.

Medieval buildings frame Assisi's Roman temple of Minerva.

Many shrines nowadays seem positively unworthy of the saints they commemorate, in their vulgarity or their overblown magnificence. Though St Francis would surely have deemed himself unworthy of the great basilica raised to his memory at the northern edge of Assisi, he would certainly have loved its extraordinary atmosphere of a shared joy, of the pleasure which its painters, sculptors and architects clearly felt in proclaiming the abiding validity of his work in the world. The place is not a museum, neither is it dedicated to exploiting tourism with jingling cash registers; it is still holy ground where awe and devotion are made possible. Perhaps, at the close of the twentieth century, this achievement may be called St Francis's most remarkable miracle.

Begun in 1228, just two years after the saint's death, the Basilica of San Francesco represents one of the most astonishing feats of medieval architecture, in terms both aesthetic and technical. The name of the architect is unknown, though it may well have been the combative, domineering Fra Elia di Buonbarone (1171–1253), Francis's successor as Vicar general of the order, who actually inspired the design. It was certainly he who set the work on foot, armed with the blessing of Pope Gregory IX (1227–41), who had canonized the saint. The operation of building two great churches, one above the other, was made far more difficult by the site, a rocky precipice on the fringe of the city. Undaunted, the builders created a system of massive arcades underpinning the whole structure, at its most impressive when viewed from a distance, and completed the entire basilica, with the aid of donations pouring in from as far away as Jerusalem and Morocco, in a mere thirty years.

Within this unique creation, powerfully marked as it is by the influence of French gothic churches (so much so that a French provenance has been suggested for the anonymous architect), the finest painters of the age were commissioned to decorate the walls and vaults with lavish frescoed panels which have since come to represent a kind of basic grammar in the language of Western art. Much as the early friars may have resented Elia's project for what seemed more like

a nobleman's palace than a memorial to their Christ-like founding father, they can hardly have objected to so splendid a celebration of the Franciscan spirit in the wider context of Christianity.

In the Lower Church, which you enter through Francesco di Pietrasanta's porch of 1487, sheltering twin gothic doorways with a rose window above them, you will find frescoes by five major Tuscan artists at work during the early fourteenth century. Immediately to your left are perhaps the most beautiful of all, those by Simone Martini (1280–1344), appropriately adorning the chapel of San Martino and representing scenes from the saint's life. Painted in 1317, they show the influence of Giotto in their realism and handling of brilliant colours, while retaining the poetic delicacy so typical of Simone's native Sienese style. Contrast, for example, the chivalric splendours of *St Martin Renouncing his Life as a Soldier*, all tents, lances, warriors and steeds, with the dramatic variation of the figures, some praying, some tenderly solicitous, posed around the saint's deathbed.

In the left transept another Sienese, Pietro Lorenzetti (1280–1348), was engaged in 1320 to portray scenes from Christ's Passion. Here it is not just the tonal subtleties of the artist's palette which catch the eye, or the sense of fluid movement in the composition, but his interpretation of every moment in the story in terms of complex, mingled reactions from those present. In the *Entry into Jerusalem*, how confident the disciples look, how eagerly the children scramble to throw down their clothes, yet what a quietly sinister note is struck by the two bearded Pharisees standing conspiratorially in the crowd.

The vaults of the sanctuary were always said to have been frescoed by Giotto, but scholars now believe them to be by a pupil known therefore as 'the Master of the Vaults'. They glorify Franciscan virtues, showing Chastity as a girl at prayer within a tower, Poverty as a marriage ceremony between the saint and his 'Lady', and Obedience as a friar accepting a yoke, in the presence of Prudence and Humility.

The right transept contains the gravely beautiful *Madonna Enthroned among Angels with St Francis*, the work of Giotto's master Cimabue (1240–1302). Very few frescoes by this first great name in Florentine painting survive, and this one has been much damaged over the centuries. Most striking is the way in which Cimabue obviously attempted to recapture Francis's exact likeness from contemporary descriptions of him, right down to the thin nose and sticking-out ears.

Equally lovely are Simone Martini's five saints, on the lower portion of the right-hand wall, studies in serene visionary abstraction. Giotto himself, if he did not paint all the vividly realized scenes on the left side of the ceiling arch, surely assisted in the overall design of each panel, and his vigorous sense of the dramatic is powerfully apparent in the two *Miracles of St Francis*. One of these shows a child of the Sperelli family falling from a tower, after which he is restored to life through the saint's intercession; the other tells the story of a boy retrieved from a house which had collapsed on top of him. The man standing on the far right is said to be a self-portrait by Giotto, and the hawk-nosed man next to him is traditionally held to be Dante (who remarked that the painter was exceedingly ugly and had six children equally hideous in appearance).

Underneath the Lower Church, in a crypt which used to be called 'The Third Church', lies St Francis himself. For centuries nobody knew where Fra Elia had placed his master, until in 1818, after some fifty nights of tunnelling (secrecy was necessary in case someone made off with the precious relics), the sepulchral urn was discovered, walled up in travertine blocks taken from Assisi's Roman rampart and still surrounded by a handful of the earliest offerings from the faithful. Mercifully, the neo-classical mausoleum has been removed and the plainness of unadorned stonework accords with the true Franciscan simplicity.

Where the Lower Church is characterized by candlelight and shadow and the gentle curve of wide-vaulted ceilings, the Upper Church, with its round, slit-windowed buttresses and tall clustered columns,

The basilica of San Francesco at Assisi, above its stupendous medieval arcading.

presents you with an entirely different visual experience. The fact that you need to go out into the daylight from one to the other allows you an essential interval. Most guidebooks tell you to enter the Upper Church from the sanctuary, but though the fifteenth-century double-arcaded Cloister of Sixtus IV which you pass on your way is indeed beautiful, I recommend climbing the stairs from the porch at which you came into the Lower Church, so that you can enjoy the noble breadth of the gothic façade and get a better impression, by a view from nave to apse, of the importance of space and light in relation to the most famous of all Assisi's fresco cycles.

This is the series of 28 scenes from the life of St Francis, traditionally ascribed to Giotto, who probably began it in 1296, at the age of 29. His basis for these episodes was St Bonaventure's biography of Francis (1263), derived from accounts by founder members of the order. Even if you have never seen these paintings before, you will certainly be familiar with some of them, for they are among the most popular images in the whole of Christian art. Here is *The Sermon to the Birds*, with its clustering finches, doves, thrushes and magpies under a bushy-branched oak tree, *The Miracle of the Spring*, where a poor peasant laps eagerly at the water Francis has made to flow for him, the wonderful *Expulsion of Devils from Arezzo*, in which bat-winged demons flit angrily off from the clustered roofs and towers of the Tuscan city, and *Francis Giving his Cloak to a Poor Knight*, amid a rocky Umbrian landscape with a hilltop town in the background.

Nobody questions either the significance of these frescoes in the development of Italian medieval art, or the intrinsic impact made by their combination of grandeur and human warmth, but art historians continue to rage furiously at one another over exactly who painted them. Certainly not Giotto, says one school of thought, which has devised a 'St Francis Master' to cover the lot. Perhaps Giotto here and there, says another, unwilling to deny his claim at least to the prevailing mood of naturalistic immediacy.

The most likely answer is that, though a good deal of what we see here is by his assistants (the stiffly drawn figures in *The Simpleton Honours St Francis*, or some of those in *The Saint Returning his Clothes to his Father*, for instance), much else is by Giotto alone. The frequently made objection that the workmanship is far less sophisticated here than in the later fresco cycle in the Scrovegni Chapel at Padua takes no account of the possibilities of artistic development, for Giotto as for any other creative spirit.

Sadly, many of the once superb paintings by Cimabue which covered the walls of the choir and the transepts have perished owing to the fatal interaction of damp with their lead-based pigments. Their ghostly remains possess the terrible fascination of irrecoverable ruin. Below them runs a fine set of inlaid wooden choir-stalls, the work of a team of craftsmen from Sanseverino in the Marche, led by Domenico Indivini (1445–1502), who included portraits of notable Franciscans among the intarsia panels.

From the basilica walk up towards Via San Francesco, where the old city of Assisi actually begins, laid out along the hillside in a series of roughly parallel streets joined by flights of steps. On your right, next to the large Palazzo Giacobetti, home of a literary academy founded in 1554, is the Oratorio dei Pellegrini, a former hospital chapel built in 1431 by members of the Pious Confraternity of St Anthony Abbot. The highly appealing frescoes of musical angels and tall saints are, as you might guess, by an Umbrian master, none other than Matteo da Gualdo; another of his compatriots, Pier Antonio da Foligno, known as Mezzastris (1430–1506), portrayed scenes from the miracles of St James and St Anthony Abbot, who, as Mezzastris reminds us, caused a providential camel caravan to cross the Egyptian desert bringing food to his starving fellow hermits.

A little further along, the ancient loggia with its ox-head cornice once housed the Monte Frumentario, a place where peasants could come to pawn their grain.

Assisi's Rocca Maggiore seen from Via del Comune Vecchio.

TRATTORIA
DA ERMINIO

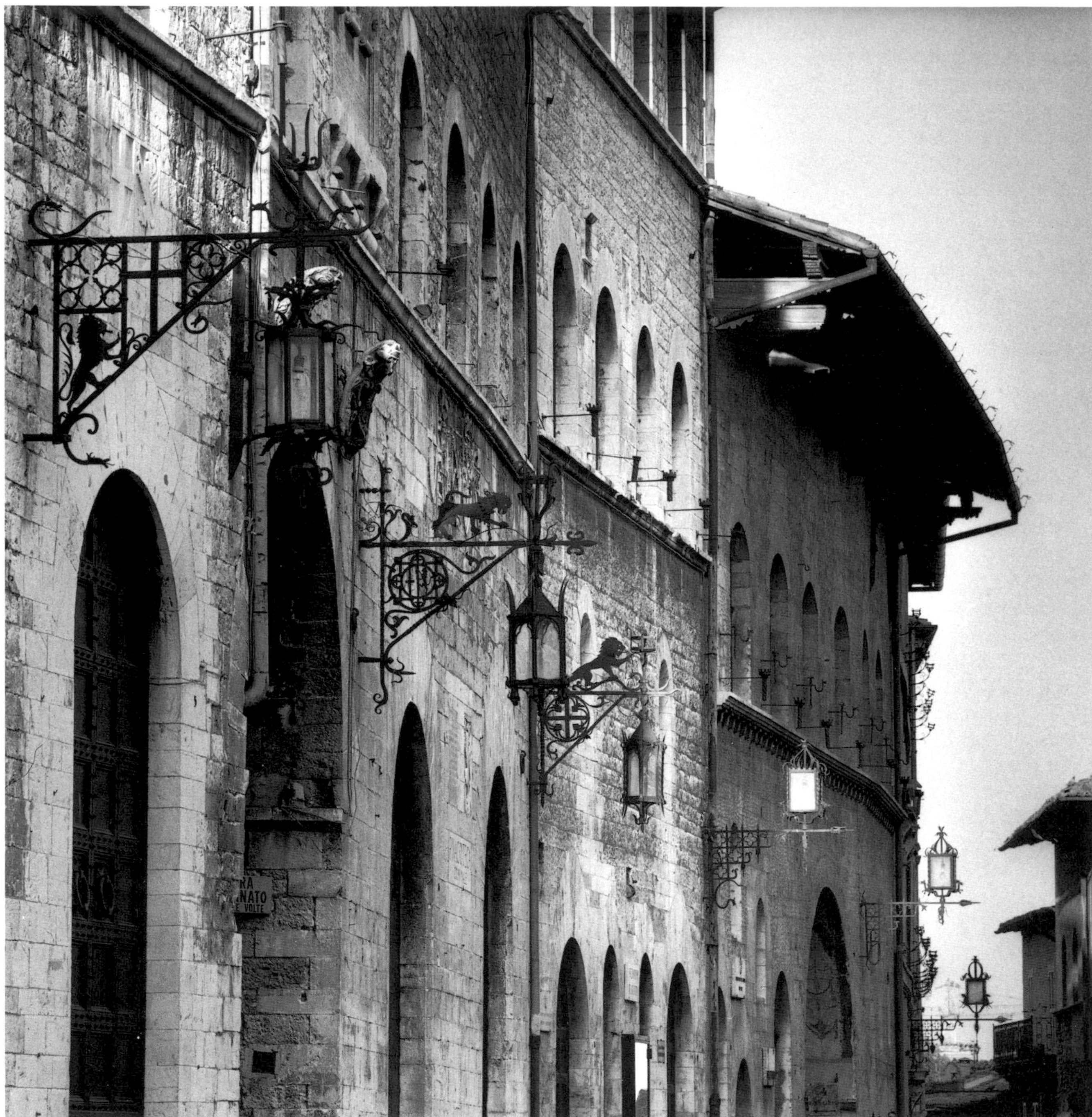

Speaking of the staff of life, it is worth sampling some of the wares in the excellent Assisian bakeries, which produce Umbria's best biscuits, always delicious, infinitely varied in colour and flavour, but more apt to be crunched than crumbled.

The street now becomes Via Portica, and here the crypt of the former church of San Nicolò has been turned into an archaeological museum, rich with evidence of life in Roman Assisium. Poor Cottiedius Attianus of the Pretorian Guard lived for only twenty years but left us a finely chiselled tombstone. Several of the fragments of mural painting come from what is said to have been Propertius's family house, and the headless toga-draped figure, if not the poet himself, was perhaps a member of his patrician clan.

The corridor leads you on into a paved subterranean space which was once the forum of the city, over and around which successive occupational layers have since risen. The forum actually extended across the whole area of the modern Piazza del Comune above it and of many surrounding buildings besides. Inscriptions here tell us of a temple to Castor and Pollux, and there are the remains of the seats where the civic magistrates once presided.

Most remarkable of all Assisi's Roman survivals is that of the Temple of Minerva, erected on a somewhat cramped site during the first century AD and dedicated by brother magistrates Cnaeus Caesius Tiro and Titus Caesius Priscus. Though the body of the building was transformed in 1539 into the church of Santa Maria sopra Minerva, and given its once cheerful, now rather dusty baroque interior a century later, the splendid pronaos or portico of six Corinthian columns with a triangular pediment was permitted to remain, and handsome it certainly is. The temple was the only thing in Assisi which really impressed Goethe, whose *Italienische Reise*, one of the best travel books ever written, describes his visit here in October 1786. He had turned aside on his way to Foligno specially to see

Wrought-iron brackets enliven sober medieval palaces in Piazza del Comune, Assisi.

Classical renaissance harmonies in a doorway at Assisi.

this 'modest temple, exactly right for a small town, yet so ideally designed that it would be a showpiece anywhere', and he was not disappointed. His rhapsodic account ends: 'I cannot describe the feelings the building aroused within me, but I know they will always bear fruit.' As for the basilica, Goethe had 'turned away in disgust from the huge substructure of the two churches built on top of one another like a Babylonian tower', and was quite peeved when some 'rude fellows' took offence because he had not gone to pay his respects to 'the dull Duomo of Saint Francis'.

On the other side of Piazza del Comune, in the medieval Palazzo dei Priori, a not especially interesting little civic picture gallery is enlivened by one or two worthwhile paintings by Nicolò Alunno and an engaging *Madonna and Child* within a landscape from the hand of the Assisian master always known as L'Ingegno ('The Genius'), whose real name was Andrea Aloigi (1484–1516).

Behind the square, with its tall fountain and ring of

The church of Santa Chiara, Assisi, supported by its heavy stone buttresses.

rough-hewn stone façades, stands the domed baroque Chiesa Nuova, built in 1615 at the expense of Philip III of Spain to a design by the local architect Giacomo Giorgetti (1603–79), whose work you will already have encountered in Santa Maria sopra Minerva. The object of this pretty little classical tabernacle, and of the Franciscan convent attached to it, was to preserve the remains of St Francis's family house. A friar shows visitors the cell in which Francis was imprisoned by his father, angry at what he considered the young man's religious eccentricities, and to one side of the church you can see the stable in which, as an angel disguised as a pilgrim prophesied to Pica di Bernardone, her son was to be born. The Latin inscription tells us that 'this oratory was a stall for oxen and asses, in which was born the Blessed Francis, mirror of the world'.

Pica was by no means the only woman to play a significant part in Francis's life. He had none of that frightful, zealous misogyny which is always paraded before us as such a tremendous virtue in male Christian saints, and thus it can hardly have surprised him that pious women as well as men should have wished to follow his example. The first of these was a young girl, born in 1194 in Assisi, whose noble family probably knew and had dealings with Francis's father. Chiara, St Clare as she is known to us, was the daughter of Count Favorino Scefi, who, on discovering her disinclination to marry, her desire to follow the newly-constituted Franciscan rule and her influence over other members of her family, made life as difficult as he could until the stubborn girl should yield to those who knew best. Francis meanwhile responded to her appeals for guidance and helped to build the earliest cells for the sisters of what was to become the Order of the Poor Clares (in Italian, *Le Clarisse*), one of the most influential of all female congregations.

Clare was a woman of deep spiritual resource, whose friendship with Francis undoubtedly enriched his final years, though the notion of a platonic love-affair between the pair is supported by nothing but romantic wishful thinking. Dying in 1253, she was canonized two years later, and her order, over whose active function she had defied the Pope, was forced into a strictly contemplative life and still pays a pound of candles to Rome on St Francis's day (4 October).

She lies in the austere gothic church of Santa Chiara, with its banded pink-and-white stone courses and immense flying buttresses, the work of Filippo da Campello (1255), which lies on the southern edge of the old town. Much of the medieval fresco once adorning the nave has gone, whitewashed owing to the preposterous officiousness of a seventeenth-century German bishop who felt that the nuns were looking too curiously through their gratings at visitors to the church, whom he thus sought to deter. Nevertheless, some lovely things remain, most of them from that world between byzantine and gothic in which

The *duomo* of San Rufino at Assisi has a romanesque façade and campanile.

Cimabue and Giotto sprang to maturity. The primitive blue-and-red striped twelfth-century crucifix in the Cappella del Crocifisso is the one which, according to tradition, bade Francis 'go and rebuild my house which has fallen into ruin', and in the left transept is a majestic icon of the grey-robed Clare, with little scenes from her life, very byzantine in feeling and probably not by Cimabue to whom it is always ascribed.

Leave Piazza Santa Chiara and climb the steps to Piazza San Rufino, where you will find one of Assisi's least visited buildings. Few travellers bother to consider that the city had a bishop and a cathedral long before the basilica gave even greater ecclesiastical significance to the community, but San Rufino, dedicated to a Roman pastor martyred under Diocletian, is still officially the premier church of the town.

A charming story attaches to the cathedral's foundation by Bishop Basileus in AD 412. When the clergy and people met to ask divine guidance towards a site for a suitable shrine to the canonized Rufinus, an old man of venerable aspect suddenly appeared and bade them 'take two heifers which have not felt the yoke, harness these to a cart whereon the saint's body is laid, follow them and where they stop, build a church'. The heifers stopped at a place known as 'the Good Mother', where the goddess Ceres was said to lie buried, and refused to move. When the Assisians, not content with this, started to build higher up the hill, the stones themselves moved back to the pagan holy place, where the church now stands. Archaeology has since shown that there was indeed a large Roman building here, and that, like nearly all legends, this one has a core of truth.

The façade of San Rufino, set off by the tall, blind-arcaded campanile behind, is one of the most impressive examples of Umbrian Romanesque. It was begun in 1140 by Giovanni da Gubbio and plays for its effect on the contrast between tall pilasters, a central horizontal line of arcading and a lower storey divided into squares surrounding three exquisitely refined portals. The largest of these has a lunette showing Christ in Glory between St Rufinus and the Madonna suckling her Child, within intricately carved semicircular bands, while the small doors to right and left show boldly incised reliefs of lions and birds.

Inside, the cathedral is mainly a sixteenth-century reconstruction by Galeazzo Alessi, who, for all his skill, simply messed about to very little purpose. The Cappella del Sacramento is an enjoyable essay in baroque by Giorgetti; the agreeably pompous paintings are by Andrea Carlone (1639–97). In the oratory to the left of the apse St Francis prayed before preaching, and in the ancient font he, St Clare and the Emperor Frederick II were all baptized. It is worth getting the sacristan to show you the crypt, with its traces of the eleventh-century church built by Bishop Ugo, and the outstandingly good third-century Roman sarcophagus, carved with the tale of Diana and Endymion, where Rufinus's relics once rested. So admired was this, indeed, that one of the bishops wished to keep it for himself, until a fight broke out between his servants and the townsfolk, which the latter won.

From San Rufino it is a short step up to the very top of the town, dominated, as always in Italy, by the *rocca* (called Rocca Maggiore to distinguish it from the smaller citadel inside the bastion on the south-east corner of the ramparts). Visually the *rocca*, with so many of its walls and towers still intact, makes the ideal culmination to any distant prospect of Assisi, commanding as it does a tremendous vista across the mountains of eastern Umbria and a southwards prospect of distant Spoleto. The earliest castle, strengthened by Frederick Barbarossa, was torn down in 1198 by citizens resentful of Conrad of Swabia's rule, and the present structure formed part of a defensive system thrown up around the town by Cardinal Albornoz in 1367. Allowed to decay during the seventeenth century, 'the chief fortress of Umbria', which once formed part of the dowry of Lucrezia Borgia (1480–1519), is now a quiet place to sit above the town and feel the hillside breezes lifting the heat from its huge masonry blocks.

Assisi is surrounded by places associated with St

Romanesque fantasy breaks free among the carvings on San Rufino, Assisi.

Francis, and the most unmistakable of these, by virtue of its commanding position on the plain, is the Basilica of Santa Maria degli Angeli, which you reach by taking the dead-straight road down to the *superstrada*, into what is essentially a small industrial suburb. The church was built in 1569 by Galeazzo Alessi, whose graceful cupola and outer walls survive, though the vast interior is a nineteenth-century rebuilding after an earthquake, and the façade is an extremely clever twentieth-century essay in pastiche.

The whole thing was designed to enclose the tiny church of the Porziuncola, which means 'small portion', referring either to its site or to the lump of stone from the Virgin's tomb incorporated within its walls. Here in 1211 Francis established what he called simply a 'place' for his followers. They built small huts around it and gathered inside for worship. Here St Clare made her vows as a nun, and here, on 3 October 1226, Francis died in the little cell next to the church, lying naked on the ground, covering only the wound of the Stigmata in his right side.

The contrast between the basilica's cavernous superfluity and this elementally simple stone shed, disfigured by a bad painting over the doorway by the nineteenth-century German 'Nazarene' master Friedrich Overbeck (1789–1869), is unutterably grotesque, and I recommend a turn in the garden outside to get over the dispiriting effects of what the French so aptly term *bondieuserie* ('good Goddery') . Into the rose bed St Francis threw himself naked one snowy night to conquer an unspecified temptation. The leaves, bloodied from his contact with the thorns, assumed a perpetual scarlet stain, the prickles themselves miraculously disappeared, and these thornless roses continue to flower each spring.

Not everything in Santa Maria degli Angeli is dull or hideous. In the museum, within the former refectory, you will discover one of those mournful, lank-limbed crucified Christs so typical of early Italian painting. This one is by Giunta Pisano, a Tuscan master at work during the mid thirteenth century. In the Cappella del Transito, where Francis died, he appears to us in a magnificent statue of enamelled terracotta by Andrea della Robbia (1435–1525), who perfectly caught the note of melancholy introspection in his features. Also by Andrea is the polyptych in the crypt, a set of eloquently modelled scenes showing the Coronation of the Virgin and moments from the Nativity story, under a characteristic frieze of garlands and fruit.

If you leave Assisi by the road up onto Monte Subasio (one Italian guidebook speaks of its 'varying gibbosities'), you arrive at what many feel is the perfect spot for a hermitage. Embowered in thick woods, the Eremo delle Carceri (*carceri* now means 'prisons', but originally just implied any sort of enclosed space) was one of various places to which St Francis, eager to refresh himself with contemplation between his missionary wanderings in the great world, used to retire for prayer and solitude. The small monastery that you see here was basically the creation of San Bernardino during the fifteenth century, but Francis's hermit's cell is still preserved, along with his stone bed and wooden pillow and the ancient ilex tree which shaded him as he spoke to the birds each day. Under the bridge next to the monastery, the river-bed was dried up at the saint's behest because its gurgling drowned his prayers. Now it only fills at the approach of some public disaster.

Life in the Eremo delle Carceri has never been anything but tough, yet this did not discourage its only female inmate, a remarkable fifteenth-century nun from Lucca known as Beata Anonima. 'Fired with an ardent desire to fight under the seraphic standard', she fled disguised as a man, arrived at the monastery and demanded to join the friars. Impressed by her piety, they allowed her to do so, and only when she lay dying, after many years of pious devotions, was the anonymous Tuscan discovered to be a woman.

Leaving Assisi by the south-west, from Porta Nuova, you reach what remains of the monastery of Sant'Angelo in Panzo, which has strong associations

Time and the Umbrian landscape have softened the effect of Assisi's Rocca Minore.

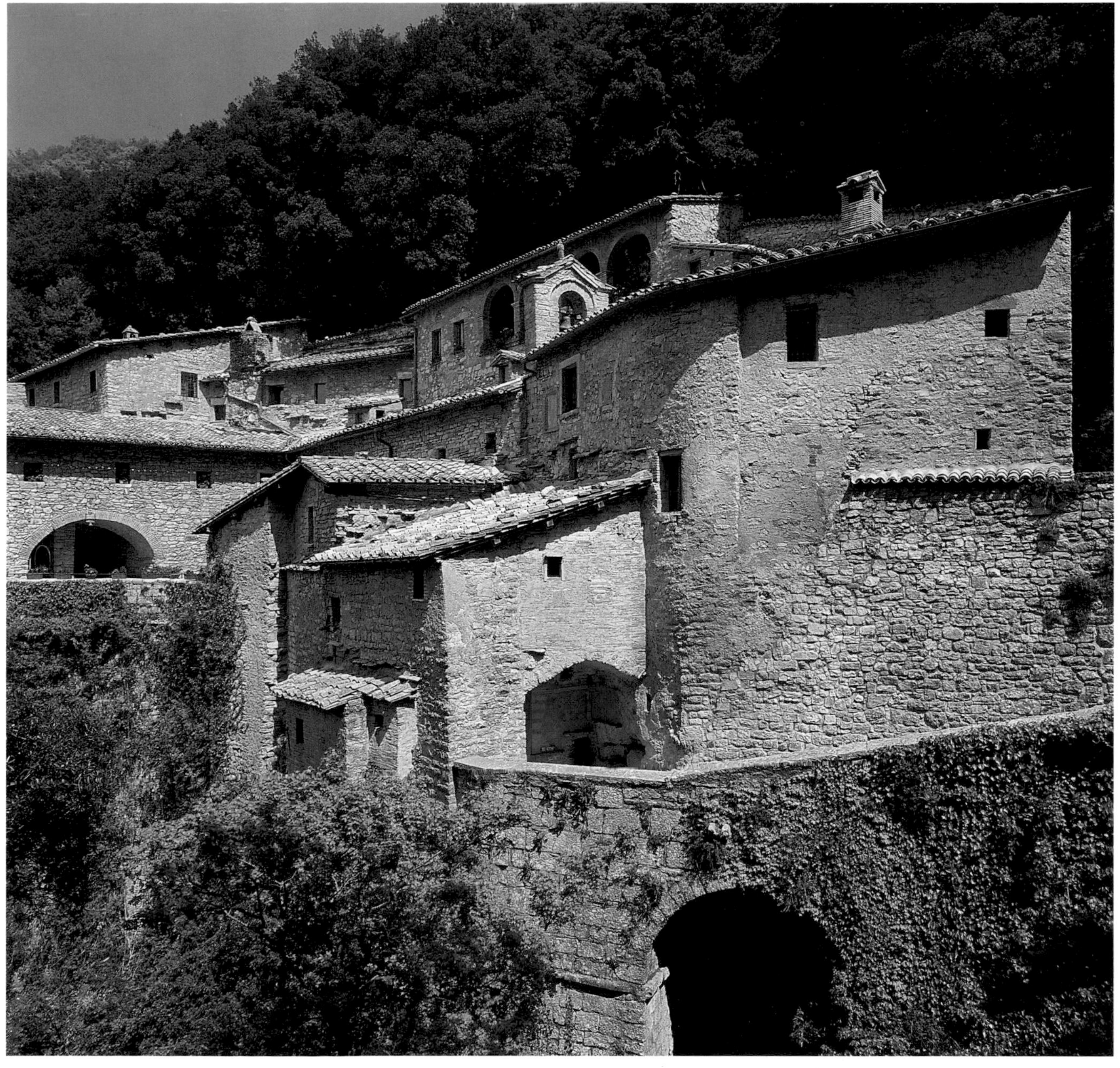

Left An angel guards the elegant façade of Santa Maria degli Angeli, Assisi.

Above The Eremo della Carceri, Assisi, overlooks a wooded valley.

A grandiose doorway to one of Nocera Umbra's noble palaces.

with the early friendship between St Francis and St Clare. Further along the road lies an even older abbey, San Benedetto, probably begun around 900, with a beautiful double crypt of late romanesque design, though the conventual buildings were restored in the seventeenth century.

Another short drive from Porta Nuova leads up among the olives and cypresses to the thirteenth-century convent of San Damiano, once a poor church where Saint Francis is said to have heard a crucifix (now kept at Santa Chiara) order him to 'Go and repair my house'. The young saint took merchandise from his father's clothing warehouse to Foligno, sold it and gave the money to the priest of San Damiano, who refused it, whereupon Francis threw it in at the window. Later he raised money himself from charitable donations and worked as a labourer on the rebuilding. Here Saint Clare died and here her nuns kept their society until the church of Santa Chiara was finished. The church and convent preserve Clare's apsidal oratory, with relics including the little bell with which she summoned the sisters to prayer, and her tiny garden overlooking the plain. In the refectory the place where she sat at table is marked by a vase of flowers.

Those in need of even fresher breezes than Assisi can offer may drive up the back road to Gubbio into the high mountains, via Pieve San Nicolò to Valfabbrica, with its medieval walls and towers, and thence to La Barcaccia, where a left turn takes you into rugged, wooded remoteness. Through Coccorano and Biscina you rejoin a main road from Perugia and soon catch sight of the noble ensemble of the fourteenth-century castle and abbey of Vallingegno, where St Francis once sought temporary refuge. At the head of the pass, which brings you almost to Gubbio, turn right and return to Assisi through Carbonesca and Casa Castalda. The journey may be more scenic than art-historical, but who, amid the unstinting beauty of the Umbrian landscape, will seriously complain, especially if they have taken care to provide themselves with a good Assisian picnic before setting out?

From Assisi you can either climb right up onto Monte Subasio, along the road running all the way along its spine, or go back down the hill and join the road to Gualdo Tadino, which carries you through the wild valley of the Tescio. This is true Umbrian hill country, with very little in the way of villages or churches to mark a strong human presence upon the landscape. Follow the line of the river for as long as you can, then, just before it peters out into a mountain stream (it is never actually more than what in Italian is called a *torrente*), turn up towards Santa Maria Lignano. An extremely minor road will bring you to a right turn for Nocera Umbra.

Nocera is one of the pleasantest small Umbrian towns. Though you can see it for miles in many directions, lying along the gentle slope of its hill, it always seems surprising both in its utter remoteness and in the sturdy vivacity of its people, evidently

Olive tree and poppies in a meadow north of Assisi.

determined that 'the back of beyond' should not necessarily mean a city of the dead. Far from it, indeed, since nowadays Nocera claims to be among the fastest-growing communities in the region. There are winter resorts on nearby Monte Pennino, and the waters of the Sorgente Angelica at the spa of Bagni are reputed to work miracles on your kidneys and intestines.

As an inhabited site, Nocera is very old. The Umbrians knew it as Nuceria and the Romans called it Cammellaria, making the town into an important staging-post on the Via Flaminia. If you arrive here by train, you can catch a glimpse near the station of the so-called Ponte Marmoreo, a Roman bridge made of large unmortared stones, crossing the River Topino. The Longobards incorporated Nocera into their dukedom of Spoleto, but its exposed position on the junction with the main highway to Ancona made it continually vulnerable to attack, and it was devastated first by the Saracens, then by marauding Hungarians. In 1248 Frederick II, at the head of his own Saracen troops, sacked the town, and by the middle of the fifteenth century it had become part of the Papal domains.

One of the main reasons for the place's existence becomes clear when you park your car at the foot of Viale Matteotti, beside a modern fountain energetically playing. Nocera calls itself 'the city of the waters', and springs of one sort or another well up all over the town, deliciously cold and memorably refreshing, so that a walk through the streets is the best sort of temperance outing.

The Viale has cheerful cafés, serving their own excellent ice-cream, and the pleasure of sampling this and watching Nocera, bustling yet relaxed, going about its affairs may keep you happily engaged for some time. Yet you should absolutely not miss the experience of walking up through the Porta Vecchia and into the old town, whose air of silent, rather battered dignity has only recently started to change, owing to a programme of patient and painstaking

The splendidly sited *duomo* and *rocca* at Nocera Umbra.

Sweet water flows from one of Nocera Umbra's many fountains.

restoration that is slowly recovering Nocera's palaces and churches.

This is a spot where you notice small but telling details, the ornamented cornices of a late renaissance façade, the half-destroyed inscription that tells you how somebody whose name has disappeared rebuilt the house of his forefathers, the blocked-up medieval *porta del morto*, the subtle fading of paintwork and the mottlings and blotchings of weather-stained stone. In Piazza Caprera, at the top of the winding main street, there is, sure enough, a fountain of magical coolness and sweetness, and the fourteenth-century gothic church of San Francesco, which contains a surprisingly good small art gallery. Most of its frescoes, uncovered in recent decades, are from the energetic brush of Matteo da Gualdo, painted probably during the 1460s. The oldest work here is a primitive crucifix by an Umbrian follower of Cimabue, and the gem of the collection is a majestic polyptych (1483) by Nicolò

Above The romanesque church of San Filippo, Nocera Umbra.

Right Vigorous reliefs show symbols of the four evangelists on the façade at San Filippo, Nocera Umbra.

Alunno, incorporating a *Nativity* and a *Coronation of the Virgin* within an opulent gilded frame.

Finally, walk up spacious Via San Rinaldo, rendered the grander by the presence of the bishop's palace, to the cathedral, originally a romanesque building remodelled in 1448, with an eighteenth-century interior. There is little of interest inside, but to the right of the church is a terrace with a stunning glimpse of the Topino valley. In the adjacent *rocca* (a tower is all that remains) on 10 January 1421, the castellan Pasquale di Vagnolo invited Nocera's powerful Trinci brothers to supper after a hunting expedition. His wife, as he knew, was involved in an amorous liaison with one of them, and that night she and her lover were murdered on Pasquale's orders. The combination of good-mannered hospitality, illicit love and cold-blooded revenge makes the story typical of its period and its nation.

Leave Nocera by the Foligno road, which takes you through some spectacular walking and birdwatching country along the Topino, under the shadows of Monte Faeto and Monte Burano. This is the Via Flaminia, named after the unfortunate Gaius Flaminius, commander of the doomed legions at Trasimeno, (see p. 45), who instigated the project in 220 BC. The village of San Giovanni Profiamma, just outside Foligno, preserves a garbled form of his name, since it was originally Forum Flaminii, and various Roman remains survive in and around the church. At Vescia, on the opposite bank of the river, the church is embellished with frescoes by Mezzastris and some naively attractive seventeenth-century scenes from the life of St Martin beside the high altar.

The little town of Spello, which you reach from a right turn at the junction with the *superstrada*, is among the loveliest in Italy. I know of nobody who, visiting it for the first time, has not wanted to remain here for ever. Several of my acquaintance are now chronically affected by a nostalgia for the place, and we have all, at one time or another, declared that if there were any spot on earth in which we should desire to pass our last years, this would surely be it.

The charm of Spello is not solely that of its people, who are courteous, affable and good-natured in the best Umbrian tradition, nor is it in the plain yet remarkable fact that the town holds no obvious mark of ugliness or misery inscribed upon its features. Perhaps the pleasure of Spello derives simply from the curious feeling of warmth, security and calm which embraces you as soon as you enter within its enfolding walls.

The earliest of these are Roman, for Spello is still in essence Hispellum, the town founded at the beginning of the first century BC and enriched with territory confiscated by Octavius from such contumacious cities as Assisium and Fulginium (Foligno) who had allied with Lucius Antonius in the civil war against him in 41 BC. Throughout the imperial period 'Colonia Julia Hispellum' enjoyed mounting prosperity and importance, crowned in the fourth century AD by the Emperor Constantine (337–40), who dignified it with the title 'Flavia Constans', gave it a new temple in honour of his family and allowed it the right, formerly the privilege of Volsinii in Latium, to celebrate the annual Umbrian religious festival.

In the Middle Ages, divided into three districts called Pusterola, Mezota and Porta Chiusa, it was the seat of a bishop and governed by a mayor elected half-yearly by twelve *boni homines*. These 'good men' also maintained a little army, which made its presence felt in fierce fighting against neighbouring cities. (To this day the Spellans bear a strong resentment towards the Folignates.) After a series of rulers whose names strike a more famous, or infamous, echo elsewhere in Italy, such as Gian Galeazzo Visconti of Milan, Guido da Montefeltro of Urbino and the Baglioni family of Perugia, the town became a papal possession in 1583.

Spello has five surviving Roman gates, and you can inspect two of the most imposing as you drive in from the Foligno road. Somewhat to your left is the Porta Urbica, an Augustan archway of large masonry blocks. The phallus carved on the inner wall was explained by

Cypresses and the tower of the *rocca* against the Spello skyline.

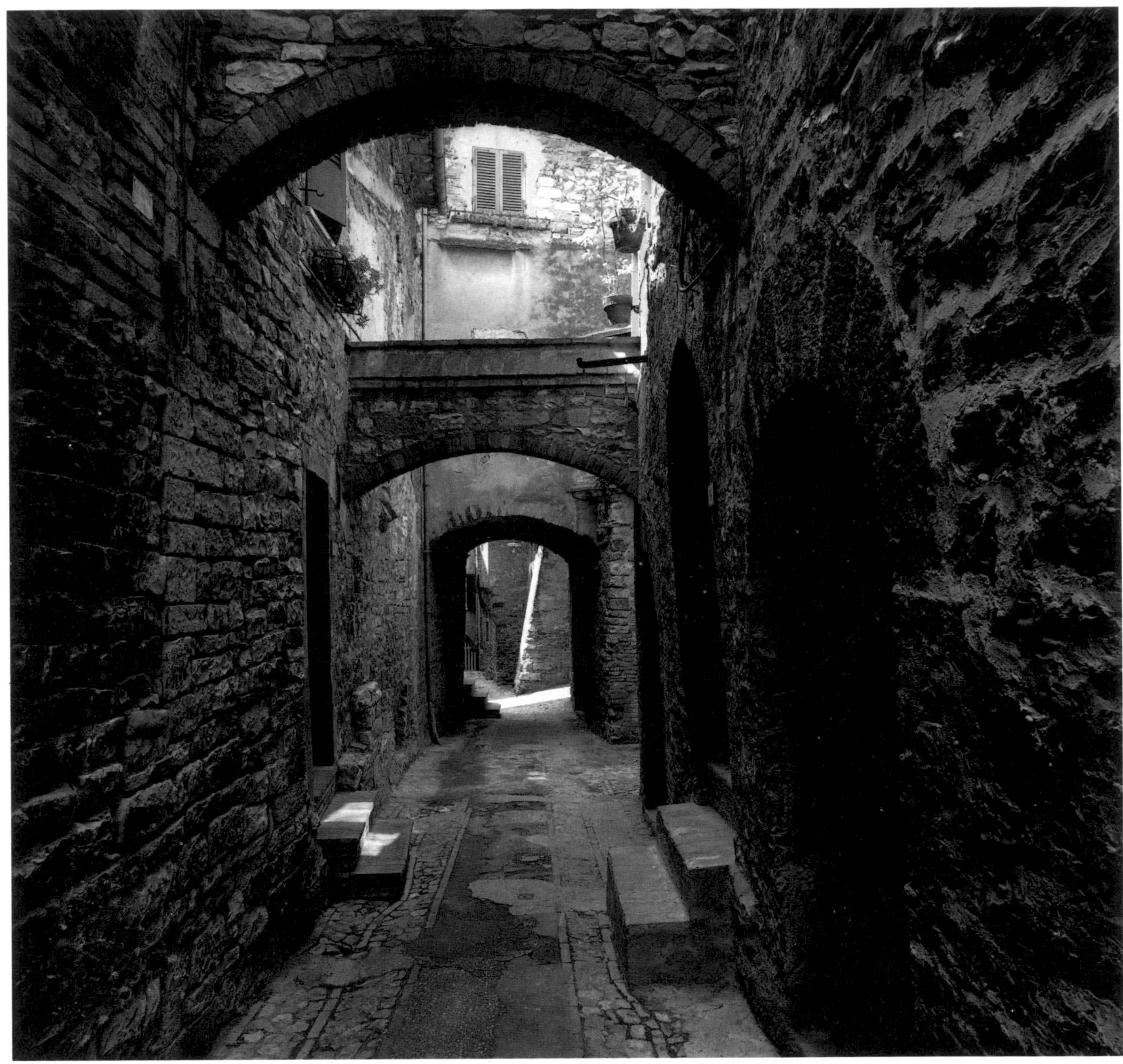

Above **The look and layout of Spello's lanes has changed little since Roman times.**

Right **An effective fusion of romanesque with baroque at Santa Maria Maggiore, Spello.**

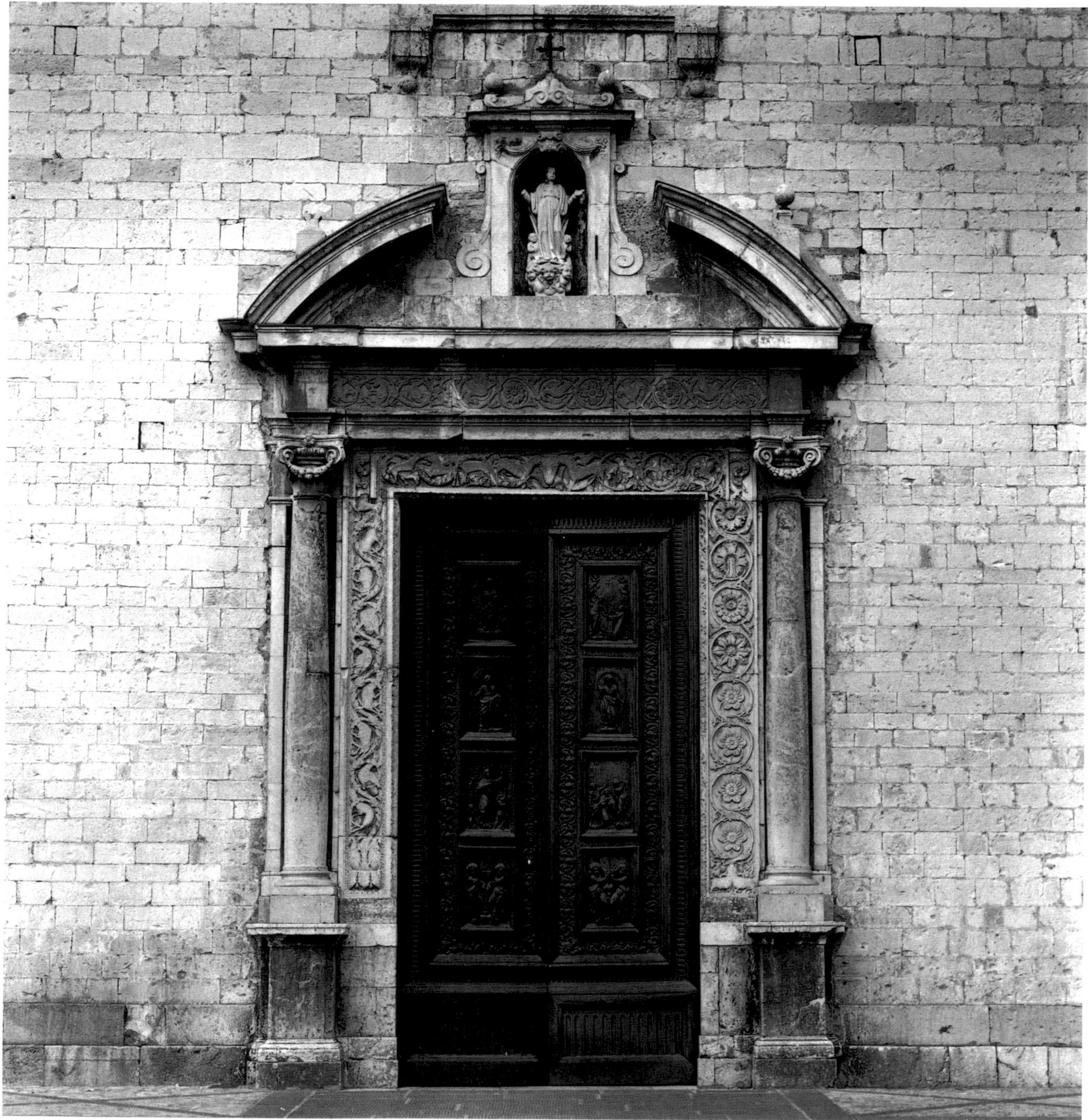

medieval Spellans as a memorial to the chivalric hero Orlando (Roland) who, while a prisoner here, was said to have demonstrated that his capacity was greater than other men's even in the act of making water (*actus mingendi*). The statues over the tall Porta Consolare, to your right, came originally from a Roman tomb, but the tower next to it, with olive trees growing out of its top, belongs to the twelfth century.

From here you enter the old town via the curving Via Consolare. Most of the houses in Spello incorporate medieval work utilizing roman masonry, but the foundations of many must actually go back to the days of the empire. On your right the Cappella Tega contains a much damaged but movingly depicted fragment of a *Crucifixion* (1461) by Nicolò Alunno. The street now becomes Via Cavour, and set somewhat away from it with a plain façade and small campanile stands Santa Maria Maggiore, the town's most remarkable church.

On a site once occupied by a temple to Juno and Venus, the present building, begun in 1285, was much altered in succeeding centuries. The font is a Roman marble funerary altar dedicated to the magistrate Caius Titienus Flaccus, whose equestrian portrait is shown in bold relief upon one of the panels, while the others are decorated with scenes of birds pecking fruit from the branches of a tree. Over the high altar stands an ornate domed marble canopy, the work of Rocco di Tommaso. Its expressive small portrait busts of the prophets were added in 1562 by Gian Domenico da Carrara. The frescoes on either side of the apse, late works by Perugino painted in 1521, are always written off as unworthy of him, but this is hardly fair. On the left the figure of the Virgin holding the dead Christ has as tender and feeling a countenance as any he ever depicted. Among the baroque side altars, look out for the sprightly, witty stucco confection representing the miraculous aerial journey of the Holy House of Loreto, said to be the original home of the Virgin Mary in Palestine.

All these things are incidental to the real treasure of the church, the fresco sequence with which Pinturicchio adorned the Cappella Baglioni in 1501. Bernardino di Betto, always called Pinturicchio (1454–1513), was one of Perugino's most highly gifted pupils and an absolute master of fresco painting, as can be seen from his work in the Vatican at Rome and in the Piccolomini Library in Siena. Art historians have given him a somewhat rough ride. Vasari accused him of working too fast, and the American art critic Bernard Berenson (1865–1959) describes him as 'all tinsel and costume-painting, a reversion to the worst Umbrian art of the beginning of the 15th century'.

It is time this verdict was seriously challenged, and you will surely think so when you see these scenes from the early life of Jesus. The colours are rich and subtle, a mixture of deep greens, blues and reds predominating, and each composition is based on a penetrating glimpse into a distant landscape of such amazing detail that we want to know what is happening there as well as here among the Shepherds and the Wise Men. In the *Annunciation* and in *Christ Among the Doctors*, Pinturicchio's marvellous sense of theatre takes over, almost as if he had personally directed the characters on a specially prepared stage. His pleasure in sheer story-telling makes these paintings among Umbria's most genuinely rewarding.

A little further up Via Cavour is the church of Sant'Andrea, a twelfth-century building with a fine vaulted gothic apse added a hundred years later. To this period also belongs the large Giottesque crucifix with a tiny St Francis praying at Christ's feet, left here by members of a religious brotherhood on their way to the jubilee at Rome in 1400. One expert has daringly assigned this to Giotto himself. On the right side of the church is a ravishing Pinturicchio altar-piece, painted in 1508 in collaboration with Eusebio di San Giorgio, showing a gentle Madonna among opulently garbed saints, with a letter from the bishop of Orvieto to the artist actually included in the foreground. Notice also the gilded baroque casket containing the relics of the Blessed Andrea Caccioli, an early companion of St Francis and one of Spello's patron saints, who is

Pinturicchio's beautiful *Nativity*, at Santa Maria Maggiore, Spello.

particularly efficacious both when rain is needed and in making it stop.

You can find the house where Andrea was born in 1194 in Via Torri di Properzio immediately opposite. The two twelve-sided towers after which the street is named flank the roman Porta Venere, but have nothing whatever to do with Propertius (Spello long ago gave up its claim to be the poet's birthplace). If you return to Via Cavour, which now becomes Via Garibaldi, this brings you into Piazza Repubblica, with the former *rocca* on your right and at the further end the Palazzo Comunale, built in 1270 by an architect called Maestro Prode.

In the courtyard of the palace a small archaeological museum of Roman sculptural fragments has been assembled. Constantine's edict promoting Hispellum is kept in a place of honour on the first floor, in the Sala degli Zuccari, whose sixteenth-century frescoes include a distant prospect of Spello and its countryside that has not changed much since. There is a little picture collection, including a half-ruined but still noble gothic diptych by the Sienese Cola Petruccioli (1362–1408), and an extensive archive and library, whose books are kept in gorgeously decorated early eighteenth-century cases.

At the top of the street, the romanesque church of San Lorenzo contains an irresistible panel by Tiberio d'Assisi of St Anthony Abbot (1518), which features the black pigs with which the saint is always associated, but is really more remarkable for its wealth of pretty furnishings and decorative features from different periods. The renaissance tabernacle for the holy oils is bedecked with inlaid *pietra dura* panels beneath exquisite carved angels in the Florentine manner. The high altar is crowned by a Berninian baldacchino of 1631, and the carving of the choir-stalls and pulpit is lavishly detailed.

The turret of San Claudio and the ancient walls of Spello.

Now turn right and walk up Via Giulia, a long curving street with little cobbled lanes running off it. You emerge into the lopsided Piazza Vallegloria and take the left turn beside the old convent church of Santa Maria. This will lead you up to Spello's second and larger *rocca*, in front of which a terrace gives you space to pause for a comprehensive view of the town, with Perugia and Assisi on their far hilltops, and the remains of the amphitheatre and the little romanesque church of San Claudio below. The elegant Chiesa Tonda beyond is a domed building on a Greek-cross plan, begun in 1517 by architects from Domodossola, on what is now Italy's Alpine frontier. The tall, green-shuttered house immediately to the north is Villa Costanzi (sometimes called Villa Fidelia), set in a neat 'Italian' garden of clipped box hedges, parterres with stone urns and an open-air theatre. It houses an art collection, open to weekend visitors, mixing twentieth-century painters, including the Futurists, works by such earlier masters as Jacopo Bassano (*c.*1510–92) and Annibale Carracci (1560–1609), and a so-called Titian of a buxom noblewoman with a black page, obviously by a later painter but very good of its kind.

Across the valley, the church of San Girolamo with its convent, nestling in the woods, beckons the traveller. This was founded in 1474, and Rocco di Tommaso gave it a broad portico with a pilastered arcade running above it. As well as the pretty cloister, there are twin chapels, and the church itself has a Marriage of the Virgin by one of Pinturicchio's pupils.

By now you perhaps feel hungry, and Spello will certainly not fail you with her restaurants. The Bastiglia has a large terrace from which, over dinner, you can watch the night steal down across the Umbrian plain below, and the Molino will reward your ardent affection with a plate of pasta with asparagus and truffles, local sausages and a tart called *fregnaccia* made with aniseed, honey, nuts and raisins. Meanwhile, open a bottle of Grecchetto or Bianco d'Arquata and, for my sake, drink a health to Spello 'and all that therein is'.

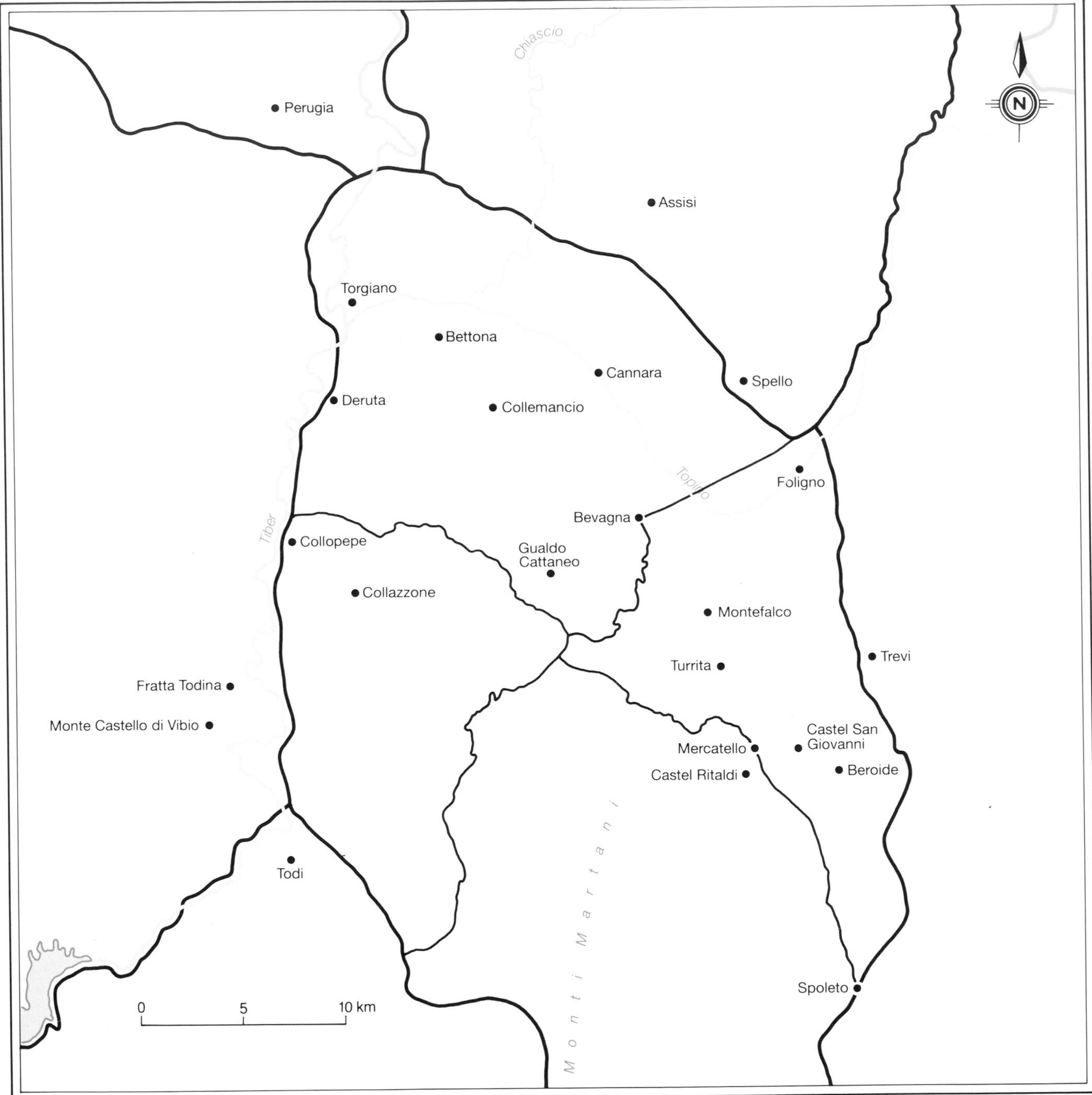
N
Chiascio
Perugia
Assisi
Torgiano
Bettona
Cannara
Spello
Deruta
Collemancio
Topino
Foligno
Bevagna
Tiber
Collopepe
Gualdo
Cattaneo
Collazzone
Montefalco
Trevi
Turrita
Fratta Todina
Monte Castello di Vibio
Castel San
Giovanni
Mercatello
Castel Ritaldi
Beroide
Todi
Monti Martani
0
5
10 km
Spoleto

4
Umbria Romana

Todi – Foligno – Trevi – Montefalco

One day someone will write – if they have not already written – a book about the foundation of cities, about why their sites were specially selected, about the importance of rivers and mountains and ancient thoroughfares in their layout and position, and about the extraordinary wealth of legends attaching to their earliest beginnings. Italian cities, some of the oldest in Europe, are especially rich in such stories, tales involving dreams, oracles, gods and goddesses, and very often the actions of beasts and birds.

Todi, high up on its three-sided hill overlooking the vale of the Tiber, is one such city. Tradition says that its founders, seeking the ideal spot to clear and prepare for settlement, sat down to eat in the valley, but had their tablecloth snatched away by an eagle, which carried it up the hillside and let it fall at the summit (hence the bird's appearance in the city's coat of arms). It may indeed have been this which led the profoundly superstitious Umbrians and Etruscans to consolidate a stronghold here during the fifth century BC and to call it Tular or Tuder, meaning 'frontier'. The Romans gave it the sonorous title Colonia Julia Fida Tuder, and made it the centre of a wealthy farming community; barbarian invaders seem to have been daunted by the sheer steepness of its hill and left it well alone.

Todi's story, during the Middle Ages, is a confused chronicle of political swings between Guelph and Ghibelline, and of domination by successive great families before it finally fell into Papal hands. Nowadays it is an extremely lively, prosperous and attractive town, a centre for Italy's antique dealers, who until recently held an annual fair here, but you can still find opportunities for agreeing with the Edwardian traveller Edward Hutton, who in 1905 praised its silence beyond everything else. 'You hear no train' he wrote, 'even in the stillest night; no tram rushes past your windows to remind you of the horrible new world that has only time for action, that has forgotten to think.'

The effect of climbing the hill from Porta Romana is indeed that of a gradual retreat into beauty, but driving and parking in Todi are difficult, so you should either park at the foot of the hill or try to find a space in Piazza Garibaldi before starting a walk through the town. The square itself, with Garibaldi's statue at the centre, is not without its attractions. On your right is a tall renaissance palace which, the Latin inscription around the frieze rather smugly tells you, 'Viviano Atti, knight, built and adorned, consulting public no less than private benefit, in 1552'. The architect was very probably Galeazzo Alessi. From the railed terrace beyond, you can look out across a wonderful prospect of gardens and roofs towards the high ridges of the Monti Martani to the east.

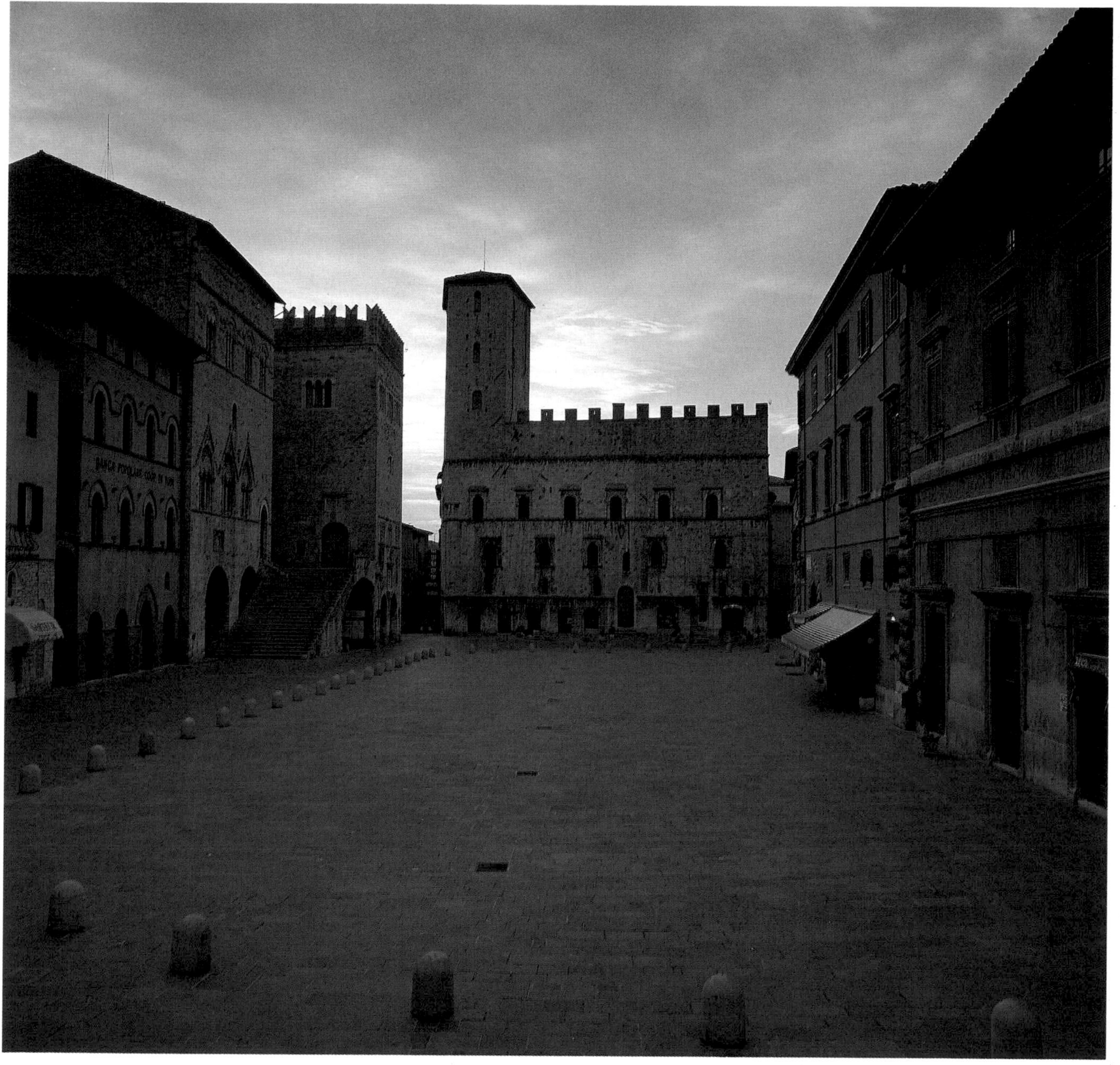

Left **A lane made of shallow steps winds up the steep hillside at Todi.**

Above **Looking across Piazza del Popolo, Todi.**

On your left stands one of the three medieval palaces which create so unforgettable an ensemble at the very heart of Todi. The Palazzo del Popolo, with its stark masonry and round-arched windows, is the oldest of these, and one of the earliest of those public buildings with which the free cities of Italy proclaimed their independence. It was begun in 1206, the upper floor being added twenty years afterwards, but the battlements, alas, are a piece of nineteenth-century fancywork. In times past, the doors over a picture of the Holy Family, attached to one of the walls, used to be solemnly opened every evening, a lamp was lit and a crowd gathered to recite the Angelus.

Next to this is the much larger Palazzo del Capitano, one of the most beautiful gothic palaces in Italy, begun in 1290. The façade carefully contrasts the rhythm of the three cusped arches over the lower row of triple-arched ogival windows with the simpler curves above the upper series. A broad flight of steps outside the palace takes you to the first floor, where the picture gallery has been closed for some fifteen years. Perhaps you will be lucky enough to arrive when the city fathers have decided that enough is enough and reopened it at last. Among its treasures I recall a gorgeous *Coronation of the Virgin*, by Lo Spagna at his lyrical best, with angel trumpeters, jubilant saints and a praying throng of bishops and friars below.

The Palazzo del Capitano dominates Piazza del Popolo, site of the Roman forum. Formerly paved with brick, in 1963 it was given its present pinkish stone paving, a questionable addition to its charms. The square, with its cafès and conversations and evening strollers, encapsulates everything you have ever learned to love about Italy, but in the Middle Ages it seems to have been a good deal less salubrious. A statute of 1275 forbade the vegetable sellers to discard rotting refuse, prohibited the tanning of hides and threatened with punishment those who left the dead bodies of animals here.

At the southern end of the square stands the long bulk of the Palazzo dei Priori, completed in 1337 but given its two extra storeys in 1513 by Pope Leo X (1513–21). From the palace, with its trapezoid tower and bronze eagle of 1339, Todi was governed, and municipal offices still occupy it.

The town had its share of early Christian martyrs. St Terentianus, the first bishop, was tried and condemned in 131 after a long interview with the Roman proconsul. At his execution in the forum, one of his accusers, a certain Flaccus, overcome with remorse, offered him water to drink and then begged to be baptized. Terentianus carried out the ceremony there and then before the amazed bystanders, and the two were promptly put to death.

Todi's earliest cathedral occupied the site of a ruined temple at the northern end of the square. The present building, begun in the twelfth century, stands at the top of a magnificent flight of twenty-nine steps, which look as though they have been set up in readiness for some thunderingly dramatic ensemble from one of Verdi's operas. The harmonies of the façade are created by three rose windows, all renaissance work of the early sixteenth century, and the gothic portals, the largest of which has a most elegant carved door; its upper panels were carved by a certain 'Maestro Antonio' in 1513 and the lower sequence added after lightning burned the originals in 1623. The carver on this occasion was a Frenchman named Charles Laurent (always called Carlo Lorenti in Italy).

The interior of the *duomo* is plain romanesque, with round-headed arches with Corinthian columns whose pilasters carry expressive carved figures of saints and a finely chiselled head of Christ. On the inner wall, if you turn round as you enter, you will see an exuberantly conceived *Last Judgment* in which the infernal regions are certainly as busy as the celestial, the work of Ferrau da Faenza (1562–1645), who was evidently inspired by Michelangelo. Most of the figures are half-clothed or nude, but in 1866 a Roman painter was commissioned to make some tactful changes 'for the purpose of covering in church certain too realistic manifestations'. Perhaps the ecclesiastical powers-that-be will

Massive brick vaults uphold the Palazzo del Popolo, Todi.

take another hint from Michelangelo, and follow the example of the Sistine Chapel in Rome, where his famous frescoes have been stripped of the prudish coverings given them in the sixteenth century by Daniele da Volterra, known thereafter as Daniele delle Braghe, 'Daniele of the Breeches'.

Among several good altar-pieces there is an appealingly primitive early fourteenth-century Madonna cradling her Child in the folds of a scarlet robe, and a sumptuously framed *Madonna with Saints Catherine and Roche* by Giannicola di Paolo (1460–1544), which came originally from a church in the village of Collepepe on the road to Perugia. The choir, whose apse has a fine primitive crucifix of the early thirteenth century, is ringed with a handsome set of inlaid stalls, executed in 1530 by the brothers Antonio and Sebastiano Bencivenni. The increasing desire of artists to represent things for their own sake, rather than as elements in a composition dominated by human figures, is often revealed by the panels in such stalls, and here the Bencivenni delighted to portray ears of barley, a birdcage, a viola da gamba or a tambourine. Some may feel it is a pity that we have lost one stall, described in a document of 1571 as *tamquam derisoria et scandalosa*, which a shocked bishop Angelo Cesi ordered to be removed.

Cesi, a figure greatly admired for his learning and generosity, was bishop of Todi for fifty years and is buried, along with several other members of his most distinguished Umbrian clan, in the family chapel to the left of the choir. The long white beard shown in the oval portrait on the tomb, by Annibale Carracci (1560–1609), was still apparently visible when the body was exhumed in 1860. Cesi it was who commissioned the famous Modenese architect Giacomo Barozzi (1507–73), always called Vignola from his birthplace, to build the episcopal palace, with its sturdy rusticated gateway, in 1593. Next to it, on the western flank of the cathedral by the staircase into the square, is the Cesi family's private residence, designed by Antonio da Sangallo the Younger.

This sober *palazzo* was the home, in his last years, of Paolo Rolli (1687–1765), one of the most gifted of eighteenth-century Italian poets, who had followed a highly successful career in England as an adviser to the intensely Italophile English nobility on everything from fashion to art collecting. He became a fellow of the Royal Society, though the one paper he delivered (on a Spanish boy said to be amphibious) was cribbed from a book. He was one of the theatre poets at the opera house in the Haymarket in London and wrote several libretti for Handel, whom he detested; perhaps that is why none of them is very good. Nevertheless his verse is highly accomplished, especially the poems he published during his last years in Todi and the witty collection of epigrams known as *Le Meriboniane*, recalling convivial evenings in London's Marylebone pleasure gardens.

Rolli's bust figures on the newly restored pink façade of the Teatro Comunale in Via Mazzini, which takes you out of Piazza del Popolo on the south side. As you might expect, the auditorium, by Carlo Gatteschi (1828–92), an architect from Arezzo in Tuscany, is a delightful confection of tiered, red-draped boxes set off by gilt medallions and cornices and a ceiling decorated with cupids and garlands. A sharp left turn at the end of the street leads you suddenly downhill, but everything here is now dominated by the expansive gothic façade of the church of San Fortunato, viewed across box-hedged lawns.

Though this north front to the church is unfinished, you will grasp at once what the effect was to have been from the nature of the surviving lower portion, whose design combines elements of gothic in the deeply incised central portal with ogival niches on either side, early renaissance in the tall classical pilasters, and romanesque in the round-arched flanking doorways. This most interesting ensemble was the work of Giovanni di Santuccio, assisted by his nephew Bartolo di Angelo, but the death of the former in 1458 put a stop to the project (the local story that the architect was the famous Lorenzo Maitani of Orvieto, whom

The romanesque nave of the *duomo* at Todi.

his fellow citizens blinded and maimed to stop his finishing the façade, is exploded by the simple fact that Maitani died in 1330). Before you go inside, look at the graceful statues of the Virgin and the Archangel Gabriel and at the tiny figures which the carvers have insinuated into the decoration, some of them of a distinctly bawdy cast, like characters from Boccaccio's *Decameron*.

Begun in 1291, San Fortunato is one of the great gothic churches of Italy, noteworthy not merely for the purity of line in its tall clusters of columns and ribbed vaulting, but also for the equal height of the aisles and the nave, a feature which relates it to the so-called 'hall churches' of Germany and gives it the same sense of clarity and spaciousness. Both the aisles are lined with chapels, several of which, despite the initially austere appearance of the building, retain fine sculpture and fresco decoration. The fourth along the right aisle, for instance, has a Madonna and Child with attendant angels, their golden hair frizzled and their cheeks delicately flushed, by Masolino da Panicale (1383–1447). The last chapel is an exhilarating essay in rococo, with two angels upholding a medallion relief of the Annunciation, while God the Father hovers above among scrambling *putti* and puffy clouds.

In the crypt, under the high altar, an enormous marble sarcophagus holds the bodies of five Todine martyrs, Saints Fortunatus, Calixtus, Cassian, Romana and Digna. Todi, let it be said, has no fewer than 105 saints: they include one pope, 95 martyrs, five confessors, three blessed virgins, sixteen cardinals and at least 70 bishops. Fortunatus himself was bishop of Todi during the sixth century and was particularly noted for a miracle worked during the advance through Umbria of a gothic army led by Witiza, successor to King Theodoric the Great (493–526). When the Goths took two Todine children hostage, Fortunatus went to persuade them to accept a ransom instead. The gothic captain who had carried off the children refused to give them up, and the bishop warned him that no good would come of his obstinacy. The next day the army marched through the city, the hostages defiantly bound and led on horseback. In front of the cathedral the captain's mount stumbled, he was thrown to the ground and given up for dead. When he recovered, he ordered the instant return of the children to their parents, and Fortunatus soon effected a miraculous cure of his broken bones with a sprinkling of holy water. The bones of Fortunatus himself, together with those of his fellow saints, were translated to San Fortunato on 5 May 1596 by Bishop Angelo Cesi in a jolly ceremony attended by 40,000 people, with a triumphal arch in front of the church holding a band of musicians, and the fountains of the town running with wine.

To the left of the sarcophagus, a simple memorial stone marks the grave of the Blessed Jacopone da Todi, one of the charismatic religious figures of the

San Fortunato at Todi is one of Umbria's finest gothic churches.

A sculptural detail from the main doorway at San Fortunato, Todi.

Madonna with Angels, a fresco by Masolino da Panicale at San Fortunato, Todi.

thirteenth century and a poet of singular intensity and brilliance. Born in 1230, he practised as a lawyer until the death of his wife Vanna, when the wooden platform on which she was dancing at a wedding collapsed. Hitherto Jacophone had been cynical about those who showed too much enthusiasm for the practice of piety, but after discovering the dead Vanna to be wearing a hair-shirt, the remorseful attorney joined the Franciscan order and championed its most radical wing against the worldly and ambitious Pope Boniface VIII (1294–1303). His poetry, written in Umbrian dialect, is by turns ecstatic, lyrical and witheringly satirical, as potent in his *Stabat Mater*'s heartrending vision of the Virgin seeking her son at the Crucifixion as in a diatribe against the hated Pope who had flung him into prison. He died in 1306, three years after his release by the new Pope, Benedict X.

Leave the crypt and walk down the left aisle. Here the chapel of the Assumption has a stuccoed cupola and frescoes by Andrea Polinori (1586–1648), a local painter with a cheerful, uncomplicated, early baroque style, and the chapel of the Santissimo Crocifisso preserves interesting fourteenth-century fragments, including a *Banquet of Herod* with a lavishly spread dinner table. The absence of any decorative objects in the church, by the way, is partly explained by the shocking behaviour of the Emperor Louis the Bavarian (1328–47), who, during the fourteenth century, looted the treasury, assisted by his protégé Pietro Rainalducci of Rieti, who had appointed himself Pope with the title of Nicholas V (1447–55). The pair, loathed by the Todines, who called them 'two old crooks', liberally helped themselves to gold and silver before making off with their crew of drunken, dissolute followers.

Behind San Fortunato, you might get a glimpse of the broad, brick-arched cloister of the old Franciscan convent (now a school) dating from the late thirteenth century, where Jacopone lived as a friar. At the back of this lies the so-called Carcere di San Cassiano, the remains of a Roman cistern, and beyond, inside a park with shady walks and hedges, stands the stump of one of the towers of the *rocca*, demolished in 1503, with yet more of those spectacular Umbrian distances in the background.

The church in the valley immediately below, with its four domes clustered around a central cupola, is the temple of Santa Maria della Consolazione, one of several similar buildings placed at the entrances to Umbrian and Tuscan hilltowns by the great architects of the Renaissance, and a work of memorable beauty in the harmony of its details and the 'frozen music' of its lines and masses. It was raised to commemorate the miraculous restoration of sight, in 1508, to a workman blind in one eye, who had wiped his face with a cloth he had used to dust off a holy picture.

Experts cannot agree as to how far the great Bramante (Donato di Pascuccio, 1444–1514), architect of St Peter's in Rome, had a hand in the design, but

The church of Santa Maria della Consolazione outside Todi.

there can be no doubt that he inspired the initial concept, which also has links with similar ideas by Leonardo da Vinci. A host of other leading architects are known to have been involved in the work at various stages during the sixteenth century, including Antonio da Sangallo the Younger, the Sienese Baldassare Peruzzi (1481–1536), Vignola, Alessi and the prolific Orvietan Ippolito Scalza.

Much of the impact of Santa Maria della Consolazione is due to the respect of those who worked on it for the integrity of the original design. Even the little pendants at the four corners of the vaults under the dome, showing the Evangelists seated amid garlands of fruit and flowers, play their part in varying the sobriety of the stone and stucco around them. The black-painted wooden statue to the left of the main door is of Pope Martin I (649–655), born just across the Tiber at Pian di San Martino. He was arrested by the Byzantine Emperor Constans II (641–68) and kept a prisoner in the Crimea, where he was ultimately pushed off a cliff into the sea. Russian sailors used to believe that he appeared during storms in the Black Sea to gather the drowning into his arms. As for the miraculous picture of the *Mystic Marriage of Saint Catherine* which the church was built to house, you can find this almost hidden within the gorgeous marble and gold of the high altar, like a chocolate inside an expensive gift-wrapped box.

Todi has other sights – or 'lions' as nineteenth-century travellers used to call them – with which to beguile visitors. In Piazza del Mercato Vecchio, just below Palazzo Atti, stands one of the most impressive relics of Roman architecture in Umbria. This is the so-called Quattro Nicchioni, four tall curved niches, flanked by pilasters, under a most elegant carved frieze adorned with little reliefs of animals, human faces and weapons. Nobody seems quite sure of the purpose behind the original building, clearly inspired by Hellenistic architectural styles and roughly dated to the first century BC, but the most convincing theory is that it formed part of a large temple complex of which few other traces now survive.

From here go south along Via Matteotti, pausing at the church of San Silvestro to look at two paintings by Andrea Polinori of St Teresa and St Joseph, which convey the liveliness and accomplished grace of this impressive local talent. Beyond the medieval Porta della Catena, at the very end of the street, is the handsome late fifteenth-century church of San Filippo, whose interesting shape owes much to later additions. Buried here is Filippo Benizzi, a Florentine born in 1233 who became a medical student at Padua before entering the Servite order of monks. His reputation for holiness earned him a candidature for the papacy, which he rejected, preferring to live humbly in Todi, where he died in 1285 and was canonized four centuries later by Pope Clement X (1670–76). His statue, over the high altar, is always said to be the work of Bernini (1598–1680). Even if there is no firm evidence for this, it is still a noble essay in baroque sculpture.

Leaving Todi, take the main Perugia road northwards, from which there are several worthwhile diversions if the Tiber valley should start to bore you. Monte Castello di Vibio was formerly part of Todi's defensive system and its narrow medieval streets still give you that sense of absolute safety essential to these hilltop refuges. They have been restoring the little eighteenth-century theatre here, and perhaps it will soon resound again to the cheerful strains of Cimarosa and Paisiello which delighted its earliest patrons. You may be astonished to find such a building in a tiny village, but Umbria is full of them, and I find myself dreaming of a time which will surely never come again, when you might cross the region from hill to hill and hear a string of operas along your journey.

Nearby at Fratta Todina, amid its tobacco plantations, the walls of the medieval castle survive. It once belonged to the Florentines and was then ruled by the *condottiere* Braccio Fortebraccio, before passing to Todi in 1452. The stately palace built by Cardinal Altieri, bishop of Todi from 1643–54, has an ornamental well-

Saint Peter flourishes his keys in Santa Maria della Consolazione, Todi.

head in the courtyard and frescoed rooms. At Collazzone, on the opposite side of the valley and into the olive-clad hills, the medieval walled *borgo* was the scene of Jacopone da Todi's death, at the convent of San Lorenzo, on Christmas Eve, 1306.

You will probably not wish to linger in Deruta, the centre of Umbria's majolica industry, whose approach roads are lined with shops selling all manner of hideous ceramics, so take the road to Torgiano, which lies on a kind of peninsula between the Tiber and its tributary the Chiascio. Here in an old Baglioni palace you will find a museum devoted entirely to wine, from its production in ancient times to the most modern methods of viticulture. There are drinking vessels, amphoras, jugs and glasses; the work of the cooper, the basket-maker and the innkeeper is shown; the botanical development of the vine, and winemaking in Umbria are illustrated. The whole praiseworthy initiative was instigated by the firm of Lungarotti, which created the Torgiano wines that have attained such celebrity throughout Italy in recent decades. You can drink these with a first-rate luncheon at the Tre Vaselle before driving up the hill towards Bettona.

On your way about Umbria you will surely have been struck by just how close to the surface its Roman remains lie. The presence of emperors, consuls and legions is constant, and we meet their ghosts once more at Bettona, still girdled by ancient sandstone walls, Etruscan in origin but reconstructed in the early years of Roman rule and strengthened anew in the Middle Ages. The town itself, perched on a hill amid the olive groves, is the very archetype of what the Italians like to call *oleografia*, meaning – with a touch of gentle sarcasm – the kind of visual image which cries out for a picture postcard or a slightly soft-centred landscape painting. There is an agreeably lopsided piazza, with another abutting onto it which contains a campanile so venerable that you can fancy a crowd gathering apprehensively each day in expectation of its imminent collapse. In the little gallery of the Palazzo del Podestà is a Perugino of the *Virgin with Saints Maurus and Jerome*, and a fresco fragment showing St Michael, by Fiorenzo di Lorenzo.

The road winds on along the edge of the hill, whence you can clearly see the cities of Spello and Assisi across the broad valley. Cannara, to your left, also retains its walls and towers, and the churches of San Francesco and San Matteo contain work by the ever arresting Nicolò Alunno. If you take a turn in the opposite direction, the road comes to a full stop at Collemancio, where, near the romanesque church of Santa Maria della Fontanella, lie the remains of a Roman town, the former Urbinum Hortense. You can make out the foundations of temples, bath houses and a forum, as well as traces of the amphitheatre. The inhabitants abandoned it for Cannara during the fourth century AD, for the purely practical reason that the plain was more fertile and accessible than the hills.

Back on the road south, you pass somewhere near the spot (not positively identified in the original story) where St Francis first preached to the birds. We are told by his early biographer in the *Fioretti* ('Little Flowers') that 'at a place between Cannara and Bevagna, the saint saw some trees by the roadside where roosted a great company of birds' and bade his companions: 'Wait for me here while I go to preach to my little sisters.' The stone upon which he stood is preserved in the church of San Francesco in the old town of Bevagna.

Mentioned by Propertius and Virgil, who tells us that white oxen were sent from here to be sacrificed at the springs of Clitumnus, Mevania, as the Romans called it, was a place of considerable importance and noted especially for its pottery, which, in one form or another, has remained a regional speciality to this day. Pliny the Younger says that its walls were of brick, but the medieval stonework of its surviving ramparts incorporates Roman masonry, and you can find intriguing traces of an ancient town that has not quite disappeared beneath the fabric of later ages.

The church of San Vincenzo in Via Matteotti (now a cinema) is called after Bevagna's first bishop, Vincent,

Collazzone looks down on waving barley fields.

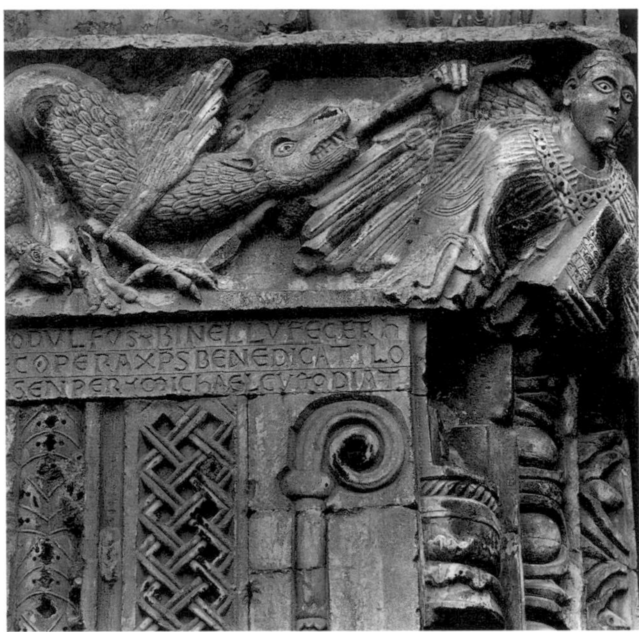

Primitive vigour strikes the keynote at San Michele, Bevagna.

martyred in 303. There are classical fragments in its façade, and beyond, in the semicircular line of houses and gardens, the remains of the theatre are traceable. In Via Crescimbeni, to your right, is the blocked-in colonnade of a temple, and nearby, in Via Porta Guelfa, a black-and-white mosaic floor shows a marine fantasy of dolphins, lobsters and a sort of sea centaur, with a trident and a curly tail.

At the end of Via Matteotti is the neo-classical Palazzo Comunale, housing the art gallery, and here you can gather some idea of Bevagna's ancient significance from the details of the various Roman inscriptions. We know, for instance, that the town was much visited for its temples to various deities connected with health and medicine, and that the merchants and artisans were divided into guilds, along lines much more familiar in Italy during the Middle Ages. There were the *centonarii*, who made coats and blankets, the *fullones*, who were launderers and dyers, the *sagarii* who kept tailoring businesses, the *plumbarii*, plumbers as their name suggests, and someone with the resounding title of *negotiator gallicus et asiaticus*, a kind of commercial agent for trade with Gaul and the East.

It hardly needs saying that the forum lies under the town's main square, Piazza Silvestri, and a most fetching ensemble this provides, especially if you arrive early in the morning and watch it slowly spring to life. The gothic Palazzo dei Consoli, with its double-arched windows and substantial loggia, was built around 1270, probably by the same Maestro Prode who designed the Palazzo Comunale at Spello. Despite my passion for small Italian theatres, I have not yet succeeded in getting into the Teatro Francesco Torti, within this palace, but my appetite is whetted by assurances that it is the most beautiful auditorium in Umbria.

Of the piazza's two romanesque churches, both by a twelfth-century architect named Binello, your preference for either must depend entirely upon your current mood, for each has its own austere grace. San Silvestro's intricately carved portal ushers you into the simplest of interiors, while San Michele, whose façade is pierced by a thirteenth-century rose window, is a more self-consciously imposing affair, with fine carving on the stonework of the apse.

A relentlessly straight road fairly catapults you down off the hills, over the plain and up to the very gates of Foligno. Why is nearly every writer on Umbria so grudging in praise of this city? Why do some not praise it at all? Even Murray's *Handbook*, which can normally stir itself to say something encouraging about far less interesting places, can only get as far as lauding the station's 'first-rate buffet, where the traveller will find an excellent dinner on arriving'. The answer to such lukewarm responses must probably be that most of us have been rendered too fastidious by the wealth of strikingly attractive small towns in the region. Thus the appearance of anything like a perfectly ordinary

The simple romanesque beauty of San Michele, Bevagna.

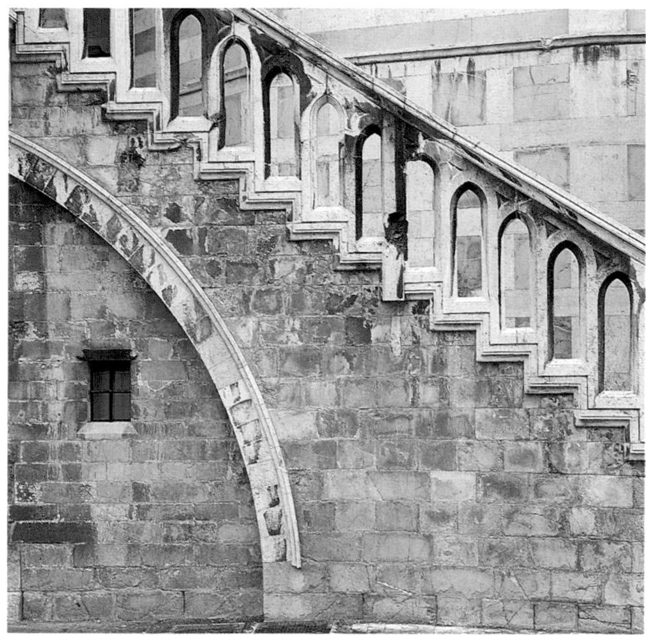

A medieval staircase beside the *duomo* of Foligno.

Lions guard the eastern portal of Foligno's *duomo*.

Italian city, with an old centre, peripheral boulevards and industrial suburbs, a place we might be perfectly pleased to find, say, in Lombardy or Emilia-Romagna, is here greeted with utter disdain.

This is quite unjust. Yes, there is industry, there are suburbs, a steady procession of traffic winds through the tree-shaded arterial avenues, but who can deny Foligno its place in history or its more than merely occasional charms? The Romans named it Fulginiae, and when St Felicianus, its first bishop, was martyred here in 251, Christians began calling it Castellum Sancti Feliciani and later built a small pilgrimage church here. First the Saracens, then the Hungarians, then the papal troops fell upon the town, but the Holy Roman Emperor Frederick II, who loved the *folignati* for their loyalty to him, called it his 'shining city', making a pun on the Latin word *fulgidus*, 'bright'.

For two centuries it was dominated, not necessarily to its detriment, by the ruthless Guelph clan of the Trinci, until in 1439 Pope Eugenius IV sent an army under Cardinal Vitelleschi to crush their power for ever and had Corrado Trinci and his son strangled in a castle near Viterbo.

Against the background of Frederick's Ghibelline triumph during the thirteenth century, Foligno's most arresting personality, the Blessed Angela, achieved spiritual fulfilment. As a married woman she had enjoyed a life of unrestrained vanity and pleasure when, as seemed to be happening all over Umbria in that 'Franciscan spring' following the death of the Assisian saint, she experienced a summons towards a better life. When she discovered that her desire to become a nun could not be granted while her husband and children were still alive, she promptly prayed for

The archetypal simplicity of romanesque at San Silvestro, Bevagna.

their deaths and was given her wish. Married to God, she remained in a trance-like ecstasy until she died in 1309, leaving a book of mystical rhapsodies entitled *Divine Consolations*.

Entering Foligno by the Bevagna road, you cross the river Topino and pass the red-and-white gothic church of San Giacomo, with its ogival porch. Turning right into Via Gentile brings you to Piazza della Repubblica, dominated by the majestic, if decidedly muddled, façade of the cathedral of San Feliciano. The original design, dated 1133 on an inscription around the main doorway, was by a certain Maestro Atto, but later centuries added the ogival windows and the pediment. Renaissance architects pulled the interior about, and it was further altered during the last decades of the eighteenth century. On the opposite side, in Piazza del Duomo, it is worth looking closely at the building's other façade, the work of the same Binello who designed San Michele at Bevagna. This front has the customary couchant lions and bands of deftly carved relief around the arch of the portal.

Inside, not all is quite as disappointing as some guides will lead you to believe. Have a look for the Crucifixion in the sacristy by Nicolò Alunno, whose native town was Foligno, a painter who knew the pain and suffering which lie at the heart of spiritual ecstasy, of the kind the Blessed Angela must have experienced. The Cappella del Sacramento, in the left transept, was specially designed in 1527 by Antonio da Sangallo the Younger, and you can follow the main incidents in the life of St Felicianus here, in frescoes by the Roman painter Vespasiano Strada (1582–1622).

Around the open space outside the cathedral (essentially three squares joined into one) is an array of medieval and renaissance palaces. The gothic Canonica dates from the late thirteenth century, while the Palazzo Comunale opposite belongs to the same period, but was rebuilt during the sixteenth century. Linked to it is Palazzo Orfini, where in 1470 Emiliano Orfini, the Master of the Papal Mint, set up Italy's third printing press (the first two were at Rome and Subiaco). Under technical guidance from the German Johann Neumeister he produced, on 11 April 1472, the earliest printed book in Italian, the *Divine Comedy* of Dante. At right-angles to this palace, Palazzo Trinci houses the city's museums and library. Built in 1407, it has a grand staircase and a series of rooms frescoed by anonymous painters working in a style heavily influenced by the French late gothic manner. In 1424 Ottaviano Nelli decorated the chapel with naively exuberant scenes from the life of the Virgin.

Both Palazzo Trinci and Palazzo Comunale were given new façades during the early decades of the nineteenth century, reflecting a notably developed enthusiasm for the neo-classical style which had flowered in Umbria around the time of the French invasion. Italy has recently started to take a deeper interest in architects of this period, such as Giuseppe

Frescoed fragments still adorn the basilica of Santa Maria Intraportas, Foligno.

The sublime cloister of the abbey of Sassovivo.

Twisting columns in the cloister of the abbey at Sassovivo, near Foligno.

Pistocchi of Faenza and Antonio Selva (1751–1819), designer of Teatro La Fenice at Venice, and Foligno produced one of the very best, in the person of Giuseppe Piermarini (1734–1808), who rearranged the interior of the *duomo*. His most famous achievement is not here, but in Milan, where, as well as palaces and churches, he built the theatre of La Scala in 1776.

The *folignati* are very proud of their architecture, and have affixed to all the surviving noble palaces discreet little plaques with the names and dates of the architects and sculptors who worked on them. There is plenty to enjoy in the details of their façades, the masks and caryatids and *atlanti* (herculean male figures), the pilasters, window frames, balconies and portals, as you take any of the various streets leading down towards Piazza San Domenico. Here the venerable church of Santa Maria Infraportas has fragments of fresco in the byzantine style of the early twelfth century, and a stumpy romanesque campanile. The nearby churches of San Tomaso dei Cipischi and San Nicolò, built slightly later, remind us of Foligno's importance and prosperity in its thirteenth-century heyday as a free city under the patronage of the Holy Roman Emperors.

Taking the road leading out of Foligno to the east and turning right, you climb the gentle hillside, and discover, embowered within its woods, the Benedictine abbey of Sassovivo, founded around the year 1000. Though the church itself is of no account whatever, the cloister, the work of a Roman master named Pietro de Maria and dated 1229, is among the most unforgettable in this land of sublime cloisters. Its various elements, the mosaic decoration, the coloured marbles and the columns, were the labour of five craftsmen in Pietro's workshop in Rome. Who would not seek the *vita contemplativa* in such a spot as this?

Go back onto the main highway south to Spoleto, which, about five kilometres on, brings you to Trevi. Rivalled only by Spello in my affections, Trevi is one of those 'cities of the heart' of which Italy contains scores; if you are lucky enough to pay your first visit at exactly the right moment, they will hold you to them in perpetuity. I arrived here at the end of a hot July day, when the shadows of the cypress trees on the road up the hill were lengthening and the people of the town, young and old, were beginning to gather in Piazza Garibaldi for a stroll and a chat. The harsh sunlight had softened, and the stucco and stonework assumed a kind of idealized glow, as if Trevi, which might at other times seem humble and provincial and decayed, had decided that this was the appropriate point at which to present itself as the object of every traveller's romantic reverie, a place that a mere flicking of the fingers would cause to dissolve into air.

Nobody knows whether this really was the Roman Trebiae, but it was certainly in existence as a town by the time the Longobards established their dukedom of Spoleto. In the early Middle Ages it became a refuge for the local Guelphs, and in 1392 the Trinci of Foligno assumed control, yielding forty years afterwards to the Church. You can easily trace the growth of Trevi from a fairly small fortified *borgo* on top of the hill to a somewhat more sprawling settlement whose line of medieval walls reached out around the lower town, known as Piaggia, meaning 'slope'.

Leave your car in Piazza Garibaldi and walk up Via Roma, which ushers you into the old town like some friendly major-domo. On your left is the Teatro Clitunno, by the nineteenth-century Perugian architect Domenico Mollaioli, which is slowly being returned to useful life. Under the archway you emerge into a delightful old piazza, with all its components intact. To your right is the medieval Palazzo Comunale, its walls studded with marble plaques bearing sonorous inscriptions to the heroes of the Risorgimento and World War I (the glory of its small picture gallery is a *Coronation Of The Virgin* painted by Lo Spagna in 1522). There is a respectable-looking café and an attractive cluster of houses and shopfronts next to it. Down Via San Francesco you glimpse the eponymous thirteenth-century church, whose nave has a simple roof of uncovered beams and a scatter of appealing little fresco fragments.

Climbing the steep Via Placido Riccardi (drink from the fountains for luck; the water is clean and divinely cold) brings you to the church of Sant'Emiliano, an Armenian martyr who died in 302. He is shown between two lions in the relief sculpture of the tympanum over the romanesque doorway, which has three little apses bulging out of the wall to the right of it. The interior was much tinkered with in the eighteenth and nineteenth centuries, but the ornately architectural renaissance altar in the second chapel to the left will always find its admirers.

The American novelist Nathaniel Hawthorne (1804–64) noted of Trevi that 'It was the strangest situation in which to build a town, where I suppose no horse can climb, and whence no inhabitant would think of descending into the world after the approach of age should begin to stiffen his joints.' He himself did not turn aside on his way northwards, but if he had, he would surely have deemed the Madonna delle Lagrime worth the effort of ascending the hill. This handsome renaissance church of 1487 stands on your left a little

Above A gothic doorway on a Trevi street corner.

Right The town of Trevi makes a spectacular impact on its high hill.

PETRVS·DE·CASTRO PLEBIS·PINXIT
A INTERRIS GENITRIX ET VIRGO FVISTI
A INCELIS TV QVOQVE SOLA MANES

way down the road from Trevi into the plain, and was built, as you might guess from a single glance at it, by a Florentine architect, Antonio Marchisi (1451–1522) of Settignano, assisted, in the carving around the porch, by a Venetian sculptor named Giovanni di Gian Pietro. The patrons of this enterprise were the greatest family of Trevi, the Valenti, who clearly projected it as a kind of memorial church for members of the clan. Their grandly patrician monuments, dating mostly from the sixteenth and seventeenth centuries, dominate the interior, the best of whose paintings (second altar to the left) is a late Perugino (1521) of the *Adoration of the Magi with Saints Peter and Paul.*

South of Trevi lies one of the favourite haunts of those travellers to Italy who concerned themselves with seeking out the exact sites mentioned in the pages of the classical authors. The springs of Clitumnus (Fonti di Clitunno), a celebrated sacred place in antiquity, received their immortality from Virgil, who apostrophized them in his *Georgics* as the waters in which the war horse and the white flocks and the sacrificial bull were all bathed. In the nineteenth century Corot painted them, and Byron hymned:

The grassy banks whereon the milk-white steer
Grazes; the purest god of gentle waters!
And most serene of aspect, and most clear;
Surely that stream was unprofaned by slaughters –
A mirror and a bath for Beauty's youngest daughters!

Nowadays the tourist buses and the gravel pathways among the poplar trees planted around the pools somewhat undermine the air of rustic poetry which our ancestors found so magical, but there is something alluring and mysterious in the limpid clarity of their bluish depths, in which trout dart and flash.

Pliny the Younger tells us of the cult of the god Clitumnus, who delivered oracles and was represented in the manner of Jupiter, standing upright and dressed in a toga. Scattered through the sacred wood surrounding the springs were numerous small temples and shrines, but these have all disappeared with the exception of the so-called Tempietto di Clitunno or church of San Salvatore, an early Christian building made out of materials taken from its pagan companions. With its pediments and columns overlooking the water, it looks not unlike a folly from some eighteenth-century English country estate – something it may well have helped to inspire. Within are the remains of an eighth-century fresco from the days of the Longobard dukes, showing Christ between Saints Peter and Paul.

Turn right, just south of the springs, towards Beroide (whose unusual name sounds like an Italian abstract noun), with its castle built by Cardinal Albornoz and a gothic parish church. Albornoz, being the sort of man who takes absolutely no chances, also built the fortress at Castel San Giovanni, with its round towers, more sophisticated in design than the grim old keep of Castel Ritaldi on the other side of the valley to the west. From here, follow the signs to Mercatello, then go northwards to Madonna della Stella, a sanctuary church founded in 1862, following the discovery by a local shepherd of a miraculous image of the Virgin.

The building, designed by Giovanni Santini of Perugia, is by no means lacking in distinction, even if the reliefs on the façade appear a trifle fussy. Santini's specialized skill as a theatrical architect rather gives him away here, for the church might quite easily pass for an opera house. There are some more than merely passable nineteenth-century frescoes within, and the paintings include a *Visitation* by the German 'Nazarene' Overbeck, who so obtrusively decorated the front of the Porziuncola at Assisi (see p. 95).

While the sanctuary was being built, the priest of nearby Turrita, Don Abdon Menicali, was continuing the studies he had begun as a boy into the possibility of manned flight. I wish I knew more about the glider which he attempted to launch from the top of Santa Maria della Consolazione in Todi, or the machine known as the 'Telaquilio' which this enterprising aviator constructed here from 1857–60, but the local histories are notably vague on this intriguing figure.

A detail of Perugino's radiant *Adoration* in the Madonna della Lagrime church at Trevi.

The countryside here is some of the most attractive in Umbria, and the church of San Fortunato, on the outskirts of Montefalco, seems merely another element of this subtly harmonized landscape. One of the oldest religious foundations in central Italy, it was originally built by a soldier named Severus and consecrated by Bishop Spes of Spoleto in 422 to house the body of St Fortunatus, the evangelist of the district (not to be confused with the Todine bishop of the same name). This Fortunatus was a ploughman, called from his team to become a priest, who died in 395. The ox-goad he had thrown aside when he went towards his new vocation was found miraculously to have burgeoned into an ilex tree, whose shoots were used as charms against devils.

The church was rebuilt in 1422, and Benozzo Gozzoli (1420–77) was subsequently commissioned to paint the frescoes surrounding the main doorway, including the charming lunette of the Madonna and Child with Saints Francis and Bernardino and two angels, as well as others inside which now survive only in fragments. Tiberio d'Assisi was responsible, in 1512, for the naively colourful scenes and characters on the walls of the Cappella delle Rose, all devoted to Franciscan themes. San Fortunato is now a Franciscan convent, and if you seek the saint's bones, in the sarcophagus behind the high altar, you will not find them, for they were removed in 1829 on the orders of Archbishop Mastai Ferretti, who later became that most famous, controversial and long-reigning of nineteenth-century popes, 'Pio Nono', Pius IX (1846–78).

Montefalco, on whose outskirts San Fortunato stands, is always known as *la ringhiera dell'Umbria*, the balcony of Umbria, though its views are not necessarily any more stunning than those of Spoleto, Assisi or any other hilltown. It is one of those places from which, once arrived, you can see no reason to move, and you can easily find yourself echoing the

A last flush of sunset over the waters of Clitunno.

Summer roses bloom in a Montefalco street.

rhapsodic outburst of the early twentieth-century travel writer Edward Hutton, who declared: 'Her unfrequented streets seem still to shine with the beautiful footsteps of the saints; her aspect is that of some mystical hermit whose face is flushed with some marvellous sweet thought of God, whose eyes search heaven for His advent.'

For once, we do not not know for a certainty that there was a Roman town here, though the entire nature of the place has a hauntingly primeval quality, as if it had been on this spot since the earliest traceable origins of settled habitation, before Romulus and Remus were ever thought of. In the early Middle Ages it was known as Coccorone, and only assumed the name of Montefalco in 1250, after it had revolted against the authority of Emperor Frederick II, who, it is thought, left one of his falcons in the citizens' possession. For a time Montefalco was governed from Spoleto, then the Trinci of Foligno took over, and

when the Pope annihilated them, it enjoyed a limited freedom, guaranteed in 1560 by the intervention of no less a figure than the great St Charles Borromeo (1538–84), Archbishop of Milan. This independence under four elected 'presidents of the people' lasted until 1820, when the deeply reactionary papal government, under the thumb of the Habsburgs, finally decided that even such token independence was too dangerously democratic.

You enter Montefalco through the fifteenth-century Porta Spoletina, passing, on your left, the dull neoclassical church of San Leonardo and, almost opposite, the much more interesting renaissance Santa Illuminata, begun in 1491 and completed in 1553. The side chapels demonstrate the range of discerning patronage extended by the citizens to Umbrian artists in the early sixteenth century. As well as the work of Tiberio d'Assisi and Mezzastris, you will discover, in the second and third chapels on the right, frescoes by Montefalco's own master, Francesco Melanzio (1460–1519), who shows the influence of Perugino on a technique formed from a study of such earlier masters as Nicolò Alunno and Fiorenzo di Lorenzo.

At the top of the street, Santa Chiara commemorates one of the town's eight saints, Chiara di Damiano, an Augustinian nun who died in 1308. Built in 1600 by Fabio Tempestivi, a *montefalchese* who was Bishop of Ragusa (modern Dubrovnik), the dignified brick structure, with its felicitous little lantern above the cupola, incorporates the much older Cappella di Santa Croce, frescoed in 1333 by an anonymous but highly distinctive painter. This unknown artist included the French donor, Jean d'Amiel, in the upper panel on the right-hand wall, showing him being introduced to Christ by St Blaise and St Catherine. In the adjacent convent you will be shown Chiara's mummified heart, the tiny surgical instruments which extracted it from her body and a crucifix set with three of her gallstones.

The green of early summer tints a valley near Montefalco.

Now you can see the town's old ramparts and, by turning right, the Porta San Bartolomeo, built in 1244, as its damaged inscription indicates, under Frederick II's patronage (his double-headed imperial eagle spreads its wings above the arch). Behind the romanesque church, follow Via Melanzio up to Corso Mameli, where the delicate ogival cusps and column-clusters of Sant'Agostino confront you, work dating from 1279. There is plenty of absorbing fifteenth-century fresco here, mostly by unnamed Umbrian masters reflecting the styles of such Gubbian painters as Ottaviano Nelli; my own favourite is half-way up the left side of the nave, where Giovanni Battista Caporali (1476–1560) placed a rough-looking St James and a suavely classical St John as attendants to a throned Madonna backed by a landscape with a seaport and a towered city.

The street takes you up into the Piazza del Comune, once known as Campo del Certame (literally 'field of the contest') after the tournaments which took place here. The fascinatingly irregular shape of this 'square', so different from the carefully planned rectangles we are accustomed to finding at the heart of an Italian city, suggests something truly ancient, the clearing in the forest, the open space among tribal huts, from which the concept of the piazza derives.

On the west side, the Palazzo Comunale, with its gothic windows and renaissance portico, houses a library based on manuscripts from the town's religious houses, suppressed, like those throughout Italy, in 1860, and its tower looks out towards Perugia in one direction and Spoleto in the other. Close by is Montefalco's little theatre, which began as an eighteenth-century oratory and was adapted to secular uses only in 1869. Opposite this there is an excellent wine shop, which seems to sell every kind of Umbrian vintage you could possibly wish to sample, including the *montefalchese* Sagrantino, Piegaro and the appropriately named Scacciadiavoli ('chase away devils').

From here turn right into Via Ringhiera, where the large medieval church of San Francesco has been turned into a picture gallery. Built in 1336–38, it witnessed the first miracle of St Bridget of Sweden,

A renaissance doorway at San Francesco, Montefalco.

whose children, Karin and Birger, were taking her dead body back to their native country in 1373. For some reason they had not wished to speak with a hermit who had been among her devoted companions, but the corpse, lying in this church at Montefalco, rose from its bier, embraced the pious anchorite and signed to its recalcitrant offspring to do the same. After the suppression of the Franciscan convent, the building had to wait forty years for conversion, in 1895, into a gallery; the simple 'preaching barn' structure remains flanked by a series of fifteenth-century chapels which create a sort of south aisle.

The wealth of different schools and styles here cannot easily be discussed in detail, but among individual paintings you should seek out Francesco Melanzio's lavish altar-piece of 1488, with saints – a swaggering squire, a demure nun and a fleshy-faced monk – like characters from Boccaccio, and a sublime saintly trio by the Roman painter Antoniazzo (1435–1508), whose work you will also find at Amelia and Perugia.

Most beautiful of all are the frescoes on the life of St Francis in the first chapel on the right and in the apse of the choir, executed by Benozzo Gozzoli in 1452. A Tuscan best known for his work in Florence and San Gimignano, Gozzoli is one of those painters who seem to exist for the purpose of having patronizing remarks made about them by experts in the field of renaissance art. It is always implied that he was, in the end, little better than a gifted decorator, and account is rarely taken of his evident enjoyment of colour and narrative for their own sake. He was not a subtle artist, and his range was decidedly limited, but I encounter him with pleasure. At Montefalco he is at his cheerful best, whether in such details as the pair of prattling children in the scene of Francis stripping naked before his father, and the clothes at the bedside of the sleeping saint, or in the enchantingly individualized portraits of the great Franciscans which run in a garlanded frieze beneath the panels of fresco.

Out of Montefalco, a pretty stretch of road to the west will bring you to a right turn towards Gualdo Cattaneo, a little walled *borgo* from which you can return to Todi. At least you will not run the risk nowadays of the great scourge of this area in the early nineteenth century, which was brigandage. The whole countryside around Todi was a haven for bandits of all kinds, the most famous being one known as La Strega, ('The Witch'), for whose successful operations the local priests apparently used to ring the bells and sing the Te Deum in gratitude, since he kept their offertory boxes well lined.

Gualdo Cattaneo, perched on its steep hilltop.

Pontechiusita
Preci
Val Castoriano
Campi Vecchio
Monti Sibillini
Castelluccio
Triponzo
Cerreto
Borgo Cerreto
Piano Grande di Castelluccio
Norcia
Valnerina
Piedipaterno
Tessino
Grotti
Spoleto
Sant'Anatolia di Narco
Savelli
Vallocchia
San Ponziano
Monteluco
Corno
Cascia
Nera
Sambucheto
Monteleone di Spoleto
San Pietro in Valle
Ferentillo
Montefranco
Arrone
Terni
Velino
0
5
10 km

5
The Refuge of the Saints

Spoleto and the Valnerina – Norcia – Cascia – Terni

Spoleto is justifiably proud of its Latin title, *Caput Umbriae* ('the Head of Umbria'). Once upon a time it really was one of the most important cities in central Italy, commanding an extensive territorial allegiance, but its civic pride, so far from diminishing together with its political status, tended to increase, so that nowadays the traveller is invariably struck by the love of the townsfolk for their native walls and streets. Though Umbria is by no means the wealthiest of regions, and though there seems almost too much in the way of historic monuments for any municipal authority reasonably to care for, no effort ever seems too great for the Spoletans when the survival and restoration of their patrimony is at stake.

Ideally sited on mountain spurs above the Via Flaminia, it was a prosperous and influential town by the time Hannibal threatened its walls in 217 BC. Omens of military disaster, including a woman who was observed to have changed her sex, had already been noted, but the gallant defenders repulsed the Carthaginians and used this gesture of loyalty to Rome as a bargaining counter for more civic privileges.

Spoleto's moment came, however, not with the Romans but under the Longobards, who in 574 made it the capital of a dukedom, one of a pair of states (the other was the duchy of Benevento, east of Naples) intended to act as levers on either side of Byzantine imperial territory in Italy. Only in 1138 did the last duke, Conrad of Lutzen, surrender his authority to the church, to whom Spoleto largely remained faithful until the absorption of the Papal States into the Kingdom of Italy in 1860. Several of Spoleto's bishops went on to become popes, including Giulio Giacomo Mastai Ferretti, who as Piux IX was one of the key figures in the struggle for national unity, and the town's loyalty was demonstrated by the bravery of the papal garrison, led by the Irish Major O'Reilly, who held out in the *rocca* against a superior army fighting for King Vittorio Emanuele.

As befits the setting for the prestigious annual 'Festival of Two Worlds', an Italo-American cultural venture pioneered by the composer Giancarlo Menotti (*b.* 1911), Spoleto has a distinctive theatricality in its position and in the ways whereby the steep hillsides have been used to maximum advantage by successive generations of architects. The ideal place in which to appreciate this is Piazza del Duomo, an open space, cleared during the last fifty years, between the sloping Via dell'Arringo (another version of the English and French 'harangue') and the façade of the cathedral of Santa Maria Assunta, which echoes on summer nights to the voices of playing children.

As the inscription tells us on the mosaic of Christ blessing the Virgin and St John adorning the upper

CLEMENTI XII · P · O · M ·
QVOD
LVDOVICO DE VALENTIBVS PATRIC · SPOLET
PROTON · APOST · ET FIDEI PROMOT ·
ROGANTE
AQVAEDVCTVM VETVSTATE DEHISCENTEM
SINGVLARI MVNIFICENTIA
PVBLICAE COMMODITATI RESTITVERIT
PROVIDO BENEFICENTISSIMOQ · PRINCIPI
S · P · Q · S ·
ANNO DOMINI MDCCXXXVII

Left The Fontana del Mascherone in Piazza Campello, Spoleto.

Above A roman sarcophagus now forms a fountain basin at Spoleto.

level of this façade, 'Solsternus, greatest of living masters in this art, made this in the years which you will find out by adding one thousand and seven to two hundred.' The portico, fusing grey with pinkish stone, was completed in 1504, but the original romanesque doorway survives below, though only one of the customary couchant lions supports a flanking pillar.

Surprisingly, the interior is a majestic baroque basilica, the work of Luigi Arrigucci, a Florentine architect who began its reconstruction in 1638. An earlier building had been systematically pillaged by Fulvio Orsini, bishop from 1562–81. His successor Maffeo Barberini took Spoleto to his heart, and when a nephew, Francesco, became Pope Urban VIII in 1623, plans were initiated for a restoration. Arrigucci was Urban's court architect and, whatever the hostile criticism of the greedy, ambitious Barberini family in Rome, nobody could deny the splendour and lavishness of their patronage of the arts. Appropriately, though you cannot see it very well, the bust of Urban high above the main entrance is by that most famous of all his protégés, the sculptor Gian Lorenzo Bernini.

To your right, the chapel of Bishop Costantino Eroli has an apse and vaulting decorated in 1497 by Pinturicchio, and though the frescoed *Madonna with Saints* in a romantically envisaged landscape is much damaged, the painter's grace and tenderness shine through. Who created the enthralling mixture of biblical themes, motifs from pagan mythology and symbolic elements in the nearby Cappella dell'Assunta is not known for certain, but it was probably the Palermitan painter Jacopo Siculo (1508–44).

In the north transept you will find the tomb of the great Florentine artist Filippo Lippi (1406–69). He may not have been the most exemplary of personalities, but he was certainly most engaging, as Robert Browning clearly felt when in 1853 he wrote his *Fra Lippo Lippi*, a dramatic monologue in which the painter divulges his artistic credo. An unwilling Carmelite monk, Lippi had trouble in controlling his 'animal lusts', as Vasari tells us, and escaped from a room in which Cosimo de' Medici had locked him (so as to get a picture finished) by knotting his bed sheets together. Invited to Spoleto with his pupil Fra Diamante to decorate the cathedral apse, he is said to have been poisoned by relatives of a woman with whom he was conducting an affair. When the Spoletans asked Lorenzo de' Medici whether they might keep his body, as their city lacked 'the ornament of eminent persons', that great-hearted Florentine paid for a tomb to be placed here, designed by Lippi's bastard son Filippino (1457–1504), and commissioned a Latin epitaph by the poet Angelo Poliziano.

The apse frescoes themselves, recently restored, were begun in 1467. Celebrating the Blessed Virgin's life, with scenes of the Annunciation, Nativity, Dormition and Coronation, they underline Filippo Lippi's irrepressible liveliness and humanity. Note, for example, Mary's demure confusion, expressed by her downward-tilting head and awkwardly turned hands as Gabriel greets her, or the throng of rejoicing angels which offers lilies to the kneeling Madonna.

Outside the cathedral, to the right as you look across the piazza, is the seventeenth-century octagonal church of Santa Maria del Manna d'Oro, built to commemorate the Virgin's benevolence in sparing the city from the Holy Roman Emperor Charles V's ravaging German mercenaries in 1527 and in showering upon Spoleto instead the 'golden manna' of successful commercial dealings with the imperial troops. Next to this stands the Teatro Caio Melisso, a positive gem of an old theatre, originally built in 1660 but given its present appearance in 1880 by Giovanni Montiroli (1817–91), a Spoletan whose most important earlier work was in England for the Victorian aristocracy. If not actually attending a performance, you can look at the theatre (where Rossini once played the double bass in his own *L'italiana in Algieri*) by ringing the custodian's bell next door. The original Caius Melissus, incidentally, was the Emperor Augustus's versatile librarian, a poet and dramatist and author of a treatise on bee-keeping.

At the top of the brick-paved steps sweeping up out of the square, the Bishop's Palace was probably once

The cathedral of Spoleto seen across its broad piazza.

the residence of the Longobard dukes, and the very simple romanesque church of Sant'Eufemia, on the right of the courtyard, may have started life as a Palatine chapel before being made the nucleus of a Benedictine monastery founded in 980 by a pious noblewoman named Gunderada. Try to see the diocesan museum next to the church, set out in the fancily adorned state rooms of the palace and incorporating pictures in every conceivable style and of all levels of technical competence, together with a gorgeous textile archive of sumptuously wrought seventeenth- and eighteenth-century vestments.

From here, follow Via Aurelio Saffi as far as Via dello Spagna, named after the painter Giovanni di Pietro (1450–1528), called Lo Spagna, a Spanish pupil of Perugino hounded by the xenophobic Perugines towards a refuge in Spoleto. This emerges into a pretty little square shaded by lime trees, with a very good restaurant to one side of it, and below this, just behind Palazzo Zacchei-Travaglini, is the unassuming romanesque church of Santi Giovanni e Paolo. Many of the frescoes here, including an energetic depiction of Salome dancing before Herod, were painted soon after consecration in 1174. Most interesting of all is one of the earliest known representations of the martyrdom in 1170 of St Thomas Becket at Canterbury, whose details, such as the knight's sword cleaving the archbishop's skull, suggest that the outlines of the story were very soon known throughout Europe.

Despite the nineteenth century's attempts at thrusting roads along the various levels of the hillside on which it is built, Spoleto's essential character is still that of a medieval town. Stone arches tack together buildings huddled along steep, cobbled lanes, some still bearing the name *vaita*, a Germanic word for the twelve wards of the Longobardic community, related to the English 'watch', or French *guetter*. You can follow an agreeable walk down these streets past the gothic church of San Nicolò, wedged into the city walls, towards Via dell'Anfiteatro and one of the most obvious traces of the grandeur of Roman Spoleto.

The ruins of the amphitheatre, dating from the second century AD, give us some notion of the town's economic and social importance during the empire. At least half of it was subsequently absorbed into the fabric of nearby buildings, but its overall dimensions, some of the grandest of their kind in Italy, can be gathered to some extent when looking at the ruined eastern section beside the almost dry riverbed of the Tessino, onto which Via dell'Anfiteatro debouches.

Many Christians were martyred here, and one of them, Pontianus, was to become the city's patron saint. On his feast day (14 January), pious Spoletines are supposed not to cut bread, so as to preserve a memory of his execution with a sword. The convent dedicated to him stands on the other side of the Tessino, behind a series of ghastly flyover loops carrying the traffic of Via Flaminia. Of the former twelfth-century church, only the outer shell, with its three apses, and a campanile have survived. The interior was reworked in 1788 by Giuseppe Valadier (1762–1839), but the crypt retains some of the Roman masonry of the original structure, founded by the devout matron Syncleta for a group of Syrian monks. While you are looking at the traces of medieval fresco here, including a lovely *Angel with Kneeling Suppliants* attributed to the fourteenth-century Spoletine painter known as the Maestro di Fossa, notice the graffiti from the same period scratched and painted on the plasterwork.

North of San Ponziano stands the Basilica of San Salvatore, generally thought to be among the oldest Christian buildings in the world, and once dedicated to the two Roman martyrs Concordius and Sentia. Behind the façade, whose ensemble of pilastered and pedimented windows and carved doorways makes it look oddly like some village church on a Greek island, the interior seems dramatically stark, its elegant lines disclosed by recent restoration. The presbytery has a cornice, frieze and entablature crowning finely carved Corinthian columns, a far more sophisticated architectural language in its grandeur and purity than the higgledy-piggledy romanesque idiom which succeeded it.

The interior of Sant'Eufemia, the most perfectly preserved romanesque church in Umbria.

Below the terrace outside the church, the town cemetery slopes down the hill, with Spoleto's nineteenth-century 'good families' commemorated by overblown epitaphs and clustered under an amusingly fanciful portico like a veranda. The roads back into town lead you into Piazza della Vittoria and the Ponte Sanguinario, a Roman bridge of travertine marble whose name derives from Christian martyrdoms which took place there. One of the martyrs was Bishop Gregory, dedicatee of the church on the northern side of the adjacent Piazza Garibaldi. His body was brought here from the arena and was buried by a pious widow named Abundantia, whose namesake founded the present church of San Gregorio Maggiore around AD 800. Its portico, however, is renaissance, added in 1520 as an obvious echo of the arcading in front of the *duomo*, and the brick-arched cloister was built some seventy years later. Sensitive restoration has uncovered much older workmanship, expecially in the crypt, where a very plain sarcophagus holds the first Abundantia's body.

From the square, follow the long Corso Garibaldi up through Porta Fuga, where Queen Christina of Sweden (1644–54), as an inscription over the gateway tells you, made a triumphal entry into the city in 1655, following her abdication. Passing the church of San Domenico, where some elegantly stuccoed baroque chapels relieve a not notably interesting interior, you reach Palazzo Collicola (1717). The tactful reserve of this imposing façade suggests that its builders, the descendants of Pope Urban VIII's doctor, were chary, as wealthy parvenus, of making too much of a splash in the face of the local nobility. The Collicola had the typical Spoletine *amor patriae*, an enthusiasm which later brought about the project for a new theatre, grander in scale than the cosy little Caio Melisso. This is the Teatro Nuovo, in Via Giustolo north-east of the palace, conservatively classical in form. It opened in 1864 with a specially composed opera called

Inside the ancient church of San Salvatore, Spoleto.

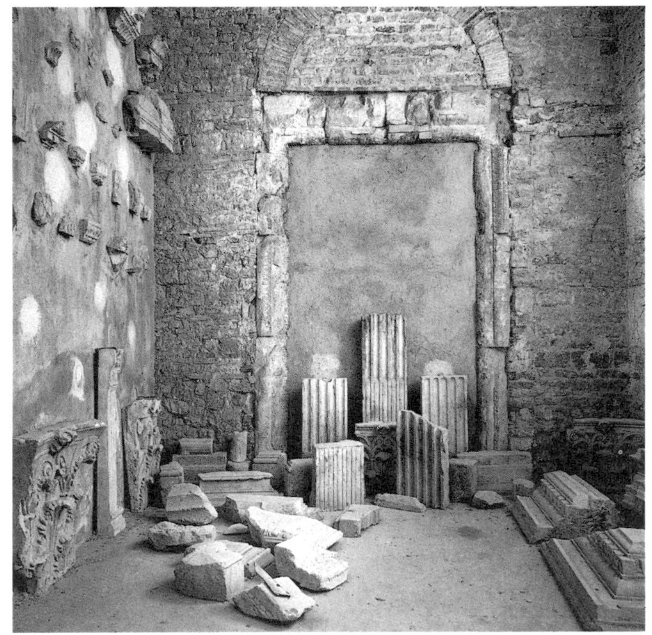

Roman fragments in the ancient church of San Salvatore, Spoleto.

Guisemberga di Spoleto by Filippo Sangiorgi, of which, so far as I know, nobody has heard a note since.

Just beyond the theatre, Via Filliteria (its name comes from the Byzantine Greek *phylakteria*, roughly equivalent to *vaita*, 'a military division') joins Via Minervio, which opens into Piazza Mentana, dominated by the church of San Filippo Neri. This very accomplished essay in Roman Baroque was completed by the local architect Loreto Scelli in 1644, and the dome added in 1671. Inside, seek out the marble bust of St Philip Neri by Alessandro Algardi (1595–1654) and the *Presentation of the Virgin* by Gaetano Lapis (1706–58) in the second chapel on the right, a modish provincial echo of the highly polished style which so entranced eighteenth-century foreign visitors to the painters' studios of Florence and Rome.

Fascinating as Spoleto's townscape always is, we should lament the loss of a substantial portion of the medieval city in the nineteenth century with the

creation of Corso Mazzini, the boulevard linking Piazza Mentana with Piazza della Libertà. The latter admittedly closes the prospect handsomely, though, with the seventeenth-century Palazzo Ancaiani, whose north side is flanked by the entrance to the Roman theatre; here the auditorium and the restored stage and 'orchestra' are regularly put to use on summer nights during the festival. Next door, in the former convent of Sant'Agata, which retains its grimly beautiful romanesque portico, is a regional archaeological museum.

Walk up Via Filippo Brignone into Piazza Fontana, where the rather battered seventeenth-century Palazzo Mansi houses the Accademia Spoletina, which, at its foundation in 1600, was given the far more original name of Accademia degli Ottusi ('Academy of the Dunces'). The church opposite is really two buildings, with the eighteenth-century Sant'Ansano on top of an early Christian chapel dedicated to the Syriac monk Isaac who came here during the sixth century. From one side springs a Roman arch, whose inscription tells you that it was built by the Spoletan senate as a tribute to the Emperor Tiberius's son Drusus and his nephew and adopted son Germanicus, and which was evidently intended as a spectacular entrance to the forum.

The original open space at the heart of Spoletium must have been much larger, but the Piazza del Mercato is still the core of the city, the very archetype of an Italian town square, with its restaurants, cafés and vegetable market and a grandiose fountain at the north end, designed in 1746 by the Roman architect Costantino Fiaschetti. Above this, on a broad, raised terrace, stands the Palazzo del Comune, built in 1784–6, apparently amid much local discord. This now houses the civic art collection, recently rearranged so as to show off its treasures to full advantage. Underneath the colourfully patterned ceilings by two nineteenth-century painters called Mercatelli and Peruzzi, an arresting display is laid out, featuring works as widely disparate as Lo Spagna's ingenious allegorical paintings, a crucified Christ among buoyant cherubs by the mid seventeenth-century artist Francesco Refini, and a genre painting of a druggist's apprentice pounding away with a pestle and mortar, by Paolo Antonio Barbieri (1603–49), brother of the great Emilian master Guercino.

Beyond, from the tree-shaded Piazza Campello, you can climb up to the massive *rocca*, one of the key fortresses of the Papal States. Built by Cardinal Albornoz in the fourteenth century and in use until recently as a penitentiary, it is now being turned into a cultural centre for the city. Out from its eastern ramparts, your view over to the slopes of Monteluco takes in a handful of medieval dovecots among the trees. Once there were many more of these dotting the landscape, and their builders were summoned much further afield than Italy, for you can find similar pigeon-lofts in the Greek islands, made by Umbrian masons for the Venetians and Genoese.

Travellers have always admired the colossal limestone aqueduct spanning the valley, known as the Ponte delle Torri and designed during the fourteenth century, probably by the Gubbian architect Gattapone, working to a commission from Cardinal Albornoz. Crossing this (it can still, if necessary, be used to carry water to the city), you find yourself on the hillside of Monteluco, where a dense forest (*lucus* is the Latin word for grove) preserves the atmosphere which encouraged St Isaac and his Syriac anchorites to establish their cells here. The hermitages remained independent of monastic rule until Napoleonic times, and though they are now private dwellings, you can occasionally get a glimpse of the Eremo delle Grazie, substantially restored in 1727, together with its little church, by Cardinal Camillo Cybo, assisted by an anonymous architect.

North-west of Monteluco, above the noisy Via Flaminia, the church of San Pietro offers a final romanesque flourish. It was founded around AD 600 on the site of an Iron Age necropolis by Bishop Achilleus, who had brought from Rome one of the chains which held St Peter in prison. The sculptor of the remarkable

A highly theatrical staircase in Spoleto's Piazza Mentana.

sequence of romanesque panels on the façade is unknown, but their arrangement is as singular as their workmanship. No merely decorative idea lies behind the presence of a ploughman with his team, a deer suckling her fawn, or Aesopian scenes of wily foxes and wolves. Each is carefully linked with a symbolic scheme of human redemption through faith and good works, and the Spoletans thought so highly of the whole façade that they left it alone when the interior of the church was rebuilt in frigid baroque idiom in 1699.

Spoleto is one of the best places in Umbria from which to explore the various areas of the region, and its position on the edge of the Valnerina district makes a journey across those rugged, lonely eastern ridges and uplands absolutely imperative. This valley of the River Nera, and the Monti Sibillini beyond it, form a hauntingly beautiful series of gaunt, grand, romantic prospects, their farms and villages perfectly integrated into the colours and contours of the landscape.

So take the road marked 395, due east from the city, winding up among the olive groves and oakwoods into the high hills. If you fancy something a little more genuinely remote (and are prepared to risk your car), a right turn takes you to Vallocchia, which has a romanesque church and a fourteenth-century fort. Close by, up a track, is the Villa della Genga, built in 1783 by the Perugine architect Francesco Amadio (1755–1817), a member of one of Spoleto's old noble families. One of his relations, Annibale, became Pope Leo XII in 1823. If you stay with the road, you come to Grotti, where the church possesses early renaissance frescoes by an anonymous local master.

At the Piedipaterno crossroads, turn left and follow the line of the swift-flowing, boulder-strewn river as far as Borgo Cerreto; fish caught here can be eaten at the Panorama restaurant near the bridge. The area was always famous for its tasty truffles, and the inhabitants of Cerreto itself (of which Borgo, perched with its towers and bastions on top of a bluff, was a defensive outpost) formerly specialized as herbalists and dealers in spices.

The breathtaking medieval acqueduct of Ponte delle Torri, Spoleto.

Romanesque scenes from the life of Christ, San Pietro, Spoleto.

When you reach Triponzo, you are indeed presented, as the name implies, with three bridges: one across the Nera, another over the River Corno, which has come down from the Monti Reatini in Latium, and a third which spans the confluence of the two streams. Triponzo still has its medieval girdle of fortifications, and just outside the village to the east are the remains of an attempt by one of the bishops of Norcia during the Middle Ages to develop the sulphur springs here as a spa. Follow the road as far as Pontechiusita, on the frontier with the Marche, then turn right along the gently curving Val Castoriano to Preci, a walled *borgo* substantially rebuilt under papal patronage during the early sixteenth century. At the same time this tiny place achieved renown for its school of surgeons, some thirty families in all, who specialized in eye operations and the removal of kidney stones, carrying

Left The rugged landscape of the Valnerina, south-eastern Umbria.

Above A fine fifteenth-century loggia at Campi Vecchio.

This gothic portal and rose window form part of a pair at San Salvatore, Campi Vecchio.

their skills to the courts of Elizabeth I of England and the Sultan of Turkey.

At the abbey of San Eutizio, up the hill south of Preci, St Benedict established one of his earliest monastic communities by bringing together an already existing group of hermits within his rule. Its importance and prosperity can be gauged by the size of the romanesque church, built by a certain Maestro Pietro in 1190. There is a bulging polygonal apse, the ceiling of the crypt is carried on immense squat columns, and the campanile is impressively sited on top of a rock overlooking the line of conventual buildings and the fourteenth-century cloisters.

Further down the valley, at Campi Vecchio, the church of the Madonna di Piazza has frescoes on the life of the Virgin's father St Joachim, a most recherché subject in Christian art, by the Sparapane brothers Giovanni and Antonio, members of a Norcian family of painters who flourished during the fifteenth century. More of their work can be found in the gothic church of San Salvatore, set slightly apart from the village, where the nave crossing has the feature, unusual in Italian churches, of a decorated iconostasis (a screen dividing the presbytery from the body of the church).

This entire area of mountainous border country has been severely affected by a recent series of earthquakes, and their results are visible everywhere, but more especially in Norcia, the sturdy little town cradled in the green folds of the mountains that is one of the oldest and most revered in all Umbria. *Frigida Nursia*, as Virgil called it, was a city of the Sabines which offered help to Scipio, commander of the Roman army in the Second Punic War of 218–202 BC, and was later to be punished by Octavius for having taken Antony's part against him in the civil war of 41 BC. Extensive conversion to Christianity took place when St Felicianus, bishop of Foligno, arrived here in AD 250, and it is as the birthplace of one of the most influential figures in the story of the Church that Norcia has its niche in European history.

Just as St Francis is inconceivable without Assisi, so St Benedict is quite unimaginable without his Norcian context, that of a town somewhat removed from the great world, a fortress and a refuge that even the all-conquering barbarian armies found hard to get at, in the midst of a countryside which fostered a life of religious contemplation for countless hermits amid its caves and woods. Benedict was born here in 480 and sent by his fairly prosperous parents to study in Rome, accompanied by his nurse Cyrilla. Attracted by a life of prayer and meditation, he eventually retired, aged twenty, to a cave on Monte Subiaco, in the mountains of Latium, where he lived in isolation for three years.

Only when others, impressed by his example, began to seek his advice as to how they should pursue a contemplative life, did Benedict consider the possibility of establishing a monastic community on the

Saint Benedict, father of monasticism, commemorated in his birthplace at Norcia.

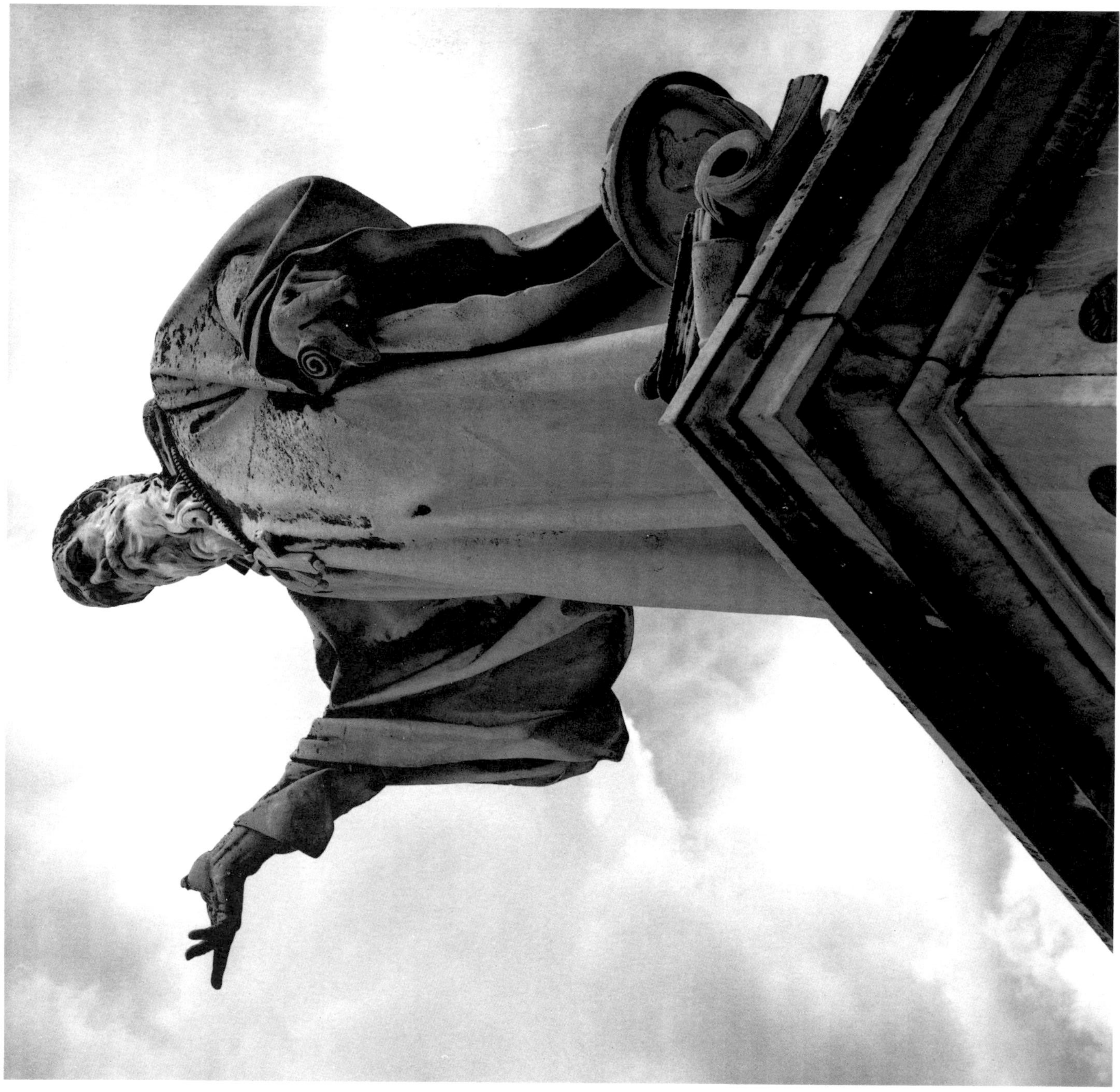

mountain, going on to found its larger and more famous sister monastery at Montecassino, and crowning his achievement with the formulation of his famous Rule, the principles by which a life of prayer, study and labour were to be governed.

Benedict's initiative had a dramatic effect on a world bruised by the collapse of the Roman empire and the ravages of a century of barbarian invasion. Women as well as men sought the order and security of monastic life, and the saint's sister Scholastica, herself later canonized, joined him at Montecassino, gathering round her a group of nuns. The siblings were ultimately buried side by side (Scholastica died *c*.543 and Benedict in 547); between them they had laid the foundations of a religious life which, in one way or another, was to remain a dominant element in European society for the next thousand years.

Leaving your car outside the fourteenth-century ramparts, you enter Norcia through Porta Romana and walk up Corso Sertorio (named after a Roman general, Quintus Sertorius, born here in the second century BC and killed in a conspiracy against the dictator Sulla) to the main Piazza San Benedetto, whose charm is heightened by its asymmetry. The Palazzo Comunale, to your left, looks wholly renaissance in character, but the elegant loggia actually belongs to the late nineteenth century and the tower was built in 1713. To your right stands the Castellina, one of Vignola's most functional, no-nonsense fortresses, with nothing to relieve the plainess of its façade but the diagonal thrust of two flanking turrets. Begun in 1554 on the site of an earthquake-shattered church, it is now an art gallery currently undergoing slow restoration, but said to contain a fine *Deposition from the Cross*, formed of carved wooden statues and dating from the thirteenth century.

At right angles to this is the *duomo*, very disappointing, alas, since, following its foundation in 1560, it was many times rebuilt as the result of earthquakes. Much more interesting is the church of San Benedetto, set slightly askew on the piazza's north-east corner. Though the loggia on its right side is renaissance in design (it was originally a corn market), the main building was actually started in 1389, with a gothic façade incorporating a rose window above a porch flanked by little statues of Benedict and Scholastica in ogival niches. Inside, the various altars and their paintings have an agreeably homely, unpretentious air. The best altar-piece is in the left transept, by Filippo Napoletano, an early seventeenth-century artist of whom practically nothing is known, and shows St Benedict being visited by Totila. We might be tempted to dismiss as fiction such a meeting between two figures representing the very incarnations of peace and war, along the lines of the supposed encounter of Elizabeth I and Mary Queen of Scots, one of those historical confrontations which ought to have happened but never took place. Yet apparently the saint and the warrior really did come face to face. Totila, wanting to find out whether Benedict had the gift of prophecy, dressed a servant in his general's panoply and sent him to the monastery, where he was promptly told: 'Take off those robes, for they are not yours.' Totila was so impressed that he went and threw himself to the ground at Benedict's feet and would only rise at his bidding. The saint told him he would conquer Rome, cross the sea, reign nine years and then die, all of which happened exactly as foretold.

If you go down to the crypt, you can see the substantial remains of Roman buildings, part of whose masonry is in the so-called *opus reticulatum* or herringbone style. This is said to be the house of Euproprius Anicius and Abundantia, the parents of Benedict and Scholastica, and the actual birthplace of the saints, though modern sources are somewhat sceptical on the subject. I can see no reason why they should not have been born here, and evidently many people would like to believe it, judging by the coins flung into these ruined foundations.

Knocked about by seismic tremors and racked, especially during the mid nineteenth century, with famine and cholera, the people of Norcia have had to be

The staircase of Palazzo Comunale, with the church of San Benedetto, Norcia.

tough, and they quote without shame the verdict of Pope Paul II (1464–71) that the *norcini* of his day were 'the wickedest men on earth'. Living here has not been easy, and as you wander through the area north of San Benedetto you will see a reflection of this in the building styles of the houses, aiming less obviously at grandeur than many another small Italian town. The streets in the angle formed by Via Anicia and Via Umberto were indeed abandoned altogether during the Middle Ages, and shepherds from the Piano Grande, on the edge of the high eastern mountains, came here to live. Known as Capolaterra, this part of Norcia still retains its sheep pens built into the houses, and a kind of 'here today, gone tomorrow' quality contrasting noticeably with the rest of the town.

From Capolaterra, you return to the main piazza along Via Anicia, where the church of Sant'Agostino is steadily being restored to its former beauty. There is an attractive fusion between the Renaissance, in some handsome fresco work by such local painters as Ansovino da Camerino and Giovanni Battista da Norcia (both working in the early sixteenth century), and the Baroque, in fine decoration on the organ case, gallery and gilded altars. The chance of lunching in Norcia, either at the Grotta Azzurra in Via Alfieri or at the Posta in Via Cesare Battisti, should on no account be missed. Not only is this one of the great pilgrimage centres for truffle enthusiasts, but it is also traditionally the place where the world's first sausages were created. Whether this is true (and it can hardly be proved), the wandering pig-killers and salami-makers of Italy were always known as *norcini*, pork butchers still advertise their shops as *norcinerie*, and the ham and sausage of Norcia, whether *capocollo*, *scalmarita*, *mazzafegato* or *sopressata*, are very good indeed.

East of Norcia is some of the most spectacular country in the whole of central Italy, much more striking, I always feel, than any in the Apennines further north. Take the straight road due south into the plain, then turn left into the hills towards Forca di Santa Croce. This region was, and in part still is, the haunt of shepherds and cowherds who moved their flocks up here each summer as part of the annual 'transhumance', involving a migration from the parched and fever-blighted Roman Campagna. The sheep were driven through the very heart of Rome itself, and there are still a few old people alive who can remember this strange nocturnal journey of bells and bleating through Via del Babuino and Piazza di Spagna, a tradition maintained until the 1920s. This custom dated from Rome's earliest days as a city, when the great patrician families were proud to bear shepherds' names and called their money *pecunia* after the sheep, *pecus*, which constituted their most precious property.

The sheep are still shifted to and fro, though scarcely over such vast distances, by a head shepherd known as the *vergaro* and his assistants, called *pastoricchi*. Presumably, too, the *caciere* and the *buttero*, men whose job it was to carry the ewe's milk cheese and ricotta, the sheepskins and the yearling lamb carcasses to Rome, no longer need to go quite so far for a good market.

A vast natural grazing ground for sheep, cattle and horses is provided by the Piano Grande di Castelluccio, crossed by a single road running down off the mountainside to the north. Within a surrounding amphitheatre of bare hillsides deeply scored with the marks of ancient glaciers and the courses of streamlets running into the pools known as *mergari*, this is an exceptionally haunting spot, in which you can feel close to the very springs of life in Italy a thousand years before Rome itself was named. In the summer these plains are thickly strewn with wild flowers, but in winter, 'when snow the pasture sheets', the church bells of Castelluccio, the little *borgo* on the hill at the end of the plain, are occasionally rung to help travellers find their way, in accordance with a papal ordinance of long ago.

The snow-capped Monti Sibillini here form Umbria's eastern frontier, with their highest peak, the 2476 metre Monte Vettore, dominating the Piano di Castelluccio. These Sibylline Mountains gave rise to a

Some local specialities on display in a Norcia shop.

COGLIONI
DI
MULO
PANINI
A
PIACERE
2
ANNI
£1000
TU SAPE
BUONA LA MIA
RICOTTA DI PECORA
DURA 2--- ANNI
SENZA FRIGO..
2
ANNI
£1000
L'ETTO
SANU

host of folk-tales and superstitions, many of them attached to the Sybil herself, the prophetess of Roman myth who is said to have left her grotto at Cumae near Naples and retreated into these Apennine fastnesses. Ariosto brought her into his *Orlando furioso* (1516) and Wagner is supposed to have derived his Venusberg in *Tannhäuser* (1845) from the notion of the Cumaean Sibyl luring young men to her mountain cave. Various people have looked for this grotto without success, and if the local inhabitants know its whereabouts, they are certainly not telling.

There is really no alternative but to retrace your steps towards Norcia. Once there, head south on the straight road across Piano di Santa Scolastica until it starts to climb up towards Savelli and commences the familiar, if sometimes rather wearisome, series of hairpin bends typical of the Umbrian mountain road. About six kilometres further on, perched on the hillside, there is something of a surprise, the sanctuary of the Madonna della Neve, a highly sophisticated affair built in 1565–71 to a design left unrealized by Bramante and intended to commemorate the miraculous rescue, through the Virgin's intercession, of a man buried in a snowdrift for three days. This was depicted on the panels of the organ loft by an anonymous painter in 1594, and the brothers Camillo and Fabio Angelucci, who flourished during the last decades of the sixteenth century, covered the vaulting in bold fresco decoration. Most of this, alas, has been severely damaged by a recent earthquake.

Take the next turn right, over the mountain top and along a rather bleak, unfrequented road which carries you down into the Corno valley, where suddenly the stridently modern profile of Cascia becomes visible. This may not look very inviting, but no traveller in Umbria can afford to pass it by.

The object of most journeys to Cascia is the shrine of St Rita, beatified in 1628 by Pope Urban VIII but only canonized in 1900 by Pope Leo XIII (her feast is on 24 May). Her story is really somewhat pathetic, which perhaps enhances her latter-day role as one of the favourite saints of the Catholic calendar in Italy. The daughter of elderly bourgeois parents, Antonio and Amata Lotti, she was born in 1367 and betrothed to her future husband, Ferdinando Mancini, at the age of fourteen, marrying him four years later.

The pair went to live in Ferdinando's house in the nearby village of Roccaporena, and Rita soon realized that her wish to remain unmarried had been fully justified. Ferdinando was hot-tempered, aggressive and given to outbursts of drunken cruelty, but it is said that he was beginning to respond favourably to his wife's milder influence when, in 1401, he was murdered in a street brawl. Their two young sons vowed vengeance, at which Rita was so horrified that she prayed they might be delivered from the eternal damnation that would surely follow, a prayer which was answered with their deaths.

Now came Rita's chance to embrace the religious life for which she had always craved, but the nuns of Cascia's Augustinian convent rejected her on the grounds that she was not a virgin. When, after repeated requests, she was admitted to the sisterhood, the most menial and wearying tasks were assigned to her, and it is difficult not to feel that the nuns were getting their own back on somebody who had known the world in ways forbidden to them. Nevertheless Rita put up heroically with everything, including the classic device for trying her saintly patience, an order from the abess to care for a plant she knew had already died. The saint obeyed, and quietly kept on watering an old vine stump, which, as a proof of her constancy and humility, miraculously burst into leaf. Before she died in 1447, she had received a further proof of God's intentions for her when a thorn broke off the crown around the head of Christ on a crucifix and stuck itself into her own, where it remained, rather like one of the wounds of the Stigmata. Artists have since always represented her thus, with a fleck of blood on her forehead.

After her death Rita was especially invoked in cases

Early snows cover the slopes of Monte Vettore, beyond Castelluccio.

where the intercession of other saints had proved ineffective, and she is now known as 'The Patron of the Impossible', an infallible assistant to those without any obvious expectation of success. Her incorrupt body lies in the huge white basilica built at the centre of the town in 1937 by a Vatican engineer named Chiapetta. This is so completely hideous that one can only suppose the design for which it was substituted, a chaste essay in imitation Roman Baroque, would have been preferable purely on grounds of architectural consistency. As it is, something looking faintly like a provincial cinema, decorated inside with wondrously repulsive frescoes in the worst imaginable vein of kitsch, gives Cascia a slightly tacky, gimcrack air, as if the cult of St Rita were not quite taken seriously. She really deserves better than this.

The Cascia Rita knew had begun as the Roman city of Cursula, destroyed by an earthquake in the reign of Augustus and rebuilt soon afterwards, only to be wiped out once more by the Goths in 534. In the early Middle Ages it became part of the Duchy of Spoleto, and was thereafter tossed about between the adherents of Emperor and Pope, fighting a whole series of pointless little wars with Norcia, Spoleto and the kings of Naples. Its continuing rebellions against their authority infuriated the popes, and in 1517 Leo X ordered the destruction of the citadel. Nature herself took a hand in 1703, when an earthquake flattened almost the entire town and claimed some 700 lives. The nobility, all of whose palaces had been destroyed, sensibly took itself off to live at the foot of the hill.

After a prayer to St Rita, who lies in a special chapel off the left aisle of the basilica, you can visit the monastery, next to the church, which preserves the miraculous vine and the cell where she died. At the end of the street, past the Augustinian seminary, is the gothic church of Sant'Agostino, built in 1380, and beyond this are the three remaining bastions of the *rocca* which Leo's soldiers pulled down. There is little else to detain you within the town. The much restored church of Santa Maria witnessed Rita's baptism and contains a harrowingly conceived statue of St Sebastian in painted wood by an anonymous fifteenth-century carver, an amusingly pompous ciborium, with the figures of the prophets under a gilded balustrade, by Francesco Piergentili (1567), and one excellent picture, over the first altar on the right, *The Peace between Guelphs and Ghibellines*, painted by the Angelucci brothers in 1547. Here God the Father and the Madonna and Child watch serenely as a group of smiling citizens witnesses a fraternal embrace between the former enemies.

Cascia was one of the many places in central Italy visited by Giuseppe Garibaldi, as an inscription in the piazza named after him reminds us. The great revolutionary leader was on his way to Rome to take charge of the republican rebels defending it against the French and Papal troops when, on 28 January 1849, he arrived with three companions at the Tintarella inn outside the town. Recognized by the jubilant *casciani*, he was carried in triumph into this very square, the church bells ringing out. After ordering the release of all political prisoners, the hero made one of his highly effective speeches of the 'simple but moving' variety to the excited populace. Their joy was not destined to last. For all Garibaldi's stupendous efforts, Rome was taken, and when he next crossed Umbria it was as a hotly pursued fugitive.

Following the road south, above the Corno valley, you come at length to Monteleone di Spoleto, a small town whose considerable attractiveness is due to the simple fact that it has been left alone, even if recent decades have brought a healthy degree of prosperity to the place. It was founded on the remains of a fortified settlement called Brufa, built in 880 by a certain Count Atto, whose descendants, the Tiberti, gave the lordship to Spoleto. When in 1228 an imperial bully named Berthold von Ursilingen, at the head of a troop of Saracen mercenaries, sacked and burned the town, the Tiberti released all their remaining claims on the place and gave the Spoletines everything they owned.

Tough mountaineers, the *monteleonesi* had always

A field of poppies on the plain of Santa Scholastica, Norcia.

aspired to total independence, and in 1535, when they threw out the Spoletines and held them at bay for years on end, they imagined that their chance had come. A *podestà* was elected and a free commune set up on the old medieval lines which were being extinguished elsewhere in Italy. In 1559, after the armies of Spoleto had wrecked their mills, laid waste their farms and grubbed up their orchards, the brave citizens gave in on the condition proposed by Pope Pius IV (1559–65) that the lordship of Monteleone be awarded to Perugia, which it duly was.

The heart of the town is formed by the open space in front of the medieval Torre dell'Orologio, all that remains of the castle, and the church of San Francesco adjoining it. This has recently been restored, and the interior is among southern Umbria's most memorable for its synthesis of paintings and fresco fragments from different periods, none of them of spectacular magnificence, but a perfect reflection of what the taste and purchasing power of a small renaissance or baroque community could aspire to. Two altars are framed by tall gilt columns and classical pediments, there are colourfully frescoed saints on either side of the chancel arch, a striking sequence of primitive panel paintings along the south wall of the nave, and a delicately carved wooden ceiling over all.

From Monteleone, you cross the western mountain range of the Valnerina to the walled *borgo* of Sant'Anatolia di Narco and follow the road along the valley southwards, between high grey cliffs, their sides shaggy with dark fir forests. After about 10 kilometres, you catch a glimpse, up the hillside, of the romanesque abbey of San Pietro in Valle, one of Umbria's truly outstanding examples of early medieval architecture. Though it is currently private property and appears to be undergoing a rather dilatory restoration, the church, together with the conventual buildings attached to it, well deserves the journey up the rather variable track leading off the main road past Sambucheto, if only for a glance at its venerable walls

The 1930s façade of Saint Rita's shrine at Cascia.

A small lion at Monteleone, 'the lion's mountain', near Spoleto.

and the lofty, five-storeyed twelfth-century campanile in the style carried all over Italy by the architects and masons of Lombardy.

San Pietro in Valle was founded on the site of a hermitage by Faroald II, Duke of Spoleto, whose son Trasamund had deposed him and then forced him to become a monk. Faroald died here in 728, no doubt meditating on the whirligig of time and the vanity of human wishes. It would perhaps have consoled him to know that the scapegrace Trasamund was eventually chased out of Spoleto and killed for conspiring against the powerful, ruthless Liutprand, King of the Longobards. The original church was rebuilt at the end of the tenth century but it still reflects one of the great and seldom recognized achievements of the not-so-barbarian Longobards, the foundation, or re-foundation, of a whole series of monastic houses, from Bobbio in northern Italy to San Vincenzo al Volturno in Campania.

The walls of the nave retain traces of a complete twelfth-century fresco scheme, with scenes from the Old Testament (the Creation, Cain killing Abel, Noah's Ark) and episodes from the life of Christ, from the Nativity to Calvary. Those in the apse have survived the ravages of the weather fairly well (the church has only recently been given a new roof) and below the byzantine-inspired Christ and the Madonna and Child you can make out the figures of five saints, Benedict, Placidus, Martial, Eleutherius and Lazarus, whose cults appear to have been especially popular in the Middle Ages. There is an exceptionally pretty cloister and at the back a range of conventual buildings which fills you with a desire to linger, like Faroald himself, cradled within the remoteness of these mountain passes, seeking spiritual solace among the woods and rocks and waterfalls of the wild Valnerina.

Further south, the valley opens out into a broad plain, with the village of Ferentillo spreading itself along either side of the river in two distinct settlements called Matterella and Precetto. A yellow sign cryptically inscribed *Mummie* is no adequate preparation for one of the weirdest experiences in mainland Italy (I say mainland because you can find something vaguely similar, though much more celebrated, at Palermo in Sicily). In Precetto the church of Santo Stefano features a vault whose geological constituents include nitrates and calcareous salts within a porous sand which has the property of preserving corpses. The custodian will open the doors and usher you into a macabre assembly which is decidedly not for those with queasy stomachs.

Preserved in glass cases, the bodies are all naked, and a rum lot they are. There are three Chinese, two men and a woman, who arrived in Italy as part of a commercial embassy at the end of the last century and succumbed to cholera while on their way over to Ancona. There is a woman who died in childbirth, cradling her dead baby. One of the Pope's Swiss guards stands upright in what looks like a grandfather clock case, and a lawyer killed in a local blood-feud lies next to one of the peasants involved who accidentally shot himself in the stomach. Much more ghoulish than the human corpses, however, are the mummies of an eagle and an owl, straight from Edgar Allen Poe. Truly a sight not to be missed.

From Ferentillo the road carries on down the Nera valley, with worthwhile detours to be made towards Montefranco, which occupies a superb position on the mountain's edge, and Arrone, whose gothic and romanesque parish church of Santa Maria has some amusingly primitive sixteenth-century frescoes based on Lippi's great quartet of paintings in the *duomo* at Spoleto.

Terni, at which you eventually arrive, is generally bypassed by the guidebook writers, and at first it is easy to see why. 'The Manchester of Umbria', as it used to be called, was devastated by World War II bombing (there were over 100 raids between August 1943 and June 1944) and public buildings, churches and palaces were flattened. The appearance of the city is frankly discouraging to anyone not interested in plastics, fertilizers, stainless steel or the small-arms business (the revolver with which Lee Harvey Oswald shot President Kennedy was apparently made here), but the place has a long history and contains a number of features to arrest the curious traveller.

Known as Interamna ('between the rivers') it was founded, according to Roman tradition, in 672 BC, though archaeology has since shown that there was a substantial settlement here from the Bronze Age onwards. For the Romans themselves Terni was a major staging post on the road north from the capital, and provided a backdrop to several typically dramatic events in the history of the empire. Here in AD 69 the general Dolabella was murdered on the orders of the cruel and gluttonous Emperor Vitellius, who had suspected him of alienating the affections of the Empress Petronia. In 253 the Emperor Gallus, who had defused a threatened Gothic invasion by buying off the enemy and become hated in the process, was killed at Terni by his own soldiers, together with his son Volusianus.

The river Nera flows past the town of Ferentillo.

Twenty-two years later, a citizen of Terni, Marcus Claudius Tacitus, actually assumed the imperial purple. Edward Gibbon, in his *Decline and Fall of the Roman Empire*, writes eloquently of this 75-year-old descendant of the great Roman historian, telling us that 'from the assiduous study of his immortal ancestor he derived the knowledge of the Roman constitution and of human nature'. It was not, alas, to do him any good, and his reluctance to become emperor was sinisterly confirmed by events. He tried to restore the authority of the senate over the lawless, bullying Roman army, pacifying mutinous troops in eastern Greece and negotiating successfully with the Scythian tribe from the Crimea known as the Alans. The legions, as he soon realized, were interested only in short-term gains from booty won during a quick campaign, and the welfare and security of the crumbling empire meant nothing to them. 'It may be doubted,' says Gibbon, 'whether the soldiers imbrued their hands in the blood of this innocent prince. It is certain that their insolence was the cause of his death.' Tacitus died at Tyana in Cappadocia, after reigning just six months and twenty days, and his brother Florianus, who forthwith proclaimed himself as successor, was murdered at Tarsus three months later.

Terni's subsequent history is a series of destructions and rebuildings, anticipating more recent experience. The Goths, Byzantines and Longobards all sacked and burned it, and in 1174 the thuggish Emperor Frederick Barbarossa, having been snubbed by the citizens when he tried to make them feudal subjects of one of his henchmen, Cardinal Monticelli, sent Christian, Archbishop of Mainz, to seize and destroy the city.

Entering along Viale Benedetto Brin and Via Mazzini, you turn left into Corso Cornelio Tacito (this is the other Tacitus, the historian who was born in *c.* AD 55; a famous writer beats a failed emperor any day for glamour). To the right of the Corso, up Via Benedetto Faustini, is the large gothic church of San Francesco, designed in 1345 by Angelo da Orvieto. St Francis himself preached to the people of Terni here from the little stone platform in front of the third pillar on the right of the nave. Beyond this, in the Paradisi chapel, you will find a singular series of frescoes by the mid fifteenth-century Perugine master Bartolomeo di Tomaso, based on the *Divine Comedy* of Dante. Here are the Inferno, divided into its seven circles, Purgatory, with the freeing of souls, and Paradise, with Beatrice and God in majesty.

At the end of the Corso are two squares opening off one another, Piazza Repubblica and Piazza Europa, and past these is a further open space in which stands the twelfth-century church of San Salvatore, raised on the remains of a Roman temple to the sun and those of a bath house. You can still see the walls and pavements of these buildings under the nave of the church.

West of San Salvatore, at the top of Via Aminale, Piazza del Duomo is dominated by the cathedral, a mixture of romanesque and baroque, with an extremely grand high altar dating from 1762 and a lovely decorated organ and choir loft of the seventeenth century. The crypt preserves the tomb of Anastasius, an early bishop of Terni, and a pagan altar turned to Christian uses. To the south of the cathedral you will find the remains of the large Roman amphitheatre built in AD 32 by Faustus Titius Liberalis. Terni's most famous martyr, and her first bishop, was not put to death here, but in Rome, in the year 273. He was none other than St Valentine, whom a recent purge of the Christian calendar may have demoted but who still remains the patron saint of lovers.

Most visitors to Terni down the centuries have come to gaze not on the city but on the superb waterfall to the south-east, the Cascata delle Marmore, formed by the descent of the River Velino into the Nera. Flowing down across the plateau of Rieti, the Velino was originally a slow stream snaking across marshy country and frequently flooding the surrounding plain. The dramatic solution proposed and executed in 271 BC by Curius Dentatus, conqueror of the Sabines whose territory this was, involved diverting the river

A romanesque lion in the porch of the cathedral at Terni.

Terni preserves the ruins of its Roman amphitheatre.

into a fresh channel and sending it over the precipice into the Nera several hundred feet below.

The Falls of Terni, which can be seen only on certain days and at stated times (you will need to check these locally), have always been one of the wonders of Italy. If, like me, you enjoy the sense of a tradition of travel, the feeling that you are sharing and renewing the experience of ages merely by going to such places as this and seeing what the tourists of the eighteenth and nineteenth century so admired, you will find a more than merely visual excitement in the plunging stream.

When Shelley came here in 1818, he wrote: 'Stand upon the brink of the platform of cliff. . . . You see the ever-moving water stream down. It comes in thick and tawny folds, flaking off like solid snow gliding down from a mountain. It does not seem hollow within, but without it is unequal, like the folding of linen thrown carelessly down. . . . The very imagination is bewildered by it.' Eight years afterwards the Irish writer Anna Jameson, in her *Diary of an Ennuyée*, organized two carriages to bring her with friends to the cascade. 'O such equipages! – such rat-like steeds! such picturesque accoutrements! and such poetical-looking guides and postilions, ragged, cloaked and whiskered! – but it was all consistent: the wild figures harmonized with the wild landscape.' When at last she got there:

> As I stood close to the precipice's edge, immediately under the great fall, I felt my respiration gone: I turned giddy, almost faint, and was obliged to lean against the rock for support. The mad plunge of the waters, the deafening roar, the presence of a power which no earthly force could resist or control, struck me with an awe almost amounting to terror.

By 1890 Baedeker's *Central Italy* was warning that visitors to Terni 'should be abundantly provided with copper coins. . . . The patience is sorely tried by the importunities of a host of beggars and guides.' Byron, who stayed at Villa Graziani Pressio nearby, had no such problems in 1817, and we should let him have the last word:

> More like the fountain of an infant sea
> Torn from the womb of mountains by the throes
> Of a new world, than only thus to be
> Parent of rivers, which flow gushingly,
> With many windings through the vale: – Look back!
> Lo! where it comes like an eternity,
> As if to sweep down all things in its track,
> Charming the eye with dread, – a matchless cataract,
> Horribly beautiful!

Terni's Cascata delle Marmore has inspired poets and fascinated travellers for centuries.

N
Massa Martana
Monti Martani
Colvalenza
Villa San Faustino
Rosceto
Orvieto
Acquasparta
Montecchio
Monte Croce di Serra
Tiber
Bolsena
San Gemini Fonte
Guardea
San Gemini
Alviano
Lugnano in Teverina
Amelia
Monte Arnata
Montefiascone
Narni
Attigliano
Giove
Nera
0
5
10 km

6
Golden Cathedral, White River

Orvieto – Amelia – Narni

One of the most richly enjoyable of all books written about Italy, and one I am always glad of an opportunity to celebrate, is George Dennis's *The Cities and Cemeteries of Etruria*. Published in 1848, after five years of intensive journeying up and down the ancient Etruscan territory, it represents the first serious attempt by anyone in modern times to get to grips with this vanished civilization, and it is delightfully enlivened by the writer's enthusiasm, sense of humour and great narrative gifts, so that another lost world, that of early nineteenth-century Italy, springs vividly from its pages.

Naturally enough Dennis visited Orvieto, one of the oldest cities in Umbria, and already in existence as a stronghold when the Etruscans arrived in the sixth century BC. Nobody who reads his description of a first encounter with the city can fail to acknowledge its accuracy in capturing the dramatic impression created by the high yellow tufa crags above which Orvieto's walls and towers are visible from far away:

> The first view of Orvieto is one of the most imposing in Italy. The road, which is level for the greater part of the way, leads unexpectedly to the verge of a cliff where a scene magnificent enough to compensate for any discomfort bursts on the view. From the midst of the wide and deep valley at my feet rose, about two miles distant, an isolated height, like a truncated cone, crowned with the towers of Orvieto. The sky was overcast, the atmosphere dense and misty, and the brilliant hues of sunshine were wanting; yet the grand features of the scene were visible as in an engraving. There were the picturesque convent towers embosomed in groves on the slopes in the foreground – the luxuriant cultivation of the valley beneath – there was the wide stretch of the city, bristling from its broad cliff-bound rock in the centre of the scene – the background of mountains which, looming through vapour and cloud, lost nothing of altitude or sublimity – and the whole was set in a framework of tall precipices, hung with woods and with many a cataract streaking their steeps.

Nobody knows for certain the real name of Etruscan Orvieto, but the city seems to have been identical with Volsinii Veteres, which was destroyed by the Romans in 265 BC and thereafter abandoned until the time of the Byzantine wars against the Goths in the sixth century AD, when as 'Ourbibenton' or 'Urbs vetus' it was a natural rallying point for local resistance. Under the forceful Longobard king Agilulf (590–616) the town received its first bishop, and in the early Middle Ages it set itself up as a free commune, constantly rebelling against the various popes' attempts to establish their authority.

There were wars with Siena, Todi and Perugia, in futile efforts to extend Orvieto's sphere of influence, and meanwhile the great noble families of the city, the Monaldeschi, the Filippeschi, the Alberici and others, fought their Guelph and Ghibelline battles up and down the winding streets. In 1313 the Monaldeschi themselves divided into warring factions known as the Beffati and the Malcorini, so that forty years and many feuds later, Cardinal Albornoz, in his customary role as referee, had to intervene. He took Orvieto under papal control, though not all its civic privileges were entirely stripped away. The grasp of the church only closed completely in 1450, when two Monaldeschi belonging to a faction called the Viper, which had exerted a brutal tyranny over the citizens, were finally expelled.

Orvieto is one of the great art cities of Italy, on the pilgrimage route of everyone seriously interested in the development of medieval and renaissance architecture and decorative art. Yet the old town itself is small and compact, and everything within it is very easily seen – except, that is, for those buildings which are closed, notices on their doors proclaiming such time-honoured Italian civic excuses as 'shut for restoration' or 'lack of staff'. You will find it far easier to walk than to drive through the centre; you should at least get your car up the winding roads to the top of the hill, but parking anywhere convenient is far from easy.

The reason for most visits to Orvieto can be spotted before you even reach the place, and in the context of a relatively small and unassuming medieval city, it never ceases to appear utterly bizarre, one of the most extravagant of all flourishes in the religious art of the world. The founding of the Cathedral of the Assunta in 1290 was a direct response to a miracle witnessed thirty years previously by the congregation in the church of Santa Cristina at Bolsena, westwards over the Latian border. In 1263 a potentially heretical Bohemian priest named Peter of Prague, journeying to Rome for spiritual guidance, was invited to celebrate mass there and witnessed the astonishing sight of drops of blood falling from the consecrated Host onto the altar-cloth, a proof of the transubstantiation he had begun to doubt. Pope Urban IV, who happened to be staying in Orvieto, received the priest in audience, and ordered the blood-stained linen to be brought from Bolsena with due ceremony. On 11 August 1264, the Pope proclaimed the Feast of Corpus Domini, and the sacred cloth was placed in a silver reliquary, in which it is carried in a solemn costumed procession around the city on 19 June each year.

The *duomo* of Orvieto, built to house the holy relic and to commemorate the significance of the event, represents over three hundred years of architectural achievement, during which, regardless of changing tastes and styles, all those who worked on it remained essentially loyal to the medieval spirit of the original. The initial design may have been the brainchild of the great Tuscan architect Arnolfo di Cambio (1250–1302),

A leafy alleyway in the heart of old Orvieto.

Sunlight transfigures the *duomo* of Orvieto.

whom we know to have been in Orvieto, busied over a tomb in the church of San Domenico, but the three romanesque naves were the work of Fra Bevignate of Perugia, succeeded by Giovanni di Uguccione, who created an apse and a crossing.

At this point, around 1305, the first structural problems appeared, and advice was sought from the Sienese architect Lorenzo Maitani (1270–1330). He it was who shored up the external walls with buttressing, rebuilt the apse in its present gothic form, created a chapel for the miraculous altar-cloth and, most important of all, superimposed the magnificent façade we see today. Other great names in Italian art, including the sculptor Andrea Pisano (1290–1349) and the painter Andrea Orcagna (1308–68), added their contributions to the work, but the concept is essentially Maitani's and the grateful Orvietans have even named a hotel after him.

His façade, among the proudest assertions of gothic anywhere south of the Alps, depends for its spectacular effect on the vital upward thrust of the four crocketed pinnacles and the severely angled pediments above deeply incised doorways. Around Orcagna's lovely central rose window stand figures of the prophets and apostles executed between 1372–88 by the Orvietan sculptor Petruccio di Benedetto, and in all the flat surfaces between the bands of carving on either side, above and below, are vibrantly coloured mosaics showing scenes from the life of the Blessed Virgin, the earliest (over the main porch) dated 1366, the work of Fra Giovanni Leonardelli, and the latest (in the topmost central cusp) a copy made in 1842 by Roman mosaicists of a lost original. The others are essentially late renaissance and baroque, as their idiom suggests. Maitani himself modelled the superbly forceful bronze symbols of the Four Evangelists on either side of the flanking doorways in 1325, and the little pavilion containing Andrea Pisano's *Virgin and Child*, while the graceful statue of the Archangel Michael above these to the left was cast in bronze by Matteo da Ugolino da Bologna in 1356.

The most admired original feature on this façade is the series of marble bas-reliefs on the pilasters between the three doorways. The original scheme and some of the carvings are attributed to Maitani, but he was almost certainly assisted by other Tuscan sculptors, in work which occupied the decade 1320–30. In these episodes from the Old and New Testament, singularity is guaranteed by the fusion of the style of a medieval illuminated manuscript with sinuous delicacy in the moulding and grouping of the figures within their sprays and tendrils of branching vines. This creates an effect unique, so far as I know, in the art of the late Middle Ages.

After all this dramatic profusion, the interior of the *duomo* at first appears strikingly, indeed disappointingly bare. The undisturbed homogeneity of the romanesque nave, with its peppermint-humbug pillars and exposed roof beams, makes its austerely dignified impact, but I have to confess that I find its cavernous emptiness gloomy and depressing beyond description. Oh, for a gilded Madonna, oh, for a bishop's tomb, oh (yes, why not?), for a decorous nineteenth-century monument, or a few indifferent seventeenth-century altar-pieces to liven up this awful purity!

Do not give up, however, for something tremendous awaits you. Meanwhile, like some polar explorer drawing on his iron rations in an emergency, you can stay the pangs of visual hunger with the Cappella del Santissimo Corporale. Here, amid frescoes telling the story of the holy relic, painted by a group of fourteenth-century Orvietan artists, stands the gorgeous parcel-gilt reliquary itself, displayed within a gothic tabernacle. The workmanship of this miracle of the goldsmith's art is by the Sienese Ugolino di Vieri, who fashioned it with his assistants in 1338. The doors feature what is effectively an altar-piece in an array of enamel panels and an exquisite predella beneath, whose blue makes a luminous contrast with the gilded frames; seated figures of saints surround the base of the elaborate construction, which echoes the spirit of Maitani's façade.

St John the Evangelist's eagle forms part of the decorated façade of the *duomo* at Orvieto.

A further burst of colour is created by the cathedral's presbytery, dominated by a huge medieval stained-glass window begun by Maitani in 1325 and only completed in 1508 by Fabiano Stasi. The frescoes here, by the same artists who worked in the Cappella del Santissimo Corporale, are not especially noteworthy, a fair-to-middling medieval job lot. You will find yourself turning very easily to admire the genuinely remarkable early fourteenth-century choir stalls, some of the earliest inlaid woodwork of its kind in Umbria, in which the figures of the apostles are vividly picked out against a dark background dotted with stars.

I have saved until last the most compelling work of art in the cathedral, and beyond any doubt the greatest achievement of its creator, the south Tuscan painter Luca Signorelli. The Chapel of the Madonna di San Brizio, on the right arm of the crossing, contains his prodigally magnificent fresco cycle, begun in 1499. Signorelli was hired (after negotiations with Perugino had fallen through) to continue work initiated, or at any rate projected, by Fra Angelico and Benozzo Gozzoli. He was charged with the duty of respecting the conservative tastes of the Orvietans and given a sort of probation before the cathedral authorities allowed him to go ahead with his scheme for decorating the entire chapel for a payment of 575 ducats, a substantial sum in modern terms.

Whatever the scruples of provincial Orvieto, Signorelli set forth on these walls and vaults his own highly idiosyncratic renaissance vision of a mingled pagan and Christian world, touched by the profound sensibilities of an artist who loved to dress in splendid clothes and who had drawn the body of his dead son so that he might not forget him. Beauty and horror sound here with equal intensity, but each is conceived on an essentially human scale, defined by a series of studies in the nude figure which have no rival until the advent of Michelangelo.

Lorenzo Maitani's superb *Last Judgment* on the *duomo* façade at Orvieto.

As well as the painted triangles within the vaulting, there are seven frescoes around the doorway, along either wall and flanking the windows behind the altar. Over our heads floats the heavenly company of the Patriarchs, the Doctors of the Church, the Virgins and the Martyrs, picked out against a gold ground in Signorelli's distinctive pale greens, blues and reds, each a portrait highly individualized in pose and expression. Above the ornately banded arches of the entrance runs an astonishing vision of the end of the world, a wild cosmic anarchy, in which the sea floods the earth and the sun plummets towards a huddle of confused men and women, frightened animals, and an anxious group of prophets (including David and the Sybil) scanning the skies, whence demons hurl their fire at the damned beneath a moon covered in blood.

On the left-hand wall is the figure of the Antichrist, prompted by a devil whispering in his left ear. The false prophet, probably meant to represent Pope Alexander VI (1492–1503), is surrounded by scenes and images of greed, lying and cruelty, while in the background a sinister troop of black-armoured soldiers throngs the portico of the Temple of Jerusalem. Next to this, angels stoop earthwards to crown the elect and summon them to paradise, to the accompaniment of lutes, a harp and a guitar. The left-hand angel stringing a violin is a charming touch.

Here the beauty of the nudes, with their lavishly sculpted contours, is striking enough, but it is in the two frescoes opposite that Signorelli's true originality as a painter of the human form springs most vividly from the walls. What more hideous than the green buttocks of the grizzled barbarian torturer in *The Torments of the Damned*, or the monstrous pink sinews of the bushy-browed creature pulling out a woman's toe-nails as he tramples on her head? Could anything, on the other hand, have more grace than *The Resurrection of the Flesh*, in which we sense all the wonder and astonishment of humanity awakening to new life? In all these works of Signorelli's there is something deeply un-Italian, a freedom of fancy and a sense of shuddering, diabolical horror which other renaissance painters either shy away from or else do not know. It is

One of Orvieto's many magnificent palace portals.

sui generis, unique to this visionary master, set apart through his insight into the nature of mortality and the everlasting.

When you emerge from the *duomo*, you will no doubt want one more look at the façade, which Dennis, who felt he had no business to be describing medieval cathedrals in the middle of a book on the Etruscans, nevertheless could not resist calling 'the petrifaction of an illuminated missal – a triumphant blaze of beauty obtained by the union and tasteful combination of the three Sister Graces of Art'. To the right of the cathedral stands the so-called Palazzo dei Papi, also known as the Palazzo Soliano, to distinguish it from the Palazzo Papale which joins it at right angles to the church. Built in a sort of russet-coloured tufa, with severe triple-arched gothic windows, the hulking mass of the Palazzo Soliano epitomizes the secular might of the papacy, as embodied by that worldly go-getter Boniface VIII, who began it in 1297.

It contains the Museo dell'Opera del Duomo, which brings together works from the cathedral itself, including a series of massive late renaissance and baroque marble apostles which used to line the nave (and ought, I feel, to have been left there to liven up its dreary emptiness) and paintings from various Orvietan churches. These include the expressive sequence of polyptych panels painted in 1321 by Simone Martini, in which you can see the donor, Trasmondo Monaldeschi, as a tiny kneeling figure to the right of the alabaster box held by St Mary Magdalene.

A museum of a very different sort is to be found in Palazzo Faina, facing the cathedral. It was begun in 1865 by Count Claudio Faina, member of a local family of amateur archaeologists, who amassed a remarkable assembly of Etruscan artefacts, including bronzes and coins, carved heads, a splendid fourth-century sarcophagus decorated with scenes from Homer, and some of the very finest Grecian vases, signed by the most accomplished masters in the genre.

Much of Orvieto's charm is outward rather than interior, and you can do nothing better than wander through the scatter of streets leading away from the cathedral towards Corso Cavour, the single main thoroughfare of the city. The Orvietan nobility, presuming on the privileges guaranteed them under papal rule, built a whole series of restrainedly elegant palaces, the best of them belonging to the sixteenth century, when the city basked in a positive architectural sunburst.

Three great names dominate the epoch, and rather than sending you on a systematic pilgrimage in search of each, I prefer, just for once, to take them as a trio, since stylistically they form an obvious line of succession. The first is Antonio da Sangallo the Younger (1483–1546), famous son of an equally famous Florentine father, who arrived here in 1527 in the train of Pope Clement VII (1523–34), a fugitive from Rome, under siege by the army of Holy Roman Emperor

Dawn light gilds the church of San Giovanni, Orvieto.

Charles V. While the Pope gathered together a holy league against his adversary and received embassies from Muscovy and England (negotiating Henry VIII's divorce from Catherine of Aragon), Sangallo was at work designing the central cusp of the cathedral façade, building the stupendous Pozzo di San Patrizio (of which more later), inspiring the design of the beautiful cloister of San Giovanni in Via Alberici, completed in 1528, and creating the lofty Palazzo Marsciano in Piazza Marconi. The commission for the last came from a so-called nephew of Pope Paul III (actually a bastard son) named Tiberio Crispo, admitted to the Orvietan nobility in 1540 and made a canon of the cathedral.

One of Sangallo's assistants in his Umbrian commissions for the Popes was a Florentine nobleman, Simone Mosca delle Pecore (1492–1553), of whom Vasari writes: 'Since he so much liked the manners of the Orvietans, he brought hither his family, so that he might live more comfortably; and thus he quietly settled to his work, being greatly honoured in this city by everyone.' As well he might be, for the palaces he designed are some of Orvieto's most attractive. Look out for Palazzo Gualterio, on the corner of Via del Duomo and Corso Cavour, with its rusticated basalt columns, the opulently sculpted window frames of Palazzo Marabottini in Via Pecorelli, or the triumphal balconied portico of Palazzo Monaldeschi in Via Ippolito Scalza.

Scalza (1532–1617) was one of the greatest of Umbrian architects, a worthy successor to Mosca, with whom he studied initially as a sculptor in the *duomo*. A man of many talents, he claimed with evident justification to be expert not merely in building and stonework, but in the making of church organs, the surveying of landed estates and the complexities of hydraulic engineering. When he became chief architect of Orvieto in 1567, he was able, amid work ranging from mapping the city's feudal territories to designing tombs in the cathedral of Amelia, to turn his hand to palaces which combined grandeur with a certain element of fancifulness, even of fun. For what are the scalloped pediments on the lower windows of Palazzo Guidoni in Corso Cavour, or the tapering pilasters and the scrollwork above them on the gateway to Palazzo Gualterio in the same street, but the achievements of somebody with a refined sense of humour? Was there even a hint here of mockery directed at the proud, eternally quarrelsome Orvietan nobles throwing up these grandiose piles from which Scalza profited so handsomely?

His uncompleted Palazzo Comunale (1573–81) stands in Piazza della Repubblica, a square that is always crammed with Orvietans young and old, many of whom are those aged men in hats who proliferate in the town squares of southern Italy. Next to the palace is the medieval church of Sant'Andrea, less interesting within, where it has been somewhat too extensively pulled about by various rebuildings, than without, where its dodecagonal bell-tower, pitted with double-arched windows and stuck with medieval stone *stemmi* (coats of arms), is worth a look. The church, supposedly occupying the site of a temple of Juno, was the place where Innocent III proclaimed the Fifth Crusade in 1216 and his successor Honorius III (1216–27) crowned Peter of Artois as King of Jerusalem in the following year; neither initiative, it may be noted, led to anything useful.

From the square, follow Via Filippeschi and Via Malabranca, past the big Palazzo Carvajal, built by a Spanish follower of Pope Clement VII (notice the inscription on the façade, which translates as 'Carvajal de Carvajal, a master of the house for the comfort of his friends'). In the little piazza at the end are two churches at right angles to each other. Sant'Agostino is a gothic shell, long disused and undergoing a seemingly interminable restoration. San Giovenale, on the other hand, is a venerable work which has been dated to 1004, but surely belongs to a much earlier era, judging both by the external masonry and by the nature of the columns and arches of the nave and the apse, all of which are decorated with patches of primitive but cheerful fresco work by anonymous local masters of the Middle Ages and the Renaissance.

If you turn out of Piazza della Repubblica in the opposite direction and walk eastwards, right along

The twelve-sided campanile of Sant'Andrea, Orvieto.

Corso Cavour, you eventually emerge in front of the *rocca*, built for Cardinal Albornoz by Ugolino di Montemarte in 1364, with the characteristic round French bastions of the period. During revolutionary disturbances in 1831, the interior was largely destroyed, and for a while horse races were held here until, during the late nineteenth century, the space was turned into a public garden.

On the edge of the cliff outside the northern wall of the fortress, beyond the remains of a fifth-century BC Etruscan temple, you will find one of the chief curiosities of Orvieto, the celebrated Pozzo di San Patrizio. Begun during Clement VII's stay in the city, from December 1527 to June 1528, this huge cylindrical well, plugged through the tufa to a depth of 62 metres, was named after the legendary bottomless well in St Patrick's cave on Lough Derg in Co. Fermanagh, Ireland (Italians use the expression *un pozzo di San Patrizio* to mean an Aladdin's cave, an inexhaustible resource). The Pope, fearful of an imperial assault on Orvieto, commissioned the work as a safety measure, making use of the inexhaustible talents of Antonio da Sangallo the Younger.

The enterprise took ten years and involved 30,000 bricks. Contrary to what is usually supposed, it was not Simone Mosca who completed the construction, but Sangallo himself, seeing through to the end his unique project, in which the central shaft, pierced with arches, is embraced by a spiral staircase up and down which it is possible to take donkeys if necessary. You can go all the way to the bottom, passing an Etruscan tomb in your descent and bearing in mind the singular fact that the well was never actually used to furnish the city with water.

Not everybody likes Orvieto. Murray's *Handbook* (1875) roundly asserts that 'the town is very dirty, and no place can appear duller to the casual visitor', while Henry James thought it 'a meanly arranged and, as Italian cities go, not particularly impressive little town'. Whatever your feelings towards the place, you would do well to have lunch here, as there is a very wide choice of good restaurants – a gastronomic *pozzo di San Patrizio*, indeed – though you should take care to avoid the kind of small establishment which makes too many obvious gestures in the direction of fussy décor and overpriced nouvelle cuisine. Do not feel that you necessarily have to grace your meal with the pale, subtle-flavoured Orvieto, since Umbria yields such a profusion of other excellent vintages, but at its perfumed, slightly insidious best, the famous wine well deserves its popularity.

Off the main road out of the town, winding down towards the *autostrada*, a right turn leads to the abbey of Santi Severo e Martirio, easily distinguished by its octagonal belltower, whose most often sounded chime is nicknamed Viola. Founded in the early Middle Ages on a site chosen – as at San Rufino in Assisi – by a pair of heifers who had dragged hither San Severo's body, accompanied by his surviving disciple Martirio, the monastery was rebuilt by the Benedictines, from whom it passed to the Franciscans. The conventual range is now a hotel and restaurant, but the church, a mixture of romanesque and gothic, with a frescoed

Above The lush colours of an Orvieto market stall.

Right The village of Baschi in the Tiber valley.

Crucifixion by Giunta Pisano in the apse, can be visited, and the *mis-en-scène* of the buildings blending with the lush pastures and wooded tufa outcrops of the Orvietan countryside is quite irresistible.

Unless you wish to stray westwards into Latium, you will have to join the Todi road for a while, until the turn off to Montecchio brings you into what, as far as I am concerned, is the loveliest stretch of country in the whole of Umbria. Moving south in the direction of Amelia, you hang high above the Tiber valley, with exhilarating vistas across to the hills above Bolsena and Montefiascone. The roadside is lined with stretches of woodland and thickets of broom, and the whole landscape is suffused with a potent sense of unvisited loneliness.

Not, however, that there is nothing to arrest you in the way of human habitation. South of Montecchio is Guardea, where the ruins of the old *borgo*, abandoned after a series of landslips, still endure on the hilltop, and the slightly forbidding Castello del Poggio is now given over to more peaceful uses, sheltering shops selling honey and herbs, and a pottery which has revived local medieval designs.

It was Adrian IV, whose real name was Nicholas Brakspear, the only Englishman ever to be made Pope, who purchased Guardea in 1158 from a daughter of its feudal lord Reynaldo, and made it an important stronghold in the semi-autonomous 'Status Alviani', the territory surrounding Alviano, a small town to the south, superbly sited on a shaggy hilltop. The original settlement was founded by Count Offredo, a follower of the Holy Roman Emperor Otto III, in 993, but the hulking fortress, with all its round bastions complete, which now dominates the place belongs to the end of the fifteenth century. It was built by the *condottiere* Bartolomeo di Alviano, using materials from earlier structures, including the romanesque lion crouching at the foot of the entrance steps, and the bizarre gorgon's head stuck into the tower on the left of the main arch.

After a succession of feudal owners, Alviano was sold in 1651 to Donna Olimpia Pamphilj Maidalchini, sister-in-law of Pope Innocent X (1649–55). Donna Olimpia is the sort of woman whose exploits seem to have been calculated with historical novelists firmly in mind; she is still recalled in Rome for her ruthless exercise of nepotism and for the shameless fashion in which she fulfilled her greed and social ambitions. Left a widow before Innocent became pope, she lost no time in using his position to her advantage. She was the kind of female politician who scorns the company of women in favour of manipulating weak and malleable men, and her hand was detected in every political initiative. The Roman mob detested her, and when any of her more compliant allies among the cardinals passed through the streets, the cry went up 'Give us bread, not whores!'

Of course she was suspected, probably without justification, of an illicit liaison with the septuagenarian pope, and it was even rumoured that in London (where Protestants went on burning her in effigy long after her death) Oliver Cromwell had been delighted with a satirical entertainment called *The Pope's Wedding*. Whatever the case, she lost no time during Innocent's final illness in 1655 in carrying off his personal effects, actually removing treasure-chests from under his bed as he lay dying. His successor Alexander VII (1655–67), who as Cardinal Chigi had been constantly slighted and abused by her, sent Donna Olimpia to live under house arrest at Viterbo, where she died in 1657 aged 63. Now her *rocca* of Alviano is occupied by an extremely well displayed museum of peasant customs and a study centre devoted to the wildlife on the nearby reservoir, the so-called Lago di Alviano, which shelters eighty different kinds of duck, migrant cormorants and sandpipers, as well as herons and geese.

Above Alviano to the south, Lugnano in Teverina preserves the aspect of an ideal, unaltered, small Italian town, wholly unconcerned with its image and the more attractive for that reason. The one large palace, which you can hardly miss since it dominates everything around it, is the late renaissance Palazzo Farnese

Alviano's round-towered castle dates from the fifteenth century.

Left A farmhouse crowns a green hillside between Guardea and Alviano.

Above Lugnano lies along a ridge overlooking the river Tiber.

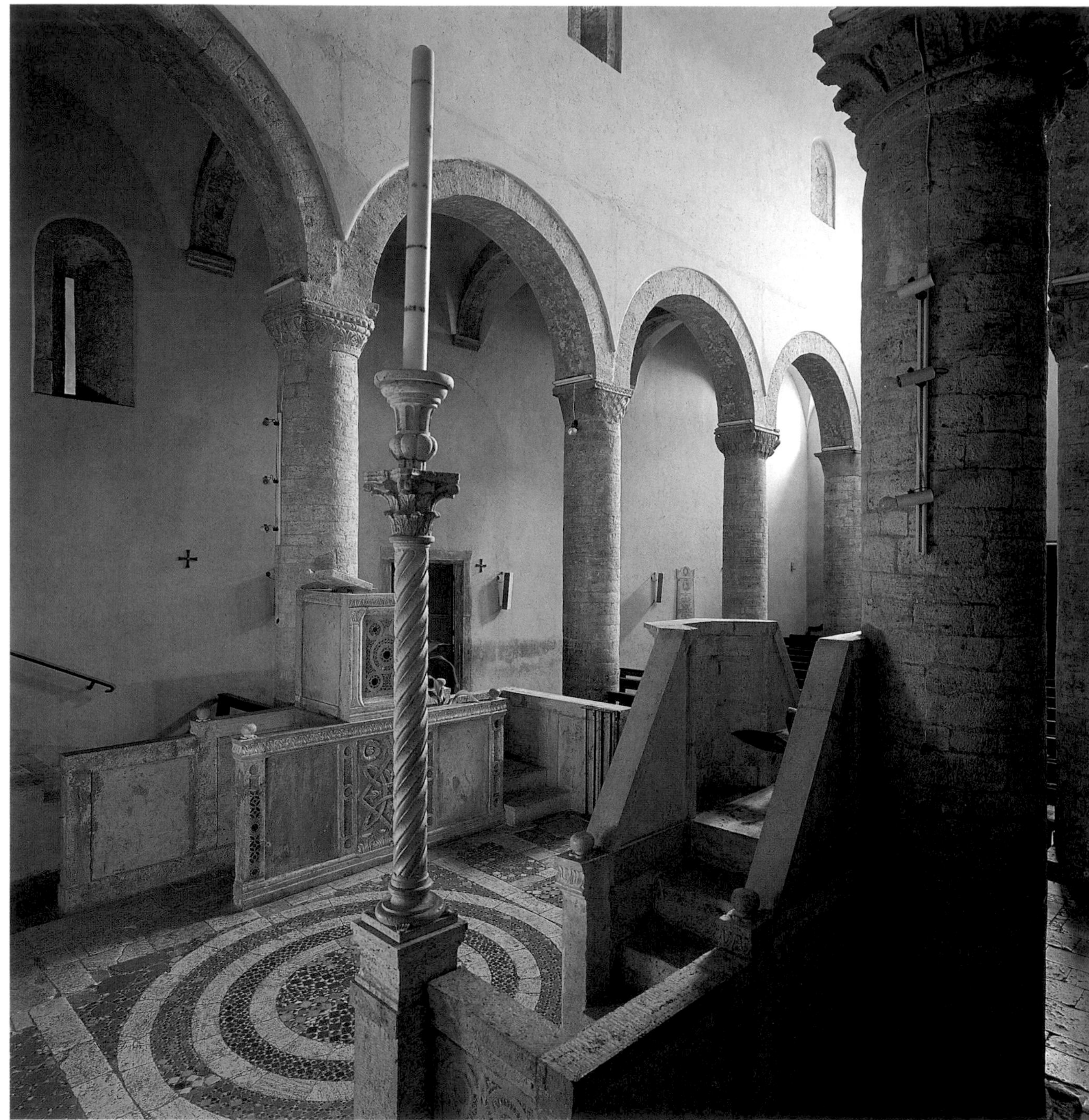

Ridolfi, known as Il Pennone, 'the spar', since it sticks out like the yard-arm of a ship. Otherwise this is still the defensive cluster of stone houses above narrow streets founded thirteen centuries ago by refugees from Gothic invasion, a settlement menaced by invading Saracens and French and squabbled over by Todi and Orvieto until, in the fifteenth century, Pius II (1458–69) made it a free commune under papal control.

The delight of Lugnano is the romanesque church of Santa Maria Assunta, standing in its little piazza at the heart of the town. Its façade has echoes of churches in Spoleto, Assisi and other parts of Umbria, but is really unlike anything else in the region in its eclectic combination of elements from various epochs. The portico, with its arches crossed by a decorated stone cornice raised on four Corinthian columns, belongs to the twelfth century, while the gothic rose window is flanked by two double-arched windows in ornately carved stone frames. The nave has preserved its floor of serpentine-patterned marble inlay, its round-headed arcades and the stone canopy of the altar behind the screen within the raised presbytery. On the altar itself the triptych, the *Assumption of the Virgin with Saints Francis and Sebastian*, is a typically poetic treatment from the hand of Nicolò Alunno.

Following the road down towards the Tiber you reach the convent of San Francesco, founded in 1229 to commemorate a miracle which took place here seventeen years earlier. On this occasion St Francis caused a wild duck to attack a wolf which had stolen the baby belonging to a woman listening to one of his sermons. Below this stands the old castle of Attigliano, with its five round towers, and a charmingly weather-beaten seventeenth-century clock-tower in the piazza (the mechanism of the clock itself still functions after three hundred years). At Giove, further on to the south-east, the Roman place-name preserves the memory of a shrine to Jupiter, though its site has not yet been uncovered. Within the village's fragmentary medieval walls stands the great palace developed from a medieval fortress by Ciriaco Mattei during the early sixteenth century. Though never completed, the exterior of the building, with its powerful contrast between warlike crenellation and the domesticity of the enchanting balcony on one corner, supported by an eagle with open wings, makes its point, and behind lie rooms frescoed by Domenichino (1581–1641) and the Perugine painter Orazio Alfani (1510–83). These are sometimes opened to the public, though the palace remains in private hands.

For the next dozen kilometres north-eastwards there is not a village in sight, and you can relish the glorious rolling emptiness of the landscape as you snake up and plunge down the hillsides, until at last Amelia, that quintessential Umbrian town, comes into view, teetering on top of its steep cone. There is something completely intransigent about Amelia; before you get close, you can have a hundred ideas of what it ought

The pure romanesque interior of Santa Maria Assunta, Lugnano.

The monumental renaissance doorway to the castle at Giove.

This balcony adorns Palazzo Mattei at Giove, south of Orvieto.

to be like, but it refuses to conform to an urban stereotype of any sort. There is no central piazza worth the name – there simply is not room for one – there are hardly any distinguished *palazzi*, the streets are murderous in their gradients and cruelly twisting just at points when the motorist might wish them not to be, and the churches have nothing of special note.

Yet it would be foolish to pass Amelia by. It is enormously old, and looks it. The Roman writer and politician known as Cato the Censor (234–149 BC) actually dated its foundation to an exact year, whose modern equivalent would be 1134 BC, and archaeology now suggests that it may be more ancient still. The walls – outside which you would be wise to leave your car – are basically splendid Etruscan masonry of huge unmortared tufa blocks, dating from around 400 BC, and scattered throughout the town are traces of Roman Ameria, a busy industrial centre specializing in tiles and pottery, which gained fresh importance during the third century AD, when the Emperor Aurelian favoured it with new baths and palaces.

Becoming a Christian bishopric in 344 (the first bishop bore the memorably uncommon name of Orthodulphus), the city was subsequently sacked by Totila and his gothic host, rebuilt by the Longobards and annexed by the Byzantines as a key fortress on their 'corridor' across southern Umbria. During the Middle Ages it was for a while a free commune before being seized by the Church in 1307. The Popes, however, ruled with a light hand, allowing Amelia to enjoy its liberties under a mayor sent every six months from Rome. A group of citizens known as the Council of Elders made the really important decisions, while a Council of Ten supervised the town's defences and the entire legal infrastructure was examined and reviewed by a body called the *Correptores*, literally 'the Correctors'.

The Porta Romana, a sober architectural gesture of 1703, with the remains of a medieval tower jammed into its pediment, ushers you into Amelia. On your right, as the Via della Repubblica starts to climb, is the very plain gothic church of San Francesco, where the Cappella di Sant'Antonio contains the handsome tombs of the Geraldini family. They were an influential clan (one of them, Alessandro, not buried here, was the first bishop of the Caribbean island of Santo Domingo) and were thus able to commission the likes of Agostino di Duccio (1418–81) to design a monument, which he did most expressively in 1477 for Matteo and Elisabetta Geraldini. The pretty two-tiered cloister next to the church dates from the sixteenth century.

The Geraldini palaces, including Alessandro's, lie further up the street, but the stateliest of these renaissance mansions is found in Via Farattini, running parallel to the south, where Bartolomeo Farattini, who was cardinal for a single day (I am afraid I cannot discover why), built his *palazzo* in 1520 to designs by Antonio da Sangallo the Younger. The architect's

Beside a secluded lake near the town of Amelia.

trademarks are all here – the windows carefully contrasted in form, the rusticated coigns, the heavily accentuated central doorway – and if the result recalls Palazzo Farnese in Rome, which Sangallo began five years earlier, this is hardly accidental, since Farattini actually asked for a scaled-down version of that great work.

Via Farattini debouches into the narrow Piazza Marconi, where the medieval Loggia dei Banditori once sheltered the heralds who proclaimed laws made by the Council of Elders. Here the fancy marble window frames of the sixteenth-century Palazzo Petrignani derive from a Roman building, and the late medieval Palazzo Nacci contains a renaissance loggia with Corinthian columns and a fine coffered ceiling.

If you are not to get hopelessly lost, since Amelia contains nothing in the way of a main street on which to orientate yourself, you had better start clambering up towards the cathedral. Should you feel adventurous, however, follow the lanes westwards out of Piazza Marconi and see if you can find the Teatro Sociale, whose auditorium is a little white-and-gold horseshoe of enormous charm, unaltered since 1783, when it was built by the local nobility. The original eighteenth-century stage machinery has been preserved, but the drop-curtain was repainted in 1880 by Domenico Bruschi with a scene showing Frederick Barbarossa besieging Amelia.

On a hot morning in summer, the scramble towards the cathedral may leave you somewhat sticky, but the cooling breezes across the terrace in front of it will soon remind you that Amelia, on its windy hilltop, is one of the highest towns in Umbria. The *duomo* was almost entirely rebuilt after a fire in 1629, and is substantially a domed baroque Latin cross, apparently based on a design by Bernini. Under a cheerful array of neo-classical ceiling frescoes hang two Turkish flags captured in a naval battle off Crete in 1665, and to the right of the main door stands the column to which the city's patron St Fermina was tied during her martyrdom. The *Last Supper* in the right transept is the work of Gian Francesco Perini, born in Amelia in 1492, who became a pupil of Raphael and received the commission for this picture in 1538 from the pious Confraternity of Corpus Christi, whose members worshipped in the cathedral. Though the stilted figure painting shows the limitations of Perini's technique, the colourful assembly of Jesus and his disciples against a grandiose architectural background, with Amelia on its hill in the distance, is not without liveliness and a sense of impending drama, especially in the morose, restless Judas seated in the foreground clutching a bag containing his thirty pieces of silver. Perini lived on until 1574 at least, when a document shows the octogenarian artist pathetically petitioning the Council of Elders for exemption from the *pontature*, gymnastic exercises in which all able-bodied male citizens were legally compelled to take part.

Mists girdle the hill on which ancient Amelia stands.

Steep cobbled streets characterize the old Roman city of Amelia.

Eastwards from Amelia, the increasingly rugged and broken country along the side of Monte Arnata gives way to the dramatic scarps and screes overhanging the lower valley of the Nera and the grizzled, romantic city of Narni. Years before I started travelling in Italy, indeed while I was yet a child, I saw an old landscape drawing of Narni on its wooded cliffs above the Roman bridge and the white river, and knew the place would not disappoint me when I finally got there. As long as you keep your back turned on the industrial sprawl which has so wretchedly or, as the Italians more aptly put it, 'abusively' been allowed to prevail in the plain around the railway station, you will catch something of Narni's haunting allure, that peculiarly Umbrian quality of the half-wild, the half-ruined, the almost forgotten, an aboriginal Italy under its dark stones.

Originally known as Nequinum, the town received the name of Narnia when the Romans took it in 299 BC, and was accorded maximum significance as a stronghold on the Via Flaminia, guarding the entrance to the Tiber valley and the approaches to Rome. Like Amelia, it prospered from making the bricks and tiles of which so many Roman buildings were constructed, and its citizens, including Pliny the Younger's sister-in-law Pompeia Celerina, acquired huge *latifundia* (landed estates) in the neighbourhood.

Narni's later history is not particularly happy. The citizens were incurably rebellious: in 1112 they rose against the Pope; fifty years later they challenged the odious Barbarossa and got sacked for their pains by the Archbishop of Mainz; and a century afterwards they successfully held off Frederick II. Their hatred of the Holy Roman Emperors lasted for three hundred years, till in 1527 Charles V's German *landsknechte*, the soldiers of his army preparing to fall upon Rome, vented some of their preparatory anger on Narni, which never wholly recovered from the wave of looting and destruction.

The city, within fragments of partly Roman wall,

A typical arched medieval street in the heart of Narni.

A sculptured lion in the Palazzo Comunale, Narni.

spreads in a narrow oblong over the spine of a high hill. Instead of entering from the first turn off the main Perugia road, you should contrive to come into the city from the Terni approach, through Porta Ternana and along Via Roma, which brings you into Piazza Garibaldi. Here, past the bronze fountain and the medieval tower to your left, you glimpse the cathedral of San Giovenale, begun in 1145. To enter the building you must walk under the arch into Piazza Cavour, where the main doorway is sheltered by a graceful renaissance portico of 1497, with a frieze of garlands above the arcade.

The interior is something of a surprise. Its original romanesque basilica layout was modified in the fifteenth century by the addition of an extra aisle to the right of the nave, and there are two fine pulpits of carved sandstone, decorated with relief panels of saints and supported by winged angels, probably the work of northern Italian sculptors. Nothing can be more unexpected, however, in the context of an

P·V
EL
LA
FER NVS

Umbrian cathedral, than the grandiose polychrome marble *confessione*, the balustrade enclosing the urn containing the bones of St Juvenalis, patron of the city, placed here in 1662. The sumptuous baldacchino of the high altar behind it, the inlaid wooden choir stalls and the baroque windows with their broken pediments under the gothic vaulting of the apse represent a triumphant flourish of Berninian splendour in the twilight years of papal authority at the close of the seventeenth century. Donna Olimpia would surely have adored it!

Juvenalis, Narni's first bishop, was a priest from North Africa, appointed in 368 by Pope Damasus I (366–384) at the request of a noble lady named Philadelphia. His missionary zeal converted over two thousand pagans to Christianity in a single day, and his eight-year episcopate was characteristically energetic in establishing the Church's significance in the life of the city. His marble funerary urn stands in the Cappella del Corpo Santo at the foot of the twin staircases sweeping down from the *confessione* to the crypt.

There are other incidental delights in this cathedral, so radiant with that natural daylight whose absence in other Italian churches tends to uplift or depress according to your state of mind. To the right of the high altar is the chapel of the Blessed Lucia Broccolelli, another multicoloured marble confection, raised by Cardinal Giuseppe Sacripanti in 1714 to the memory of a pious Narnese nun who founded a convent in Ferrara. Her body is shown on the altar, and above it is a picture of the saint in ecstasy by Francesco Trevisani (1656–1746), a highly admired and influential artist whose career led him from Capodistria (in modern Yugoslavia) to Venice and thence to Rome, where his work earned enormous praise from French and English travellers.

Further down the far right aisle you will find St Juvenalis's first oratory, much adorned in the Renaissance but retaining some of its early sixth-century decoration (note the engagingly primitive marble plaque with twin lambs). Once the saint's bones lay here, together with those of his successor St Maximus and a limb or two of a later bishop, St Cassius, whose body, together with that of his wife St Fausta – they are one of the few married couples in the calendar – somehow ended up at Lucca in Tuscany.

Next to this is an exceptional statement of renaissance classical ideals in the shape of a chapel erected by the pious Confraternity of St Anthony Abbot. It consists of two imposing triumphal arches, one in front of the other, decorated with the most exquisite relief carvings, the work of the Lombard sculptor Sebastiano di Francesco Pellegrini (1477–1532). The first arch, framed by Corinthian pilasters with angel heads in roundels next to them, may initially look simpler than the second, but its interior surface has a whole sequence of intricately devised symbolic emblems relating obliquely to elements of Christian doctrine. The second, altogether more florid, shelters a ceiling of stone rosettes above the altar.

This is not the only distinguished sculpture from this period of Italian art to be found in the *duomo* of Narni. On the opposite side of the church, seek out the lovely tomb of Pietro Cesi, who died in 1477, and whose high-relief effigy was carved by the Florentine sculptor Bernardo da Settignano. Weeping cherubs flank the inscription, and a Crucifixion scene fills the garlanded lunette. Nearby, the equally fine monument to Pedro Gormaz, a Spanish bishop of Narni appointed to the see by his countryman Alexander VI in 1498, reflects his fondness for the kind of embellishments through which he brought the cathedral treasury to near bankruptcy. The mitred effigy, surrounded by saints, with God and the Virgin above, was carved by an anonymous sculptor in the Venetian idiom in 1514.

Leaving the cathedral, you suddenly find yourself at the heart of an intransigently medieval prospect of tall, frowning old stone houses, several with defensive 'domestic towers' of the kind raised in Italian cities during the Guelph and Ghibelline struggles. Thanks to

Judith and Holofernes, a romanesque carving on a wall of Narni's Palazzo Comunale.

some fascinating recent researches into the ancient statute books, we know a lot about the values and customs of Narni's citizens during this period. Laws controlled everything from the pressing of olives in the streets to parental control of children 'committing nuisances in public places'. Anyone throwing water 'or other base substances' from the windows had to shout '*Guarda, guarda, guarda!*' and the lanes and squares were washed and swept every Saturday. Butchers were forbidden to indulge in the practice of inflating the carcasses of dead animals to make them look bigger, and sellers of drugs and spices were subjected to regular inspection by a special official who made them throw away any medicines which had passed their shelf-life.

More threatening, inevitably, were the penalties imposed for domestic and sexual misdemeanours. Families were expected to discipline their offspring adequately, but if they became 'refractory, dissipated and prodigal of their inheritance' the children could be brought before the chief justice, known as the Vicario, who would then administer a stern reprimand, or even imprison the black sheep if he saw fit. Women who cuckolded their husbands were deprived of their dowries, 'concubines' might be expelled from the city, but *bona fide* prostitutes were permitted to practise their calling in certain specially indicated areas of the town. Rapists were hanged, sodomites were burned, and the Jews were subjected to a special tax whose revenue was used to pay for the annual festivities in honour of St Juvenalis. The only really free creatures in medieval Narni were the six pigs sacred to St Anthony, permitted by law to wander in the streets, but even these, to stop them from rootling, had to wear iron rings in their snouts.

The Loggia dei Priori, from which many of these laws were issued, stands on the right of Via Garibaldi, leading up from the cathedral, and was built in the fourteenth century, possibly by Gattapone. Opposite is the Palazzo del Podestà, an amalgam of three medieval tower-houses, which contains a small picture gallery with a magnificent *Coronation of the Virgin* by Ghirlandaio (the immense crown, surrounded by a frieze bearing the inscription *Delecta Mea*, 'my delight', is purely symbolic). Beyond this, the church of Santa Maria in Pensole, dated around 1175, has doorways beautifully framed in wreaths of romanesque relief supported by a set of bizarre little gnome-like figures. *In pensole* means 'on sliding ground', though the fabric shows no obvious signs of wandering off down the hillside. For many years it was thought to have been raised on the site of a temple to Bacchus, god of wine, but in 1883 the local antiquarian Marchese Giovanni Eroli proved to his satisfaction that it was not. In his published account of his excavations in the crypt he tells us: 'Among the many curious onlookers, those most devoted to wine would keep asking me "Have you found the statue of Bacchus yet?" and I used to answer "Bacchus never lived here: these putrid bones tell us that it was the abode of death. If you truly want to find your god, go and seek him in the company of Mastro Girolamo the innkeeper, and enjoy his pleasures to your heart's content."'

Dionysiac delights, indeed, can be found in Vicolo del Comune opposite the church, where at Ristorante La Loggia you will eat one of the most satisfyingly cooked and presented meals in Italy at no very dramatic damage to your pocket. Further along Via Garibaldi, it is worth seeking out the old twelfth-century church of San Domenico, whose patches of fresco, fine tabernacle attributed to Agostino di Duccio and dignified monument to the young Giovanni Massei, 'snatched away in the flower of his adolescence' in 1494, as the inscription tells us, have all been incorporated into a museum. The display includes pieces of medieval sculpture, an Annunciation by Gozzoli and a portrait by Fiorenzo di Lorenzo.

Leaving Narni at this northern end of the city, you follow the signs towards Perugia, and descend the hill to cross the deep gorge of the Nera. Once a Roman bridge 30 metres high spanned these steep hillsides, but now only a single arch is left of the four which

Romanesque and baroque join forces in the *duomo* of Narni.

FRUTTA

made up the Ponte d'Augusto, built on the great Emperor's orders in 27 BC. The Romans were much fascinated by the whiteness of the river at Narni, created by the chalky deposits on the riverbed, and their writers keep on referring to it. Claudian (370–404), the last great Latin poet of the empire, talks about 'the strange-coloured stream which gives its name to the town, its sulphurous waters running tortuously between the mountains through the thick ilex groves'.

The road across the plain through unattractive Narni Scalo soon climbs into the hills again, to reach San Gemini, an extremely pretty little *borgo* which was elevated to the rank of a city in 1781 by Pope Pius VI (1775–1800). The gothic church of San Francesco, to the right of the principal gateway, has interesting patches of anonymous fresco in the niches along the aisles, while the *duomo* was heavily neo-classicized in the nineteenth century. In the Piazza di Palazzo Vecchio, with its pleasing ensemble formed by the medieval Palazzo del Popolo and the Oratorio di San Carlo, the latter's fifteenth-century frescoes bear witness to the primitive vigour of the Umbrian tradition even in so humble a spot as this.

San Gemini has given its name to the curative springs just off the road northwards, which provide the region's most famous mineral water. The spa is in full swing from May to September, with the usual clientele of sufferers from digestive and liver ailments wandering sedately along the shady gravel walks among the rhododendrons to drink from the springs at the centre of the park. Flung down in the middle of the Umbrian agricultural landscape, San Gemini Fonte, with its air of a slightly faded sanatorium from some time between World Wars I and II, has an incongruity which definitely needs to be savoured.

To heighten this sense of cheek-by-jowl oddity, take the track (it is not much more) up the hill behind the spa and follow it to the very end. You will find yourself among the ruins of a Roman city, an uncommon enough sight in Italy, where most towns have been continuously inhabited since the fall of the empire. This is Carsulae, founded in the third century BC on the Via Flaminia, and once a prosperous community, whose sudden end came in the early fifth century AD, when a Gothic invasion was followed by a devastating earthquake.

No wonder Tacitus and Pliny the Younger so praised the loveliness of Carsulae's location. As a ruin, it is perhaps still lovelier. Under the shadow of gentle hills, with the larks singing and the grasshoppers chirping, you wander to and fro among the green hummocks and dips, picking out the sites of the theatre and the amphitheatre, the remains of temples, shops and inns, and a scatter of crumbled arches and half-buried walls. You will even find the ruts made here by the passing of Roman chariots and carriages. Perhaps this was an inspiration for Robert Browning's beautiful poem *Love among the Ruins*, written in 1853, where he describes a romantic tryst at

> . . . the site once of a city great and gay
> (So they say) . . .
> Where a multitude of men breathed joy and woe
> Long ago.

One of those who pioneered the excavation of Carsulae in the seventeenth century was Federico Cesi of Acquasparta, a town which lies a little further to the north, on the very edge of the range of high hills known as the Monti Martani. I am very fond of Acquasparta, with its cheerful sense of bustle and prosperity, but I can never avoid the impression that the Cesi family, its enlightened rulers, wanted a destiny for the place which it never had a hope of accomplishing. Founded in Roman times, its importance grew during the early Middle Ages, and though Guelphs and Ghibellines tore it apart with their struggles, it was sufficiently attractive to appeal, in the early sixteenth century, to the powerful Farnese family, who purchased the overlordship. In 1540 they sold this to Isabella Liviani, wife of Giacomo Cesi, and it was that talented and philanthropic family,

The gateway to the little town of San Gemini.

whom we meet at Todi and elsewhere, who created what was essentially a little renaissance paradise, where the learned men and women of Italy might come and converse in the tranquillity of the Umbrian countryside.

They built themselves the magnificently sober ducal palace, with its double loggias decorated with the escutcheons of the family and its connections and a whole sequence of frescoed rooms with coffered ceilings, the work of Giovanni Domenico Bianchi (1537–1618). Here Federico Cesi, in the early years of the seventeenth century, established the Accademia dei Lincei ('Academy of the Lynxes', because they were ever watchful for new knowledge), Europe's earliest scientific society, still in existence after nearly 400 years. One of his most distinguished guests was Galileo Galilei, who spent some time here as a refugee from the Inquisition in 1624.

Federico and others of his clan are buried in the handsome chapel built by his grandmother Isabella Liviani in 1581 as an annexe to the church of Santa Cecilia. The gothic church of San Francesco nearby, begun in 1294, is impressively austere, though the columns of its cloister arches are cheerfully varied in their decoration. Successive generations of the Cesi family kept up the tradition of artistic patronage – commissioning the young George Frideric Handel (1685–1759), for example, to compose music for a Cesi daughter's wedding to a Neapolitan duke. They have now gone from Acquasparta, but their spirit lives on in the little town, under the lines of washing and the arches spanning the quiet streets, and the windowsills and balconies bright with geraniums.

The roads up to Todi lead off towards several towns and villages which once formed part of the extensive territory controlled by the city – places always known as *castelli*, even if their castles nowadays either lie in ruins or have wholly disappeared. At Villa San Faustino, for example, walls were thrown up in the early Middle Ages around a Roman settlement, and a Benedictine abbey was founded in the twelfth century on the site of an ancient temple. At Rosceto, in 1273, the entire *castello* was burnt down in local feuding between the Atti and Chiaravalle families, while at Colvalenza the fortress withstood a terrible series of sackings and sieges. In 1272 it was set on fire and the garrison was put to the sword. Thirty years later, a certain *cavalier* Savelli, leader of the Ghibelline faction in Todi, carried on a long and fruitless siege, concluded only by the Pope, who took Savelli's brother prisoner and then had the pair of them beheaded. The Atti, leading the Guelphs, were equally harsh in their rule over the town, and it was only in 1487 that the Chiaravalle drove them out – an event signalled, according to a contemporary chronicle, by the birth of a boy with a calf's head.

North of Colvalenza is Massa Martana, whose castle, some of its towers remaining, was built in 1276 by a cardinal with the splendidly tautological name of Bentivenga Bentivenga. Outside the town, across the valley, stands the abbey of Santi Fidenzio e Terenzio, founded in the twelfth century, though the masonry makes use of Roman stonework, both in the crypt and on the lovely pink-and-white striped façade – quintessential Umbria.

From here, it is only a short drive to Todi, as good a place as any in which to conclude an Umbrian journey. From its balconies, terraces and towers you can look out across marvellous vistas of that unparalleled landscape, before turning back towards the endlessly intriguing details of the old town itself, whose history is a microcosm of the Umbrian experience, mingling faith and romance with violence and joy. Over that last glass of Sagrantino or Grechetto in one of the restaurants perched on the edge of the high hill on which the city stands, you will surely agree that the expedition has been well worth it.

Among the ruins of the abandoned Roman city of Carsulae.

Index